Surviving and Thriving
in the Law Office

Surviving and Thriving in the Law Office

What Every Paralegal Should Know

Richard L. Hughes, J.D.
Attorney at Law
Paralegal Instructor
Highline Community College
Des Moines, Washington

THOMSON

DELMAR LEARNING   Australia Canada Mexico Singapore Spain United Kingdom United States

WEST LEGAL STUDIES

Surviving and Thriving in the Law Office: What Every Paralegal Should Know
by Richard Hughes

Vice President, Career
Education
Strategic Business Unit
Dawn Gerrain

Director of Editorial:
Sherry Gomoll

Editorial Assistant:
Brian E. Banks

Director of Production:
Wendy A. Troeger

Production Manager:
Carolyn Miller

Production Editor:
Matthew J. Williams

Director of Marketing:
Wendy E. Mapstone

Cover Design:
Dutton & Sherman Design

NOTICE TO THE READER

Publisher does not warrant or guarantee any of the products described herein or perform any independent analysis in connection with any of the product information contained herein. Publisher does not assume, and expressly disclaims, any obligation to obtain and include information other than that provided to it by the manufacturer.

The reader is notified that this text is an educational tool, not a practice book. Since the law is in constant change, no rule or statement of law in this book should be relied upon for any service to any client. The reader should always refer to standard legal sources for the current rule or law. If legal advice or other expert assistance is required, the services of the appropriate professional should be sought.

The Publisher makes no representation or warranties of any kind, including but not limited to, the warranties of fitness for particular purpose or merchantability, nor are any such representations implied with respect to the material set forth herein, and the publisher takes no responsibility with respect to such material. The publisher shall not be liable for any special, consequential, or exemplary damages resulting, in whole or part, from the reader's use of, or reliance upon, this material.

For Alisa, Stephanie, and Grant

Contents

Part II   Beyond Survival—How to Thrive as
a Paralegal

Chapter 5

Getting Off to a Good Start   75

Chapter 6

What Is Important to a Law Firm?   93

Part III   Taking Stock of Your Paralegal Career

Foreword

Congratulations on choosing the paralegal profession as your career! It is always difficult to be considered the "new kid on the block" in any profession, and starting in the legal profession as a paralegal is no exception. A "newbie" often comes into the profession believing he or she has had superb paralegal education and internships, knows the law, and is competent to work as a paralegal. Then the newbie goes to work in a law firm or a corporation and realizes, "This is not what I expected at all. What did I get myself into?" Fortunately, most paralegals will have a great mentor where they work, either another paralegal or attorney, to show them the ropes. If the paralegal does not have that great mentor or a support group, this book, *Surviving and Thriving in the Law Office: What Every Paralegal Should Know*, will help you.

After seven years in the profession, I still remember with horror my first paralegal position. I went to school to be a paralegal, landed my first job, and didn't realize how little I *didn't* know until I started working. Granted, I worked for a solo practitioner and learned a great deal for my specialty, but I never learned managing my workload, how to properly bill, resources to use, and all the other great tools that this book offers. I did join a local paralegal association and through that avenue made friends, met other paralegals, and built my own network of resources. However, if there had been a book about office politics, billables, assignments and all the other facets of life in a law firm, I would have purchased it gladly.

Billable hours alone is the bane of most people's existence in the legal profession, and to bill properly is a fine art, one that I never mastered and relished learning about in this book. Fortunately, in my current position I don't have to bill my hours, but for years it was a source of great angst and frustration at accurately and ethically capturing the time for my services. I also believe managing time is something every professional, legal or otherwise, should master. Your job will be much easier if you understand the ins and outs of managing your time. If you can effectively manage your time and bill properly, you will become the star paralegal in your office.

Surviving and Thriving in the Law Office provides an inside perspective of what really goes on in a law office. If you, as a paralegal, can understand the reasons and rationale as to why a law office is set up the way it is, the politics involved, time issues, and other important matters, you will be way ahead of the game.

Everyone should have goals, and I was happy to read the chapters on goals in this book. I used to groan when people asked me in interviews, "Where do you see yourself in 5 years, 10 years?" I hadn't thought that far ahead! My whole goal for a while was to be a good paralegal; in fact, only recently did I realize I need to keep adding goals to my professional life to avoid getting bored and jaded. Smart professionals are always looking down the road to create a niche or a new path for themselves. Goals keep you focused, interested, and passionate about your new profession. It is a great pleasure to wake up each day and realize that you love your job, your interaction with people, clients, and solving problems for others. Goals also keep you motivated, and *Surviving and Thriving in the Law Office* advises you how to stay motivated in a challenging profession.

Being a paralegal has given me outstanding opportunities to grow professionally and personally. It has allowed me, through my work and with the National Federation of Paralegal Associations, to meet other like-minded professionals, and it has kept me "newbie young."

Good luck in your paralegal career, and make sure to keep *Surviving and Thriving in the Law Office* beside you as you move on in this ever changing, ever challenging profession.

Janice M. Amato
Corporate Paralegal, Nypro Inc.
National Federation of Paralegal Associations,
Vice President of Professional Development

Preface

This book is full of practical advice from someone who was a supervising partner in a private law firm and later became a full-time paralegal educator. The information you are about to read has worked for others, and it can work for you too. As someone who is about to complete your paralegal education or has recently been hired as a paralegal, you can begin to put the information contained in this book to work for you today.

When I began my legal career in 1984, the term *paralegal* was not one I heard much in the law office. Paralegals seemed to be confined to large law firms in big cities. The profession was still emerging. The paralegal profession has changed considerably since then. Today, paralegals are an essential part of the legal team in law offices of all sizes and in communities almost everywhere. Paralegals work in the private, government, and nonprofit sectors.

As a member of a growing profession, you will have more opportunities to succeed than those who preceded you. Those trailblazers who came before you in the paralegal profession deserve our appreciation; they made the most of the opportunities you now have available to you. However, an opportunity does not necessarily equate to a success. There are right and wrong ways to achieve success. This book's purpose is essentially to help you define success as a paralegal, and how to achieve it. The pedagogical features of this book are in keeping with this purpose. They include:

> Key Learning Points at the beginning of each chapter that preview the main ideas of the chapter

> Paralegal Perspective text boxes that contain practical career advice and observations by new and experienced paralegals

> A Chapter Summary that reinforces the main ideas in the text

> Web Research Exercises in each chapter designed to supplement the information contained in the chapter in which a particular exercise appears

> Chapter Exercises that reinforce the material in each chapter

> An Ethical Discussion in each chapter that causes you to consider the ethical implications of your actions

> Suggested Reading at the end of each chapter for exploring career topics in more depth

> Numerous situations that actually occurred in the law office setting and the career lessons to be learned from them

> A reader-friendly format, in plain, direct language, with the use of humor where appropriate, in order to make reading this book enjoyable without sacrificing content

> An annotated sample cover letter, resumé, and follow-up thank-you letter in the appendixes that provide valuable information, nearly sentence by sentence, about how to construct the best possible end product

> Information in the appendixes about nontraditional and alternative careers available to those with paralegal training and the NFPA model code of ethics

The chapters in Part One are arranged to be read sequentially and then referred to later as needed. The remaining chapters can be read in any order, though they do follow a logical pattern. Read the Key Learning Points for each chapter. The Paralegal Perspective text boxes refer to the topics in the chapter and allow for a natural pause to consider what you have read to that point. The end-of-chapter Exercises, Ethical Discussion segments, and Web Research Exercises are designed to be completed shortly after each chapter has been read. The Chapter Exercises are conducive to both individual and small group work, with many of them asking pertinent questions or raising significant issues, and allowing the instructor to tailor the activity to the class.

In my capacity as a supervising partner in a law firm, I hired, trained, and worked side by side with paralegals, often through difficult circumstances such as acrimonious jury trials. I came to respect the importance of paralegals in the delivery of legal services to clients. I also identified what I thought made paralegals effective. I realized that the training aspect of my job was what I enjoyed most, which is why I became a full-time paralegal educator. Learning is a life long process. Any ideas that would help new paralegals in their careers are appreciated. I can be reached through Thomson Delmar Learning at westlegalstudies@thomson.com.

INSTRUCTOR'S MANUAL

Written by the author of this text and available exclusively in electronic format on our Web site, the Instructor's Manual contains course schedules, summaries, outlines, transparency masters, and test questions. To download, log on to www.westlegalstudies.com, click on "Instructor's Center," and follow the instructions.

ACKNOWLEDGMENTS

Thanks to the wonderful and professional people at Thomson Delmar Learning who gave me the opportunity to make a difference in the lives of those who read this book:

Sherry Gomoll, Editorial Director

Brian Banks, Editorial Assistant

Carolyn Miller, Production Manager

Matt Williams, Production Editor

I am also grateful to those who gave valuable ideas and information selflessly: Lillian Ai, Wendy Allen, Jennie Bigley, Linda Bolima, Debbie Ellenwood, Pamela Dayhill, Demetrius Hatcher, Hetty Grant, and Kelli Wilcox.

My coworkers at Highline Community College, Joy Smucker and Buzz Wheeler, deserve thanks for putting me in a position to continually improve as a paralegal educator.

I greatly appreciate the reviewers of my book, whose comments enabled me to write more effectively:

Michael K. Allen
Highline Community
College
Des Moines, WA

Vickie Brown
Carl Sandburg College
Carthage, IL

Dora J. L. Dye
City College of San
Francisco
San Francisco, CA

Wendy B. Edson
Hilbert College
Hamburg, NY

Leslie Sturdivant Ennis
Samford University
Birmingham, AL

Sharon Halford
Community College of
Aurora
Aurora, CO

Nance Kriscenski
Manchester Community
College
Wethersfield, CT

Konnie G. Kustron
Eastern Michigan
University
Ypsilanti, MI

Richard P. A. Lewis
Los Angeles City College
Los Angeles, CA

Janet Longus
Hamilton College
Cedar Falls, IA

Penny Lorenzo
Rhodes College
Phoenix, AZ

Melody C. Schroer
Maryville University
St. Louis, MO

Janell Spencer
College of the Sequoias
Visalia, CA

Julia O. Tryk
Cuyahoga Community
College
Parma, OK

Bobby Wheeler
Highline Community
College
Des Moines, WA

Special thanks to Stu Rees, whose "Stu's Views" cartoons appear with permission throughout this text. For more information, www.STUS.com.

Part 1
Setting Goals:
What Should You
Expect from a
Paralegal Career?

> > > > > > > > > > > > > > >

Chapter 1
Why Have Goals?

Key Success Points

> Goal setting results in a plan for your career.
> Those who do not plan are likely to fail.
> Set your goals and successful behavior will follow.

> > > > > > > > >

Part I > Setting Goals: What Should You Expect from a Paralegal Career?

4

> ## A CAREER IS TOO IMPORTANT TO LEAVE TO CHANCE

I want you to stop reading this book—just for a minute. Write down three career goals for yourself. We'll come back to your goals in the next chapter, so keep them handy. For most people, writing goals is a completely new experience. Most people never take 60 seconds to write down what they want to accomplish in their career but will spend hours a week on the Internet, golf course, or shopping. These are all wonderful pursuits, but are they more important than an activity in which you spend most of your waking hours? Of course not. Is it any wonder that the average worker does not enjoy going to work each day? Is there anything worse than getting up and going to a job you despise day after day, year after year? Yet that is exactly what most people do. Why? A lack of planning—otherwise known as goal setting—is at the root of the problem.

In my observations as a partner in a law firm, I have noticed something that is both interesting and apparent about employees. When employees do not perform well, it is usually for one of three reasons:

1. They are afraid to fail.

2. They are afraid to succeed.

3. They have little or no idea why they entered the legal profession.

Forcing yourself to articulate well-considered career goals will help you overcome these problems. Setting career goals requires you to set aside time, a precious commodity and it requires you to think—*really think*. It is more than just writing down a few ideas. It is hard work. Goal setting requires you to dig deep into your inner soul and decide what is important to you professionally and personally.

Your professional and personal goals are intertwined; each affects the other. For example, if one of your goals is to attend two paralegal association conferences this year because you want to advance professionally, by necessity you will have less time to pursue personal achievements or interests. What is the payoff for clearly defined goals? A career that is positive and fulfilling, which is something quite rare. Let's discuss briefly the reasons that employees fail and then goal setting as a way to avert failure and thrive in a law office.

> ## WHY EMPLOYEES FAIL

Fear of Failure

The employee afraid of failure is a person who would like to advance in the legal profession but does not take advantage of opportunities that would result in that advancement. This person seldom takes a risk, because with every risk comes the possibility of failure. This attitude is like a student who enrolls in a class and never takes the final exam for fear of not doing well. This becomes a self-fulfilling prophecy. The outcome on the job is equally predictable. You would not think of enrolling in a course and not taking the final exam because it is clear how poorly you would do in the course. In a job situation the consequences of risk aversion are more subtle but even more serious. Here is an example.

When I was new to the law office setting, I had the pleasure of working with a paralegal who had been employed by the firm for several years. Jim (not his real name) had graduated from a paralegal program a few years earlier. His transcript noted that he took a legal research and writing course and scored an above-average grade. What his transcripts did not indicate is that Jim never felt comfortable about his writing skills. He lived in constant fear that once an attorney saw that he was not a good writer, his job was doomed.

So, whenever an attorney needed a legal brief written, Jim found a way to avoid writing it. He would write correspondence for his supervising attorneys—after all, his job did require some writing. The problem for Jim was that in a civil litigation firm, there were *always* briefs to write. Jim would eventually be found out.

One day the senior partner wanted a "memorandum of points and authorities" prepared for an important client and gave the assignment to Jim. He froze. He did nothing until the day before the assignment was due, when he announced to the partner he "was not able to get to it." As a result, an associate attorney and another paralegal were up until the wee morning hours pounding out the memorandum (in quite an agitated state). Jim did not take the "final exam" so to speak and failed the course. Soon after this incident, he found himself looking for a new job.

Fear of Success

Being afraid to succeed sounds like an anomaly. I didn't invent this idea but I certainly observed it in my years of law practice. It is not something I learned before I became employed in the legal field. I understood that some people would be afraid to fail; that seemed somewhat natural. But being afraid to succeed? That was something I had not thought about before embarking on a legal career.

Unlike Jim, the employee who fears success knows how to do the task at hand but fears advancement because he or she believes the tasks

Part I > Setting Goals: What Should You Expect from a Paralegal Career?

6

then become more difficult and the responsibilities greater. Often this employee fears the changes in life she or he believes come with success. In a sense, this person thinks he or she doesn't deserve success and wouldn't handle it well.

In contrast to Jim, who didn't want his lack of ability discovered, a person who fears success does not want others to know she or he is, in fact, able. Returning to the college course analogy, it's as if getting an A in the course may cause the instructor to recommend harder courses that will challenge the student, yet result in greater knowledge. This type of person says, "I'll take my above-average (but not outstanding) grade, and not worry about challenging myself." How does a person who fears success end up? Unfortunately, this person is going to spend a lot of time with Jim.

Law firms are places in which success is to a great degree dependent on reaching one's full potential. Reaching this potential leads to higher self-esteem and greater interest in your job. It's a snowball effect: higher self-esteem and greater interest make you want to accomplish even more. Your legal career can be everything you want it to be, but first you have to have a game plan. In other words, you have to set goals for yourself. If you find it hard to believe someone could fear success, listen to Jodi's story.

Jodi appeared to have it all. She had attended a good law school where she earned excellent grades, and she was awarded law review membership, a feather in the cap of any law student. She was an excellent legal researcher and writer. It was only later that I learned something about her that no one else knew: she did not want to become a partner in the firm. Jodi feared success. "Making partner" was thought to be the universal goal of all new attorneys. Jodi was sure that once she made partner, she could not handle the pressure of dealing directly with clients. She was uncomfortable with the thought of driving a nice car like the other partners. She thought the trappings of success would make her a different person. These were all excuses for the real reason Jodi did not want to become partner: she wasn't suited for a law firm environment. As a result, Jodi has bounced from firm to firm, never advancing beyond the level of a junior associate despite years of experience.

Are you beginning to see why goals are important? In Jodi's case, setting goals would have caused her to ask herself whether a law firm setting was the right direction for her life to take. Jodi did what most other people do: she left her career, and thus much of her life, to chance. It's not hard to imagine what Jodi's level of job satisfaction must have been as newer employees continued to pass her on the seniority ladder.

Those Who Don't Know Why They Are in the Legal Profession

It is hard to imagine that someone would spend all the money and time to complete paralegal training and only afterward ask whether this is a good career choice. Yet I have seen otherwise intelligent people do exactly this. These employees are often unmotivated, and when the going gets tough, they fold. They do not have the determination required to see a difficult legal project through at the high level of quality expected based on their training and ability.

In order to achieve fulfillment in a career—legal or otherwise—there must be a reason other than money to enter it. That is not to say money is unimportant. Indeed, I hope that one benefit of this book will be to make you a better paid paralegal. A successful paralegal receives—and deserves—significant compensation. Money is important, but if it's the sole reason you go to work every day, the luster will eventually wear off. Any time a decision is made solely for the money, there is a good chance it is a wrong decision.

I have seen a number of paralegals and attorneys go into the law only because they have a general idea that it pays above average and carries with it some prestige. Most people are more careful about buying a car than choosing a career. They can't tell you why they went into the law.

Don't be one of the lost souls. Know not only why you went into the law, but why you chose the firm where you work. Try stating the reasons in terms other than money, although making more money is perfectly acceptable as one of several goals—for example:

> *"I went into law because I've always liked solving problems."*

> *"I went to work for this law firm because there is an opportunity for me to help those who have been mistreated at work."*

> *"I went to work for this firm because I had a back injury and know what a tough time injured people have."*

> *"I went to work for this law firm because . . ." (List all of the reasons.)*

Try filling in the blank in the last statement. Then compare your list with the career goals you set for yourself. You will be surprised how this simple exercise helps you focus on what is important to you in a career and personal life.

Most people leave one of the most important aspects of their lives to chance. Isn't your career too important for the roulette wheel approach? It's time to learn what setting career goals can do for you.

Part I > Setting Goals: What Should You Expect from a Paralegal Career?

8

> ## GOALS CAUSE THE BEHAVIOR NEEDED TO BE SUCCESSFUL

A legal career is like a long road trip. You probably wouldn't set out to drive from Los Angeles to Boston without getting a map out and plotting your route, the stops along the way, and when you expect to arrive at your destination. You would decide how far you would like to go each night. You would also want to see a few sights along the way or maybe slightly out of the way if those sights were worthwhile to you. If you didn't take these steps, it's not certain where you would end up and how long it would take to get there. You would likely spend a lot of needless effort because you got lost along the way. The trip would probably take longer if you arrived at your destination at all. You might even run out of money before you got to your destination!

If you're a conscientious person—and my experience is that most people who go into the law are—you would have your car looked at by a mechanic. Before you got onto a long stretch of deserted highway, you would want to know if your car could handle the trip. The consequences of a breakdown would not be pleasant.

Goals Are a Road Map to Success

Now let's turn to your legal career. It would not be unusual at all for your legal career to last 20, 30, even 40 years. It is a *very long* career road trip that you are taking. Indeed, your career will likely consume most of your life. Like the trip you take in your car, you will need a map to tell you how to get where you want to go. That map consists of your goals. Plotting where you want to be each night is tantamount to setting short-term, intermediate-, and long-term goals. The trip seems less daunting if you take it in shorter segments.

With the career course plotted, you know where you want to be and how you want to get there. With your goals established, you set into motion the behavior required to complete each step of your career trip. Just like filling up the tank and loading your car, your behavior automatically corresponds to the destination you want to reach. For example, a short-term goal may be to learn more about family law because you want to help those whose families are breaking up. When an opportunity arises to assist the family law attorney in your firm with a new client, you ask to be assigned to that case. Perhaps another goal is to cross-train to another job in your office because you want additional job security, and it will keep your job interesting. When the managing paralegal needs help negotiating with a vendor, you volunteer to handle this task. Once you plot your career trip you automatically know what you need to do to make that trip successful, just as you would do all of the necessary tasks on your car trip to make sure you got to Denver by next Tuesday, for example.

Why is the behavior necessary to accomplish your goals automatic? Making the effort to set career goals signifies a commitment. You have invested your time and your mental energy toward planning a successful legal career. You have further committed yourself by putting your goals in writing. Have you ever watched a TV show about the law when one person says to another, "It must be legal. He put it in writing"? It is human nature for us to consider something in writing to be solemn. When those goals are reviewed periodically, the commitment grows deeper and the behavior more automatic.

There may be some sights to see along the way on your career road trip, that is, some events or experiences that you don't want to miss. They do not necessarily get you to your destination more quickly, but they bring professional or personal enjoyment and satisfaction. When you jump in that car headed toward Boston, you may want to see the Grand Canyon even if it's out of your way simply because this wonder of nature is an experience you would not want to pass up. When you take your career road trip, you may want to attend a national paralegal conference, visit the U.S. Supreme Court, teach a legal class, or something else—like have children or climb a Tibetan mountain. It's okay. In fact, I strongly encourage you to take these "side trips." Just as it would be dull to simply drive from Los Angeles to Boston and never leave the interstate highway, it would be equally unexciting to deny yourself something enriching you really want to do in a job or in life. I find that employees who live their lives in this manner are more productive.

A word of caution is in order here. Make sure these "side trips" do not become the destination itself. A side trip can get you sidetracked. That trip to the Grand Canyon can evolve into a hike to the basin, followed by a raft trip down the Colorado River, followed by camping in the wilderness. At this rate, you'll never make it to Boston. You'll have only gone a fraction of the distance you wanted to go. Enjoy yourself, but keep your focus on the goals you have set for yourself.

Prepare Before You Go on the Career Trip

What I mean when I say to have someone check under the hood before taking your trip is that you should take care of your mental, spiritual, and physical well-being. I find it ironic that before going on a cross-country car trip, most people would take the trouble to have a mechanic

Part I > Setting Goals: What Should You Expect from a Paralegal Career?

10

look at their car but would not make an appointment with a doctor, counselor, or clergy before embarking on a decades-long career trip. A car represents a big investment for most of us, so we're careful to change the oil regularly. And we would never think of putting water in the gas tank.

Aren't you much more valuable than a car? If you make $30,000 a year (a very conservative figure) for the next 30 years, that's nearly $1 million you will generate in your career. Would you let a million-dollar racehorse smoke cigarettes, drink too much, sleep too little, and never exercise? Of course, you wouldn't! That racehorse wouldn't run very fast. Yet many people in the legal profession (and elsewhere) treat themselves in this manner. You can't get to Boston if your car breaks down on the way. You can't reach your career goals if *you* break down along the way either.

I once had a legal secretary who was one of the best secretaries anywhere. She was competent, had a great sense of humor, was hard working, and was loyal to a fault—everything a law firm would want in an employee. She also smoked two packs of cigarettes daily, drank alcohol to excess, and, in her own words, "allowed my weight to get out of control." She died of a massive heart attack at age 50, leaving behind family, friends, and coworkers who miss and depended on her.

My point is not to criticize (we could all do a better job of taking care of ourselves) but to help you realize you are your most important asset. Take care of yourself at least as well as you would take care of a nice car and hopefully as well as you would a million-dollar racehorse. You can't reach your goals if you don't take care of yourself. It's that simple.

How Career Goals Make a Difference in Real Situations

Let's return to Jim and Jodi. How could setting goals have helped them? Had Jim, who was afraid to fail, set as one of his goals becoming an excellent writer, he would have behaved differently. Making this one of his goals would have forced him to think about all of the things he would need to do to accomplish his goal. Jim would have stated his goal to become an excellent legal writer like this:

> *"I will become an excellent legal writer by preparing an inner office legal memorandum within one month, meeting with someone whose writing I admire within six weeks, preparing a client advice letter within two months, completing a night course in advanced legal research and writing within three months, and writing a memorandum of points and authorities within four months."*

Jim would now have a road map and a plotted course. Goal setting breaks an otherwise daunting task into manageable component parts. Instead of confronting all of his fear at once and failing ("I wasn't able to get to it"), he would have confronted his fear a little at a time by taking on writing tasks that were progressively more difficult. These small victories create the self-confidence to try something more challenging the next time.

Jodi's situation would have radically changed if she had well-defined goals. If Jodi had answered the question, "I work for this firm because . . . ," it is likely her answer would have been "solely for the paycheck." She would then compare this answer with the career goals she had set for herself. Jodi would realize that her place of employment would not allow her to accomplish her goals. She presumably would have found legal employment in a setting that allowed her to accomplish her goals instead of becoming a middle-aged junior associate in a firm she didn't particularly care for.

What if Jodi's goal was to become a partner in the firm? She would be forced to consider all of the tasks associated with becoming a partner. Her career goal of partnership could be stated like this:

"I will become a partner in this firm within seven years. In order to accomplish this goal, I will read one book in the next month about business ownership, establish one new client contact each month for the next seven years, talk with a partner outside the firm for advice within six weeks, try a case within the next six months . . ."

It is likely the trappings of success Jodi feared would be alleviated with a plan like this as she learned more about what it really means to be a partner in a law firm. Jodi's fear of success would decrease as she experienced a small success one goal at a time. Just as it was important for Jim not to confront failure all at once, it was equally important for Jodi not to confront success all at once by one day in the future "making partner." In effect, Jodi would slowly become a partner by preparing herself one step at a time.

What about someone who had no idea why she or he chose the law as a profession? Goal setting for this person should start with a slightly different phrase than in our prior exercise:

"I want to remain in the law because . . ."

Attempting to complete this sentence will force this person to determine what it is about the legal profession that is appealing—for example:

Part I > Setting Goals: What Should You Expect from a Paralegal Career?

12

"I want to remain in the law because I have always enjoyed reading, and as a paralegal I am required to read extensively."

Once this person knows why she or he chose the paralegal profession, it serves as a basis for goal setting:

"My goal is to become the best legal research and writing paralegal in my office. In order to accomplish this goal, I will read one book about legal research within the next two months, take a course on advanced Lexis within the next three months, . . ."

Now the person has direction rather than leaving everything to chance.

The law as a profession is full of variety. That's one of many reasons it is a wonderful way to make a living. It doesn't matter what your interest or personality, there is very likely a job just right for you. However, there will occasionally be a person who is unable to complete the sentence about why to stay in the legal profession. For this person, goal setting is especially important. Your goal may be to use your training for a career that is related to the law rather than as a paralegal. There are many opportunities for someone with your training. You might state your goal as follows:

"My goal is to find a career outside the law in which my legal training will be valued and utilized. In order to accomplish this goal, I will read one of the many books about this topic each month, visit my campus placement office each week . . ."

GOALS ARE A MEASURING STICK FOR SUCCESS

Let's suppose you've left Los Angeles for Boston and discover that all the road signs are missing. You eventually wouldn't know what direction you were headed and whether you would ever get to your destination. Your odometer may register many miles traveled, but you may not be any closer to Boston. That's a lot like a career without goals. You don't know if you're making progress. All you know is that your odometer is registering a lot of miles as you put in those hours at the office. When you set goals, you can determine whether you're successful by whether you accomplish those goals. In the next chapter, we'll discuss why the only meaningful goals are those you set for yourself. But suffice it to say for now that it is an exercise in futility to let others decide when you have become successful. Don't use someone else's measuring stick for your success. I have seen many unhappy people who let others define their success and thus, to a great extent, determine their happiness.

CHAPTER SUMMARY

Usually, when law firm employees are not successful, it is because they are afraid to fail, afraid to succeed, or have little or no idea why they entered the legal profession. Goal setting is hard work, but it is critical to success. When goals are well thought out, written down, and referred to periodically, they cause personal behavior changes that lead to achieving those goals. Think of your paralegal career as a long road trip. Just as you would not likely reach your destination without a road map, you are not likely to reach your career goals without setting goals and having a plan to achieve them. Achieving your goals is a measure of your career success.

> Web Research Exercise <

Go to http://careers.findlaw.com/ on the Internet. Search paralegal job opportunities. Find three job opportunities that appear to be a match with your career goals. Then find three job opportunities that are not a match with your career goals. What do the matches have in common? What do the mismatches have in common? What does this information tell you about the type of paralegal position you should look for?

> Chapter Exercises <

1. Finish the following sentences:
    a. I chose the paralegal profession because . . .
    b. I am working at my current law firm because . . .

    or

    I have applied [or will apply] for a position at [name of firm] because . . .
    c. What I most enjoy about being a paralegal is . . .

    or

    What I most enjoy about paralegal school is . . .

Part I > Setting Goals: What Should You Expect from a Paralegal Career?

14

    d. What I least enjoy about being a paralegal is . . .

        or

    What I least enjoyed about paralegal school is . . .

    e. Something I would really like to accomplish before the end of my legal career is . . .

    f. Something I hope I never have to do as a paralegal is . . .

    g. I won't feel successful as a paralegal unless . . .

2. In a small group, discuss your answers in question 1. What do those answers mean in terms of the goals you should set for your career? Help each other decide what are worthwhile goals based on the answers given to question 1. Make sure that the group assists you in stating your own goals rather than telling you what your goals ought to be. Write those goals down on separate sheets of paper. Be ready to discuss your answers. Alternatively, think about your answers to question 1 individually and what those answers mean in terms of the goals you should set for your career. Write down those goals on a separate sheet of paper.

3. Refer to your written goals from question 2. If working in a small group, discuss with your group what you should specifically do to accomplish those goals. Give reasonable time frames for accomplishing each goal. Write your answers next to each goal, and be ready to discuss them. If working individually, consider carefully what you should do to accomplish each goal, and write your answers next to each goal. Whether you worked in a small group or individually, seek input from those whose knowledge and judgment you respect. Ask whether they have suggestions about how best to accomplish your goals. Then write or type your final product, save it, and review it periodically to remind you to stay on track with your career.

> Ethical Discussion <

Are there ways in which your goals as a paralegal can come into conflict with your professional ethical obligations? Under what circumstances? What can you do to guard against creating ethical issues as you attempt to achieve your goals? Try to be as specific as possible with your responses.

> Suggested Reading <

Richard Nelson Bolles, *What Color Is Your Parachute?* Ten Speed Press, 2003.

Chapter 2
What Should Your Goals Be?

Key Success Points

> *Your goals should originate from your own priorities and values.*

> *Self-assessment and career research are required before you can set achievable goals.*

> *Once you undertake self-assessment and career research, aim high! You can do more than you think you can.*

> > > > > > > > >

YOUR GOALS SHOULD BE YOUR OWN

Let's return to our trip from Los Angeles to Boston. This is a trip of a lifetime, and you can hardly contain your excitement. You can't wait to make the trip, and you find yourself thinking about it constantly. Then your travel companion tells you the day before you leave for Boston that he or she has taken care of the itinerary for you, including how far you will drive each day, where you will stay each night, and what sights you will see along the way. Exciting? The trip will not be nearly as exciting as you had hoped for. In fact, the trip has the distinct possibility of seeming long and tedious. Why? You will still be traveling from coast to coast, going about the same distance, and seeing sights along the way. The answer is that you do not have an *ownership* interest in the trip now that someone else has done the planning for you.

By the term *ownership*, I mean that your goals should originate from your own priorities and values, not someone else's. That does not mean you should forgo advice and assistance in setting your goals. It *does* mean that goals must be tailor-made just for you. If you borrowed a suit from your neighbor, odds are it wouldn't fit just right. It might be tight in some places, and loose in others, and the fabric might irritate your skin. We are all built a little differently from each other, and it's great that we are. When you go to work each day in an ill-fitting job, the discomfort is just as real as when the suit doesn't fit.

Borrowing someone else's goals is just like borrowing a suit. It would be purely chance if those goals fit you just right. Yet haven't we all let someone else define our goals for us at one time or another? Have you ever felt the need to do something just because someone else is doing it? Many of us have been "borrowing" a used suit in our careers and didn't even realize it. Maybe an older sibling went into a certain profession, and your parents expected you to do "at least as well." Perhaps a friend went to work for a prestigious law firm in a big city, so you decide not to take a job with a sole practitioner in Smallsville. Maybe your favorite class in school was torts, but you're afraid of what your classmates would think if you went to work for an "ambulance chaser." Maybe you want to work in a nonprofit agency, but you're afraid your family or friends would look down on employment there.

We all feel the pull to please others, and generally that's healthy. I have noticed that those who enter the legal profession have a disproportionate desire to please others. There is a sense of duty that exists in most people who work in the legal field. That sense of duty will help you be successful and find more meaning in your career. If you are in the process of becoming a legal professional, you can harness your sense of duty to motivate you to work harder and more happily. It's well known that Albert Einstein didn't sleep much because he could hardly control the enthusiasm for what he was doing. Although I'm not advocating that you give up sleep for your job, the principle that doing something that you truly enjoy gives you more energy is unmistakable.

However, it is important not to let the desire to please that comes with a sense of duty cloud your judgment when it comes to your legal career. Are you working downtown in a prestigious law firm because someone else decided you need to make $75,000 a year? Granted, it is unlikely someone will come up to you and tell you specifically, "I want you to make $75,000 a year." It is much more likely someone will expect you to live a certain lifestyle that only a larger salary can support. Conversely, are you with that sole practitioner in Smallsville because someone else told you that's the most you should expect for yourself? (By the way, my experience is that small town law firms offer wonderful opportunities to gain broad-based, sophisticated experience.) My point is that someone else has incorrectly decided that small town law firms are less desirable than firms in larger cities, and it is wrong to act on someone else's conclusions, whether correct or not.

How satisfied can you be chasing someone else's dreams? The world is filled with unhappy workers who got that way because they let someone else decide what they should or shouldn't do in their careers. Don't be one of them.

If you find yourself in a less-than-desirable career situation, you have the ability—indeed, the obligation—to make that situation not only good but great. Your ability has already been demonstrated by possessing the ability to succeed in a paralegal education program. Not everyone has the aptitude for a paralegal profession, but you have already distinguished yourself by completing much or all of the difficult course work required. In fact, not everyone has the ability you have demonstrated in the process of becoming a legal professional. All you have to do is try to explain some of the intricacies of what you have learned in your paralegal training to a layperson to illustrate how far you have come. Chances are you didn't know any more than that layperson a relatively short while ago. The bottom line is that you made it this far because you are gifted with certain attributes and skills that most people do not possess. Your success comes from using those attributes and skills to achieve goals that you have set for yourself.

If you have the ability to come this far in your paralegal training, you have the ability to correct an unhappy career situation. How do I know this? First, logic dictates that you can overcome a bad situation.

Second, I have seen people on numerous occasions change an ugly career path into a great one.

We have already shown that you are someone of at least superior ability. If you had any doubt about your ability, it should have been erased long ago by your achievements in training yourself for a complex, demanding profession. You didn't get this far without a lot of intelligence, hard work, and dedication. But it also takes intelligence, hard work, and dedication to change your career into something positive and rewarding. It is logical to conclude that if you have the ability to learn to be a paralegal, you also have the ability to find career satisfaction. Why of all the able people who enter this wonderful profession would you be singled out for an unfulfilling career? Of course, the answer is that there is no reason for you to be singled out. To conclude otherwise makes no sense.

You need intelligence to evaluate your current situation. You have to evaluate your current situation correctly:

> Does my unhappy job situation have more to do with me or with the job itself?

> If it has to do with me and not the job, what can I do to improve myself?

> If I make those improvements in myself, will the job be one I enjoy? If the answer is no, then focus on the job.

> What is it about the job that I don't like?

> What will make the job one I enjoy?

If the answer to the last question is "nothing," then it is time to find another job, this time one that you will enjoy.

Hard work is necessary because you have to treat finding the right job like a job. This is not a task to do in your spare time. It is something that you make time for. You have to treat this pursuit like a job in that you need to have a "work" schedule just like you would in an office. Have predetermined hours and tasks to accomplish during those hours, just as you would if you reported to work in a law firm.

"Dedication" means that you don't give up under any circumstances. You report to work on time every day until the task is accomplished, despite the inevitable bad news. Do you see why goal setting is crucial? Without goals, you don't know when the task is accomplished. A goal of "finding a good job" is not specific enough to cause you to act in the methodical way required. You'll spin your wheels a lot wasting time on endeavors that may not ultimately take you where you want to go. Rather than having a goal to "find a good job," why not something like this?

> *"My goal is to find a paralegal position in a private law firm that specializes in employment law and allows me to meet with clients, conduct legal research, and attend trials, because I enjoy the private law firm atmosphere, I am a "people person" who likes to have contact with the public, and a class I took in employment law, an internship in that area, and my contact with paralegals who work in employment law convinced me that I have the aptitude and interest required to be a great employment law paralegal."*

Now that you have established the overall goal of achieving a specific employment position, you can set shorter-term goals that will result in accomplishing the longer-term goal:

> *"In order to accomplish the above goal, I will contact at least one current or former classmate each week to ask about any job openings that may be available and are consistent with my goal of becoming an employment law paralegal. I will volunteer to assist at the next paralegal continuing legal education concerning employment law because I will learn more about that area of law and come into contact with practicing paralegals in that field of emphasis. Within one month, I will identify law firms in my geographical area that practice employment law and further identify the best contact person within each firm. I will then contact one contact person a week to determine the availability of paralegal positions within that firm."*

The foregoing is not intended to be an exhaustive list of goals associated with finding a satisfactory legal position, but demonstrative of the specificity with which goals are needed. Do you see that when your goals are sufficiently specific, it is easier to act on them? (We'll discuss more about the need to be specific in setting goals in the next section of this chapter.) With action toward sufficiently specific goals ultimately comes success!

I have seen legal professionals go from a bad career situation to a great one on numerous occasions. Many paralegal students are in school because they are escaping a poor career situation. They rightfully want something better for themselves and those they care about. I often see these students go on to satisfying and rewarding careers as paralegals. I have also seen paralegals dissatisfied with their employment situation either improve their situation with the same employer or find a satisfying position with a different employer. Why in the world would they be

Part I > Setting Goals: What Should You Expect from a Paralegal Career?

20

able to find satisfying jobs and you not be able to? There is absolutely no reason that you shouldn't be as successful in finding fulfilling work from both a logical and an empirical standpoint.

An Example of the Importance of Setting Your Own Career Goals

My own career experience is an example of the importance of having your own goals and that you should never settle for a job situation that isn't well suited for you. To do otherwise is a prescription for disaster not only in your career but in your personal life as well. As we discussed earlier, your career and your personal life are inherently entangled; one necessarily affects the other. My own experience as a young lawyer should be illustrative.

One of my first jobs after graduation was as an associate with a prestigious law firm, located in some of the most expensive real estate in America. The firm members were extremely competitive, well-respected lawyers who handled high-profile cases for large companies. Of the job offers I received, the offer from this firm included the highest salary. I would make my classmates green with envy and please all those who had taken an interest in my career—or so I thought. I had made it to a big-time law firm! Those people on the TV show *LA Law* had nothing on me! In retrospect, it was clear I had no definable goals of my own. My goals were defined by others, including a TV show.

I stayed with this firm for only about a year. It turned out that along with that expensive real estate came the insatiable need to bill a lot of hours. After all, you have to pay the rent. I worked seven days a week, and most of the days were at least 12 hours. Even on rare days when I had my work caught up, I had to be in the office because a more senior associate told me "it would look bad" to do otherwise. I spent many evenings attending parties at one partner's house or another. I started noticing that many of the partners had personal lives that were not what I would want for myself. Even though I worked with great people, I was miserable. My life, and my career, were not my own. My personal life became strained.

Much of my philosophy about how one should go about a career stemmed from this experience. All of my goals were vague and based on someone else's idea of success. Since I had little ownership of my goals, they were doomed to failure. I had taken this job for the wrong reasons.

If you find yourself in a similar situation, there is still hope. Consider your situation a learning experience. I learned a tremendous amount about my own values and what I wanted in a career from this experience. If you had trouble stating why you work where you do in the Chapter 1 Exercises, there is a good chance your career goals are not your own.

When I took my next legal job, the process was completely different. I first examined myself. Self-assessment is critical in determining your career goals. What was important to me both personally and professionally? Although money was important, I had never been particularly enamored with it. In other words, money was not the main reason I liked to work, though I knew I had to make a certain amount to maintain the lifestyle that I wanted. Though I had worked hard to put myself through college and didn't mind long hours when necessary, I was not addicted to work. I would rather have some measure of balance in my personal and professional life. While I recognized large companies should have representation, I grew up with an appreciation of the struggles of the common person. Although I liked the challenge and mental stimulation of high-stakes litigation, I had fond memories of a small town attorney who helped my family through a difficult situation when my father died. Keep in mind that these were my goals, and they would no easier fit you than would a pair of my shoes. Your goals are likely different from mine.

With self-assessment in hand, I was able to set better career goals. My goals were to work in a law firm where the billable hour requirements left a reasonable amount of time for a personal life. The firm would allow me to represent individuals as well as corporate clients. I also wanted to work where there was opportunity to advance financially, although a so-called high salary was not going to be determinative as it was the first time. I was not going to let someone else's idea of success control my decision. I would not have considered myself an expert in goal setting at this point in my career, and in retrospect could have gone about it better, but at least I had goals that were my own.

The firm I went to work for was where I would stay for the next 14 years until I left to teach in a college paralegal program. I had the privilege of working with great people, including paralegals. I represented individuals as well as companies. I had time to take tennis lessons and a class on human anatomy during my first six months with the firm. I rose to partner in this 98-year-old firm in five years, which was ahead of my own schedule. I developed an employment law and personal injury practice where I could help others. Indeed, there were all sorts of reasons for me to enjoy going to work every day. Yet the starting salary of this firm was the lowest of the offers I received. I didn't intend to take the lowest offer; it just turned out that way.

Because I had set my own goals, I was extremely motivated. With motivation comes a high degree of energy. I was constantly thinking of

Part I > Setting Goals: What Should You Expect from a Paralegal Career?

22

ways to be a better lawyer, whether it was learning a new area of the law, establishing a better way to serve our clients, or something else. The end result was becoming a partner in a relatively short period of time, which more than made up for the initial low starting pay. I would not have achieved this if I wasn't motivated by my own career goals.

YOU CANNOT AFFORD A POOR JOB SITUATION

You may be asking yourself whether you can afford to be so particular about a job when you are new to the legal profession. My answer is that *you cannot afford to be otherwise.* Had I accepted the situation in my first legal position, one of two things would have occurred, neither of them good. First, I would have been condemned to a miserable life of working with people I didn't relate well with, doing legal work in which I had little interest. Second, the personal relationships in my life would have suffered greatly—if they survived at all. I would have paid the price with my health. Had I not suffered this bad job experience, the "up-or-out" policy would have me looking for another position if the firm decided not to make me a partner. The going can be rough for someone looking for a job in this situation. As a paralegal, you may also be asked to leave if you are not progressing as expected.

There are times in life when a job—any job—must be the priority. Bills are an inescapable fact of life. But do not accept any job as a permanent situation. Turn a negative situation positive by using this job as a place to learn and gain experience. Turn in the highest quality work you are capable of producing for as long as you are employed there. This job will help you focus on what you want and don't want in a career. *Above all, do not accept this situation as permanent.* I am touched and inspired by the extreme sacrifices I see my students make to become paralegals and have a better life for themselves and their loved ones. You have invested too much of yourself and your hard-earned money to work in a place you'd rather not be. You deserve to have a fulfilling and rewarding legal career.

Wherever you are in your career, from paralegal student to new paralegal to seasoned professional, you need to set goals and make sure they are yours, not someone else's. Remember the three goals I asked you to write down at the start of this book? Reexamine them. Do they need to be revised or replaced altogether? Are they truly yours? Are they based on your own values and priorities? If they are not, long-term success in the legal profession is as far away as Los Angeles to Boston for that poor soul who traveled on someone else's itinerary. Your career trip will be equally long and tedious when your goals are not your own. There is nothing worse than dreading that drive to the office each day. Set your own career itinerary. You'll get to where you want to go and have fun along the way!

≫ Paralegal Perspective ≪

> Attitude defines altitude. If you want to get anywhere in the world, your attitude is what makes or breaks you. Therefore, never forget you are a professional. Maintain a positive attitude in everything you do, whether on or off the job.

GOALS SHOULD BE SPECIFIC

What's wrong with the following statements?

"I want to be the best paralegal I can possibly be."

"I want to learn as much about the law as I can."

"I want to use my position in the legal profession to help others."

"I will be the best employee in the office."

The answer is absolutely nothing. Who wouldn't want to do all of the above? And that's the problem. These goals are so general in nature that they apply to everyone. They are not specific enough to prompt you to change your behavior or to know when they've been accomplished. Armed with these goals, you don't know where to begin or when you've finished. They are devoid of priority and necessarily lacking your own values because the latter are what cause you to set priorities in your professional and personal life. Generalized values require little in the way of self-assessment or thought. They are also the very types of statements that others will make when telling you what you should do with your career.

In my position as a paralegal educator, students often ask me about their careers. It is the exceptional person who has done any significant measure of self-assessment and job research before concluding what it is he or she wants to do with a career. A lack of self-assessment will lead

Part I > Setting Goals: What Should You Expect from a Paralegal Career?

24

to goals that are too generalized to be of much use. Insufficient job research will result in the wrong goals. Conversations with students often tend to go something like this:

> INSTRUCTOR: So you want help with your career goals?
>
> STUDENT: Well, I already am pretty sure I know what I want to do. I took a class in civil litigation [or any other class] and liked it. Could you help me find a job working in civil litigation?
>
> INSTRUCTOR: Other than taking this class, have you tried to determine what paralegals do in a law firm that specializes in civil litigation?
>
> STUDENT: Well, not yet. . . .

What is wrong with this conversation? The student has only a general short-term goal—finding a job in civil litigation—and it is based on incomplete or inaccurate information. A goal is only as worthwhile as the information on which is it based. The information may be incomplete because taking a class in civil litigation is not the same thing as working in a law firm that practices in that area. Many paralegal schools do an excellent job in teaching civil litigation (and many other types of law) but can go only so far in simulating the law firm environment. Does the student know that in many firms, a large part of preparing for trial is reviewing vast amounts of information such as deposition transcripts and medical records and putting them in accurate summary form? Does the student know that preparing for trial can involve long hours as the trial date approaches? Does the student know that litigation is by its nature adversarial?

Yet for some people, nothing compares with the thrill of working on an important case. Many litigation cases are exciting stories, with the trial being the closing chapter. However, without a lot of research, it would be pure chance if the law firm and the student are a good match.

SELF-ASSESSMENT IS CRITICAL

There must be a painstaking amount of self-assessment. What is it that you enjoy? What is it that you dread? What price are you willing to pay in terms of sacrificing your personal life to do what you enjoy? What is it that you're good at? Look back at particular aspects of jobs you have held to assist in your research. What did you like or dislike about the classes you took in your paralegal program? These classes do not provide all the information you will need, but will help. Ask people who know you well what they feel are your strengths and weaknesses. With respect to weaknesses, ask yourself whether you are willing to make the effort required to address those weaknesses that are pertinent to the career goals you have set.

There are likely to be professionals on campus or in the community who are experts in self-assessment. Career counselors often have tests to help determine your interests, aptitudes, and abilities. Seek these professionals out. There are numerous books on this topic. A word of caution: while the professionals and books will assist you in your quest to discover what it is you should be doing with your career, they are not a substitute for your own analysis and conclusions. You are best suited to answer the questions posed in the prior paragraph.

Once you are armed with an accurate assessment of yourself, do some research on careers that may be a match for you. Take an internship or temporary position in an area of the law you think would be compatible with your self-assessment. Talk with people who work in various fields of law. You will find that legal professionals, as busy as they are, will usually take time to talk about their careers. Go online and read as many articles as are available in a career field you may want to pursue. Visit a bookstore. Meet with instructors who teach the classes in fields you may want to pursue, even if you haven't taken a class from that instructor. Most instructors teach areas of law in which they have legal experience.

Once you have done a self-assessment and thoroughly researched which area of the law is a good match for you, you need to identify which employers in that field are a good match. There is definitely a difference in working for a small firm versus a large firm, a rural firm versus an urban firm, an old firm versus a newer firm. For example, large firms tend to offer greater opportunities to specialize. Smaller firms often require more broad-based job duties.

Is this all a lot of work? Yes. But the alternative is to leave your career to chance. *You should never settle for leaving your career up to chance.* Additionally, if you do not make the tremendous effort to find the right employer now, chances are you will have to do so later anyway. You only need to have one awful experience in a legal position to wish you had done your self-assessment and research before you took that ill-suited job. The cost of not doing your homework is much greater than the effort expended in finding the right position at the beginning of your job search.

Finding the right job is goal setting and, like other goals, must be based on good information and specific enough to cause you to act. That's where self-assessment and career research come in. It is difficult to be specific about the job that is right for you if you do not have the information you need. If you are already in a job that is not right for you, think of your current position as providing invaluable information about yourself and what you like (or don't like) in a job. Above all, tell yourself that you deserve to work in a job that you enjoy, and never consider a poor job situation permanent. Life is too short—and your career too important—to work indefinitely where you are not happy.

>Paralegal Perspective<

> Growing up, I had always wanted to work in the field of law, but as I found out, life events can take control and shape a career if one chooses not to be one's own director. It's rather like a dingy drifting in the current with no direction or purpose, but is set on a course dictated by outside influences. For 23 years, I was stuck in a job that I had fallen into, but didn't particularly like, because it was easy. I had the talent to do the job, and the money and benefits were very good. After wishing (a nonproductive, passive activity) for so many years for a career in law, I realized that I had allowed outside influences to control my career direction. Taking stock of my circumstances, it was obvious I had become the dingy in the current, allowing others to set my goals and shape my career. I finally left a job with a lifetime guarantee and certain financial security, and traded it in for a set of goals that will give me a shot at a career of *my* choice. Rather than drifting on the current, I have set a course constructed by and for me that will enable me to realize my goals as a paralegal.

YOUR PARALEGAL EDUCATION IS AN EXAMPLE OF SPECIFIC GOAL SETTING

Chances are you have already had experience with setting specific goals and didn't even realize it. The specificity required to have meaningful goals is similar to obtaining a paralegal degree. When you enrolled in paralegal school your long term goal was to obtain a degree. That was quite specific. You had shorter-term goals along the way, such as taking Legal Research and Writing this fall, Civil Procedure next winter, and Contracts next year. Each goal was specific. You had a plan. That plan may have been devised by consulting with educators, administrators, family members and others, but ideally the plan was yours.

Once the plan was in place, you automatically altered your behavior to accomplish the plan. You obtained a class schedule every semester or quarter. You enrolled for classes consistent with your plan. You went to class, took notes, read the textbook, and studied. You didn't have to remind yourself with each reading assignment that this was part of your plan to obtain a paralegal degree.

The same level of precision should apply to your career goals. Instead of stating that you want to be the best paralegal in your office, try these:

"I will be a supervising paralegal within three years."

"I will be a managing paralegal within five years."

"I will be president of the paralegal association within ten years."

Do you see the difference in setting more specific goals? You now have a time frame to work with, just like when you gave yourself two years to obtain a degree for example. Once the specific goals are set, you formulate shorter-term goals that ensure you complete the long-term goal.

Let's take the first example of having your goal to become a supervising paralegal within three years. Once you've set this as a goal, what are the shorter-term goals you will need to accomplish if you're to be a supervising paralegal? Just as we touched on in Chapter 1, state what you are willing to do to accomplish your overall goal:

"In order to become a supervising paralegal within three years, I am willing to. . . ."

When you fill in the blanks, you are setting your short-term goals. Your own responses will vary but could be something like this:

"In order to become a supervising paralegal within three years, I am willing to:

1. Take a class in human resources management within six months.

2. Join the local chapter of the paralegal association and attend any management classes they offer in the next three years.

3. Meet one new supervising paralegal every two months.

Part I ➤ Setting Goals: What Should You Expect from a Paralegal Career?

28

> 4. *Prepare a written report to my supervising attorney of what I have learned about managing paralegals each time I attend a class."*

Put each goal in writing and on your calendar. Each time a goal appears on your calendar, review it along with the rest of the goals you have set for yourself. For example, you are to take a human resources class within six months. When six months pass, review all of the above goals to make sure you are on track. This will also serve to reinforce those goals. The shorter-term goals (such as taking a human resources class) may need revision when they are periodically reviewed; the long-term goal (here, to be a supervising paralegal) normally will not change.

You can set reminders as you need to. If you want to take a human resources class within six months, you may want to put it on your calendar three months out to give yourself enough time to enroll and complete the course within six months. If you want to meet with a supervising paralegal every two months, you may need a reminder every month because you need to give the other person enough notice to ensure his or her availability. You will need to develop a system that keeps the time frame you have set on track. If you fail to develop such a system, your goals may languish. You tend to put your goals off, and fail to accomplish them altogether, when you do not have consistent prompting.

SETTING TIME FRAMES IS IMPORTANT

How far out should you set your goals? You should always have goals that are at least seven years into the future. My experience is that limiting yourself to goals you can achieve in less than seven years precludes you from setting goals that are high enough. In other words, there are goals that are worthwhile in your career that are unlikely to be accomplished in less time. A legal career is generally a long proposition. Some worthwhile goals take place only after years of planning. You normally can't all of a sudden decide you want to be president of the state paralegal association next month and expect that to happen. Paralegals take their jobs seriously and will want someone representing them who knows the profession intimately and has a large degree of credibility. This doesn't happen overnight. On the other hand, it seems silly to have as a goal to learn how to balance the firm's checkbook within 10 years; it doesn't take that long. *The timing of the goal depends on its nature.*

Refer again to the three goals you wrote down at the beginning of this book. Did you set time frames? A goal without a time frame is of little use. It might as well not exist. What are reasonable time frames for each goal you wrote down? You can see that goal setting in most instances requires information gathering. The source of that information depends on the goal in question. Sometimes you can gather the information independently; most of the time, it will help to have the advice of someone who is more knowledgeable than you. For example, before you set the goal of becoming a supervising paralegal, talk with those in the field to determine whether three years is realistic. My experience is that people overestimate the time it takes to accomplish a goal as often as they underestimate.

HOW HIGH SHOULD YOU SET THE BAR?

Armed with a painstaking self-assessment and the requirement of specificity, there are few, if any career goals you cannot accomplish. The process of experiencing the necessary self-assessment described earlier in this chapter, along with the necessity of making those goals specific enough to cause you to act in conformance, will naturally prevent you from setting any goals you are not capable of achieving. Knowing yourself well will cause you to set goals compatible with your own abilities and values. Having to make the goals specific will require you to assess whether the conduct in conformance with that goal is a price you are willing to pay.

Proper Application of Goal Setting Will Guide You

Here is an example of how the principles of goal setting contained in this book will assist in setting goals at the proper level for you.

You have determined by consulting with paralegals, educators, and loved ones and the results of an assessment test that you are somewhat introverted, like detailed work such as legal research, value stability in your job and your personal relationships, and need to feel that you are helping others. Would becoming supervising paralegal in a corporate law firm or corporate law department within a firm be a reasonable goal for you? Suppose you wanted to accomplish this goal within seven years?

Corporate law paralegals are highly respected and trained professionals, but most do not do a lot of legal research. They tend to prepare corporate documents, often under rigorous deadlines. They tend to work in large firms. The supervising paralegal in a corporate law department often speaks with groups of attorneys, paralegals, or other legal staff. He or she would also have to consider specifically how to reach your goal within seven years, which would involve, among other requirements, taking your personal time for extra training. Is becoming a supervising paralegal in a corporate law firm or department compatible with your self-assessment? Can you spot the inconsistencies between the person and the goal? They are rather obvious.

Now let's assume the same person has as a goal to be the chief investigating paralegal in the state attorney general's office within seven years. This job requires meeting with crime victims, among others, and preparing meticulous reports based on these interviews. Although this person interacts with others in the office, he or she does not supervise them. He or she normally has regular work hours. Can you see that this may be a better match?

Aim High in Setting Goals

Within the requirements that you set goals consistent with your self-assessment and specific enough to cause you to act in conformity with those goals, you should aim high. Most people are capable of accomplishing far more than they believe they can. They set their targets too low. Why? The root of the problem is low self-esteem, not lack of ability or desire to attain more in their career. They don't think they deserve to set lofty goals. In my experience as an attorney and currently as a paralegal educator, I have sometimes heard statements like these:

> *"I just want to find a job."*

> *"I'm okay just being a legal secretary."*

> *"I just want to get my paralegal degree."*

What's wrong with these statements? They reflect that the declarant is settling for less than what she or he would like. Take the word *just* (or anything similar) out of your goal-setting vocabulary. Using words like this indicates a defeatist attitude that will ensure you set your goals too low. (By the way, legal secretaries are wonderfully skilled professionals; the point of the statement is that the declarant is settling for a position that is not what she or he really wants.)

Low self-esteem is overcome in part by surrounding yourself with positive people who make you feel good about yourself. The inner circle of people who can help you achieve your goals referred to in the next chapter needs to include people of this type. Conversely, you should avoid pessimistic people like the plague when you are deciding career goals for yourself; they will attempt to confirm your erroneous misgivings about yourself. The process of self-assessment will often lead to greater self-esteem because you will realize you possess skills that are valuable and sought after. The axiom that "knowledge is power" is applicable here. Knowing more about what paralegals do, at the higher levels especially, will help you realize it isn't unrealistic for you to aspire to do at least as much with your own career. It may surprise you to learn that there are already people who look up to you and respect what you have accomplished.

CHAPTER SUMMARY

Your goals as a paralegal must be your own. The goals others have for you are not likely to be those that bring you job satisfaction, if you achieve them at all. Setting goals requires accurate self-assessment of your values and ability. If your current job is not consistent with your goals, consider the situation a temporary one and work extremely hard to find a job that matches the goals you have set for yourself. You deserve to enjoy your career. Your goals must be specific. Generalized goals do not cause the changes in behavior required to achieve success. Once you decide on specific goals, make a plan to achieve those goals. The plan also must be specific with realistic time frames. Have short-, medium-, and long-term goals. While goals must be realistic, remember that most people are capable of doing much more than they give themselves credit for. Do not sell yourself short.

> Web Research Exercise <

On the Internet, go to www.findlaw.com. Click the link to "Employment," then click "Professional Development Center," then click "Strategies for Self-Assessment." Once there, you will find articles and information about career self-assessment. Choose

Part I > Setting Goals: What Should You Expect from a Paralegal Career?

32

an article, and explain how it will assist you in assessing your own career objectives.

> Chapter Exercises <

1. In a small group of three to five, discuss the people and resources available to you to assist in an accurate assessment of your skills, aptitudes, interests, and values. A resource may be a web page, book, article, or any other nonhuman source of information. For each person or resource, discuss what information would be elicited. Make a master list of those sources your group considers to be helpful. Distribute a copy of that list to all your group members.

   If working individually instead of in a small group, write down every person and resource that comes to mind, as well as potential people and resources who can help you assess yourself. Then contact the potential people and view the potential resources to confirm whether they would be helpful. Create your own master list.

2. Follow up with the list from exercise 1. Contact at least one person on the list, and use at least two resources. On a separate piece of paper, describe in detail what you did, what information you obtained, and how that information assisted in your self-assessment. Then write a self-assessment based on the information you obtained.

3. Think about any job or jobs you have had in the past that you did not like. What was it that you did not like about each job? List specifically what you did not like about each job on a piece of paper. Next, consider every job you enjoyed, and list specifically what you liked about each such job. Does this comparison indicate any similarities in the jobs you did not like? Does this comparison indicate similarities in the jobs you enjoyed? What does this information tell you about what you will look for in your next job? What does this information tell you about yourself?

> Ethical Discussion <

Is it ethical to set career goals that are not in the best interest of a client, your supervising attorney, or your employer? Explain your response.

> Suggested Reading <

Louis H. Janda, *The Psychologist's Book of Self-Tests*, Perigree Publishers, 1996.

Chapter 3
Who Can Help You Achieve Your Goals?

Key Success Points

> No worthwhile achievement was accomplished alone.

> Establish an inner circle of professional relationships that will assist you in achieving your career goals.

> Establishing professional relationships is an ongoing process that should last your entire legal career.

> > > > > > > > >

YOU CAN'T ACHIEVE SUCCESS BY YOURSELF

Our culture admires independence. Popular movies showcase the hero as someone who takes on a host of problems alone, against all odds. Sports figures are promoted by the media as individuals rather than team members. This week's match-up isn't as much one team against another team as it is one superstar against another superstar. Many like to think the American West was settled by rugged individualists who braved the elements, disease, and hostility. One of our most admired presidents, Teddy Roosevelt, was practically synonymous with the notion of individual courage.

The problem is that we often admire individual moments of achievement in a vacuum. We see that great moment but forget about those behind the scenes who helped make the moment possible. The fact is that no worthwhile achievement was accomplished alone. So-called sports superstars have teammates, coaches, trainers, parents, and others who helped them rise to the top. President Roosevelt didn't charge up San Juan Hill by himself. The West was settled because many people worked together to accomplish that goal. The Wild West cowboy mentality is largely based on myth. As for movies involving action heroes, suffice it to say they are a great form of escapism for the most part.

You Did Not Accomplish Your Achievements Alone

Think about your own life. What are your achievements you consider most important? For each one, there will no doubt be others involved who made it possible. Someone taught you to ride a bike, solve an equation, complete a sentence, drive a car, and myriad other achievements that are important. Chances are that for each achievement in your life, there were multiple contributors to your success.

You are reading a book at this very moment about how to be successful as a paralegal. You have passed the stage in life where simply becoming a paralegal is something you aspire to. Now you want to be an accomplished paralegal. How did you reach the point where becoming an average paralegal was not enough? Who helped you develop an interest in the legal field and obtain the skill and confidence to know you could complete a paralegal program, and want to excel at your profession? No doubt you can name several people.

Since it is clear there were others who got you as far as you are today, it should be equally clear that you will need help from others to take you as far as you want to go in your career. I am referring to people

Part I ▸ Setting Goals: What Should You Expect from a Paralegal Career?

36

who can give you advice, information, and encouragement. This is your *inner circle*, and it consists of others whom you can consult when a career crisis or issue needs to be addressed or when a career opportunity opens up for you. These are the people who give you the tools to be successful; it's up to you whether and how to use those tools. You can share your private thoughts and concerns with those in your inner circle without fear of ridicule or retribution. They will give you constructive advice about how best to handle a particular situation and the moral support to know you are a capable legal professional who can handle any situation.

It is also important to recognize what your inner circle *is not*. I am not referring to people who will do your work or make your decisions for you. For example, your paralegal professors may have taught you what a cause of action is, how to use local court rules, and how to prepare a summons and complaint. However, only *you* can prepare that summons and complaint for your employer. Your professors helped you acquire the necessary tools, but you have to use the tools yourself. A colleague may have given you information about a certain job opportunity, but she will not be at the job interview with you. To return to the sports metaphor, the coach may have told the player how to execute a particular play, but he will not be the one who actually carries the ball.

Learning the Hard Way

Early in my career, I learned a hard lesson about the difference between someone assisting me in acquiring the tools for success and having to use those tools myself. One of the first cases I worked on after completing my education involved a horrendous accident in which several people were killed and many others were injured. The law firm in which I was employed represented one of the defendants; my supervising attorney felt this person was brought into the case on a very tenuous legal theory. The decision was made early in the case to bring a motion for summary judgment on our client's behalf. (A motion for summary judgment asserts that there are no substantial factual issues, and thus the judge can decide the case as a matter of law.)

I was assigned to prepare the motion for summary judgment. The supervising attorney, the senior partner in the firm and highly respected in the legal community, gave me instructions about how to approach this task. He explained the legal theories I should research, what I needed to be looking for while conducting my research, and some more mundane instructions, which didn't seem important at the time. These instructions concerned when and under what circumstances motions for summary judgment are appropriate and local rules that applied to these types of motions.

Because of the magnitude of the case, the client authorized me to spend many hours preparing the motion, and for several weeks, that was practically the only case I worked on. After I had produced several drafts, the motion was finally signed by the supervising attorney, filed, and a hearing date set. The motion consisted of nearly fifty pages of points and authorities. (In the points and authorities section of a motion, parties argue their positions, citing legal authority that they believe will persuade the court.) This was a big case, and I was proud of my work.

When the hearing date arrived, I went with my supervising attorney to the courthouse. He would argue the motion, and I would be there for any assistance he needed. "Assistance" at that point in my career meant carrying heavy objects, opening doors, and having certain items of evidence ready to hand the supervising attorney, all of which I was thrilled to do.

We sat in the courtroom waiting for our case to be called. Finally, the case was called, and fifteen or twenty attorneys all stood and stated their appearances, that is, they stated their names and the names of the parties they represent. My supervising attorney, sensing my nervousness, stated his and my appearances for both of us.

What I wanted to hear the judge say was what an excellent motion we had filed. What I heard instead was a reference to local rules. My heart sank. The first words out of the judge's mouth were whether we have reviewed the local rules. The judge dutifully pointed out that under local rules, any points and authorities exceeding ten pages needed a table of contents and table of authorities. I had included neither. Under the circumstances, the judge had no choice but to consider only the first ten pages of our argument and, on that basis, deny the motion. Due to the magnitude of the case, the first ten pages of my points and authorities contained nothing but the factual and procedural background of the case.

It was a long ride back to the office. I never made the mistake of failing to consult the local rules before filing a motion again. As you might imagine, the students in my civil procedure class are required to know federal, state, and local rules.

What is the point of my story? My supervising attorney had given me the tools to write a successful motion. He had specifically made reference to the local rules, but I did not use that particular tool.

Part I > Setting Goals: What Should You Expect from a Paralegal Career?

38

Certainly you need the assistance of others to achieve success, but it doesn't matter if you have the world's best group of advisers if you don't use that advice to your advantage. You can't achieve success as a paralegal by yourself, but the assistance of others is not a substitute for your own industriousness. Still, if you have the right people helping you (your inner circle) and resolve to take full advantage of their assistance, there is no reason you can't accomplish the goals you have established for yourself.

> Paralegal Perspective <

Who can help you achieve your goals? I suggest shadowing an attorney or senior paralegal in your office who likes to teach and mentor. They can usually give you real-world examples and tips to help you be successful.

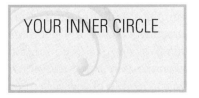

YOUR INNER CIRCLE

Your inner circle consists of individuals with knowledge or expertise in areas useful to you whom you can call on when you need assistance in your career. You know them well enough to disclose problems and concerns to them on a confidential basis. And they know you well enough to be open and candid about their advice. They will not always tell you what you'd like to hear. Yet although they will not sugarcoat their advice, they are positive in outlook. If you are new to a job, they are not likely to be anyone with whom you work. Finally, they are people you are willing to assist if needed; *you* may be a member of *their* inner circle. The group's size will likely be relatively small—around four to five members.

Tailor Your Inner Circle to Your Abilities and Goals

The fact that you can call on others for assistance with your career means they have knowledge that is useful to you and willing to share it. What knowledge would be useful? The tendency is to say "everything" when you are new to a career. There will be areas in which you know you need extra attention. And remember that everyone experiences feelings of self-doubt because they think they should know more about a certain part of their job than they do. This self-doubt is perfectly normal.

If you feel weak in technology, for example, at least one member of your inner circle should have superior knowledge in that area. If you feel you need to be better at legal research, there needs to be at least one member who can help you in that area. Perhaps you feel your weakness is not so much of a technical nature but in how to relate well to others in a law firm. For lack of a better term, your inner circle should include someone who knows about law office etiquette. Remember that what may seem obvious and even easy for someone with more experience may be difficult for you when you're just starting a new legal position. That's why members of your inner circle are those you need to feel comfortable with letting your guard down. You don't have to worry about asking what you think would be a stupid question. You also feel confident that any misgivings you have about your own ability are not for public consumption.

Here is an example of what I'm referring to. One of my former students now works as a paralegal in a business litigation law firm. From time to time she contacts me to ask about a task she is working on. Once she sent a frantic e-mail asking if I knew anything about an abstractive judgment. She had just been asked to prepare one by her supervising attorney but she could not find this term anywhere in her legal research. In fact, what she meant was an "abstract of judgment," which is a summary of the most important terms of a judgment that might be filed with a local or state agency to make it a public record. I was able to help her. I am a member of her inner circle.

Should she have been able to ask her supervising attorney the same thing she asked me without feeling defensive? Sure, but the fact is that we all have doubts about ourselves in a new position that we would rather our new employer not know about. That's why I recommend against anyone you work with being a member of your inner circle. My former student reciprocates by her willingness to speak to my current students about her experiences as a first-year paralegal, something that students are always very interested in.

Since you should be able to disclose your concerns confidentially and without fear of undue criticism, members of your inner circle are usually not someone you recently met. This is a relationship that needs trust. This means that you begin developing these relationships now. If you have undergone the meaningful assessment of yourself referred to earlier in this book, you have a good idea of your strengths and weaknesses already.

Sources of Inner Circle Members

Your professors and fellow classmates are excellent prospects for inclusion. The type of relationship that needs to be developed normally doesn't occur simply by going to class. You need to become actively involved in your paralegal program. If your campus has a paralegal association, that is a great way to become involved. If a professor provides an opportunity to become more involved, take advantage of it.

I often ask one or two students to help others in my legal research and writing course. These students who help gain expertise as they assist other students in understanding a particular aspect of legal research. These student volunteers also can tell potential employers they helped in the class, leaving the clear impression that they have superior knowledge in legal research. Also, by working closely with a professor, they are more likely to develop the kind of relationship well suited for the inner circle. This is the classic win-win situation. Every campus has a multitude of opportunities to become more involved and, in the process, establish important relationships.

Keep in mind there are reasons to be involved that have nothing to do with your career. It is important in any profession, perhaps the legal profession in particular, to use your knowledge and ability to help others regardless of personal gain. And you'll find that in the process of doing the right thing, a wonderful by-product is meeting and getting to know those who are more than willing to help you in your career.

When I was in law school, my constitutional law professor asked for students to help her do legal research for a law journal article she was writing. I was not sure I wanted to take on more work (the first year of law school is very busy without taking on extra duties), and I wasn't sure about this particular law professor, who had seemed a bit stern and unapproachable. Nevertheless, I was interested in constitutional law and wanted to learn more, so I stopped by her office after class and volunteered. Helping her was a lot of work, and some of it was mundane, like checking legal citations for accuracy, but it was well worth the effort. Later that year, she hired me to be her paid legal research assistant.

Since 1987, when we first worked together, she has become one of the premier constitutional law experts in the country, writing books and speaking to groups regularly. She has continued to give me advice whenever I ask, especially since I gave up the full-time practice of law to become a paralegal educator. In fact, when I began to contemplate leaving my law practice to teach in a paralegal program, she gave me valuable insight and wrote a letter of support to the hiring committee that eventually offered me a full-time teaching position.

Many campuses today have service-learning opportunities: students gain college credit by volunteering their time to those less fortunate. I am fortunate to work with a paralegal educator who has championed this cause where I teach and by speaking to national paralegal organizations. In the paralegal program where I teach, it means volunteering time to causes with a legal component, such as those that give legal assistance to abused women. What better way to establish a great relationship? There are attorneys and paralegals who work in organizations like these, and most make it their job to know what is going on in the legal community. You'll find it's relatively easy to discover opportunities that have a good chance of building on your inner circle if you make the effort.

There are off-campus opportunities to lay the groundwork for the inner circle too. Local, state, and national paralegal associations abound, and many of these associations have student memberships. There are numerous ways to become involved in these associations. Attending meetings is one way to begin the process of becoming involved and, in the process, meeting people who can help you. I have found that closer professional relationships usually take more than attending meetings, however. You should become involved with a project or an event sponsored by a paralegal association—perhaps helping a presenter put on a class, offering to review the association's by-laws that need updating, or assisting in planning an association lunch. Working closely with those who are considered leaders in the paralegal profession puts you into contact with those who are likely to have knowledge that you can benefit from.

When I helped the state paralegal association plan its annual conference on the campus where I teach, I asked for students who were interested to help. The students who volunteered worked closely with officers of the state association, met many of the course presenters (all attorneys or paralegals), and attended the conference for free. Several of them who have since graduated, have maintained relationships they had established from working on the conference. I suspect many of those relationships formed the basis for inclusion in the former students' (now new paralegals') inner circle. Yet when I asked for student volunteers, only five students took advantage of this opportunity. Is it any wonder so many students graduate and have hardly any professional relationships that can assist them in their careers? Don't be one of them.

A former student of mine was very interested in alternative dispute resolution (ADR) and wanted to work in a firm that did this work. When I saw a brochure promoting a class for paralegals in ADR, I told

Part I > Setting Goals: What Should You Expect from a Paralegal Career?

42

him to contact the presenters and offer to help. This student was surprised to learn that the presenters gladly accepted his offer. When he took a paralegal position with a local firm that does a lot of ADR, there is no doubt that his experience with and connection to the ADR course helped win over the employer. The student has since informed me that he keeps in touch with one of the ADR course presenters. My point is that opportunities to establish relationships with those who can help you with your legal career abound. Some of these relationships ultimately become inner circle relationships, but all have the potential to be worthwhile.

Regardless of your strengths or weaknesses, one member of your inner circle should be someone who is well connected in the legal community. These people tend to be heavily involved in a paralegal association or have been in the profession so long that they know many others in the profession. When there is a job about to open up, they know about it early because they had lunch with someone in the firm where the opening is about to be made public. When this person writes a letter of recommendation on your behalf, it carries a lot of weight with a prospective employer because of the reputation of the letter writer. These also tend to be the people who keep up with the latest trends in the profession, such as emerging or declining specialties, new legal software, upcoming changes in continuing-education requirements, and other useful career news.

How do you find someone like this? First, remember that meaningful relationships do not grow overnight, so you should not delay laying the groundwork. Leaders of paralegal organizations can be very effective inner circle members. Find out what committees they serve on, and if you have a genuine interest, ask to be a member of that committee. Notwithstanding that it may be disingenuous to volunteer for a committee purely for personal gain, chances are you will appear disinterested and make the wrong impression if you really don't care much for the committee members or its purpose. However, there are a multitude of opportunities for people with widely varying interests, and you should be able to find one well suited for you. Once you are involved in something you truly care about, your enthusiasm and ability should make the experience enjoyable and put you into contact with the well-connected person who can help.

I am a friend of the former president of the local bar association where I practiced full time before becoming an educator. I served on the board of directors of the association while Jerry was the president. Jerry is one of the most respected attorneys in the legal community. He knows all the local judges on a first-name basis and many of the officers at the state bar association and his reputation for honest and ethical behavior is well known. Jerry and I became friends not because we attended bar meetings, but because we worked on various projects together, including one that assessed the status of professionalism among local attorneys. I didn't set out to make Jerry part of my inner circle; it just worked out that way. I set out to do something I enjoyed and cared about—professionalism in the legal community—and it turned out that Jerry cared at least as much about the same subject. There have been many occasions where I have asked Jerry for career advice, and he has responded generously.

Inner Circle Members Must Be Positive People

Those in your inner circle should have a positive yet realistic outlook on life. The glass is always half-full to these people rather than half-empty. They look to the future and see more opportunities than pitfalls. They tend to be comfortable with themselves, yet motivated to improve regardless of their stage in career and life. They are not necessarily outgoing. (Indeed, I have found many outgoing people are compensating for insecurities about themselves.) These are the people who will focus on how to tackle the problem rather than give up. They view problems as opportunities to learn and grow rather than as preludes to failure.

The reason that members of your group should be positive in outlook is that most problems in your career can be overcome with a positive attitude. Of course, a positive attitude without effort is useless, but without a positive attitude, the effort required usually does not follow. In fact, a negative attitude often magnifies a problem such that it takes on a life of its own, far in excess of the problem itself. That does not mean the problem is illusory or should not be taken seriously. However, most of us tend to make problems worse than they really are. It's at those times that a trusted member of your inner circle can help you put the problem in its proper perspective.

Let's return to the example of the motion I prepared without following the local rules. After that experience many thoughts passed through my mind, all of them negative. Did I have what it took to be successful in the legal profession? Was my job in jeopardy? Would my coworkers laugh at me? At the moment, I didn't need someone to tell me the negative aspects of what I had done. Nor would I be helped by someone telling me "not to worry" and "everything will be all right." That kind of false optimism can do as much harm as good. What I needed was someone to put the issue into its proper perspective and keep me from the kind of self-destructive thoughts that could lead to equally self-destructive behavior.

I called my best friend from law school. Dave and I had been study partners in school, and we had often worked together to prepare for exams. I explained to him what had happened, and he agreed that I had made a serious mistake by not following the local rules, especially for such an important case. It would be unrealistic and dishonest to conclude otherwise, Dave said. But then he shared with me that he had made a similar mistake when he first entered the legal field. This mistake had nothing to do with failing to include a table of contents, but it was similar enough that I could appreciate the relevance of his experience. Dave said he hadn't lost his job, the mistake was correctable, and he has since had wonderful job reviews from his employer. He also never made the same mistake again.

Dave's advice was positive yet realistic. He didn't sugarcoat the problem; he admitted it was serious. He didn't gratuitously or condescendingly tell me everything would be okay without any basis to make that conclusion. His optimism about the situation was grounded in experience instead of false hope. He helped me put my problem in perspective by reminding me the problem was correctable (the motion could be refiled) and was not career threatening (provided I learned from it rather than repeat it). He didn't pour fuel on the fire of self-doubt by reminding me of what a lousy job I had done.

Do you see why it's important to have people in your inner circle who are positive yet realistic? Most of us are very good at focusing on the negative when a career problem arises, especially when the career is relatively new. Problems that arise or mistakes that we make in a new profession often cause our insecurities to come to the surface, and those around us tend to reflect our negativism rather than offer constructive solutions, even with the best of intentions. If those people are not reflecting our negativism, they are usually giving us false optimism—hoping to make us feel better (or perhaps hoping we'll bother someone else with our problems).

The fact is that there are no career problems or issues without solutions, but sometimes it helps to be reminded of this by those whose advice you especially respect. I do not mean to imply you shouldn't maintain personal and business relationships with those who may not be so positive in outlook. I know and appreciate people with decidedly negative attitudes but who have other qualities I admire. You simply do not want people like this in your inner circle giving you what is supposed to be constructive advice about your career.

What if you happen to be positive yourself? Do you need some "half-empty" types in your inner circle to complement your outlook on life? The answer is no. A career problem is much more likely to be alleviated with a positive approach. Having negative people as close advisers will almost assuredly cause you to do one of two things. First, if you follow the advice, you will be taking an approach that *creates* more problems. For example, if someone had agreed with me when I didn't follow local rules in preparing a motion that my job was likely to be in jeopardy, I might have left the law firm. What would I do at the new firm when a problem arose? Leave? What would my spotty work record suggest to potential employers? Second, you may choose to discount or ignore the advice from a "half-empty" type because it differs so drastically with how you would approach the problem. What use is it to have an inner circle member whose advice you're not willing to seriously consider?

If you have a positive approach to problems that invariably arise in your career, having positive but realistic people in your inner circle will help you determine if your outlook is based in reality or based on false assumptions about the problem or about yourself. In the example involving local rules, if I had brushed aside the situation as a rookie mistake, I would likely have repeated the mistake because I undervalued its seriousness. One mistake like this will normally not be career threatening, but multiple mistakes of the same type are another story altogether. My inner circle member Dave reminded me that the mistake was a serious matter.

Don't Let Pride Stand in Your Way

When developing an inner circle, don't allow pride exclude someone who otherwise has the qualities that are helpful. Although members of your inner circle will tend to have more experience and training than you do, it won't necessarily always be the case. There may be someone who possesses special knowledge or experience that is of use to you but who is younger, possesses less formal education than you, or has worked in the legal world a short period of time. This person could be a classmate of yours, just as Dave was a classmate of mine. The goals you have set for yourself will be difficult to achieve if you exclude those who can help out of your own pride or even jealousy.

One of my inner circle members, also a friend, was an employee of mine before I left my law partnership to teach. I trained Bill when he came to work for the firm soon after graduating from law school, and he has since left the firm to start his own successful law firm. I have asked Bill on a number of occasions for his advice about how best to teach a certain legal topic. When I began my education career, it necessarily meant I could not practice law full time. Although I had handled many cases prior to becoming an educator, I knew that Bill would be in a better position to stay current with certain law firm practices I wanted my students to know. For example, Bill is in a better position to know how long cases are "trailing" before going to trial. (A case "trails" when a courtroom isn't available on the date set for trial and the litigants are in stand-by mode expecting a courtroom to be available shortly.) I haven't tried a case recently, so I'm not current on average trailing periods, but Bill is at the courthouse frequently. On one occasion, Bill spoke to my Introduction to Law class about estate planning because, despite my being his senior in age and overall legal experience, he has done more estate work than I have. I am not envious or jealous of Bill's success. I am proud of it and glad to have Bill in my inner circle.

How is it that Bill is always willing to help me despite having a busy law practice? He has on a number of occasions told me how grateful he is that I accommodated him when he was a new attorney and learned he had cancer. He was new on the job, and his medical condition required that he miss quite a few days of work. Bill has told me that my law partners and I never once implied that we were annoyed or even inconvenienced with his situation. We wanted Bill to work through his medical condition because we valued him as a person and as an employee. I think Bill overstated our generosity; good employees are hard to find. When Bill eventually told us he had to leave the firm to seek treatment in a different state, we offered to employ him when the treatment was completed. Bill recovered, then decided to start a law practice with his brother in his new state. As fate would seem to have it, Bill's law practice is within a half-hour from the college where I now teach.

If you're asking yourself how you can possibly establish an inner circle of people who are willing to listen to your most private problems and concerns and go out of their way to help you, it is important to set out to do what is right first. Giving of yourself to important causes or helping those who need your help should be reward enough. However, the incidental benefit of establishing important relationships is often a wonderful by-product.

> Paralegal Perspective <

Networking was the most important part of finding a paralegal job, and although I was transferring skills from health care to legal, I needed every contact I could get.

BEYOND THE INNER CIRCLE: OTHERS WHO CAN HELP

In any career, you will find people who generously offer to help you when you find yourself in a difficult situation. When you consider those who have helped you get this far in your career, your list no doubt includes people from all walks of life. The great majority of these people are not inner circle members but offered help at a critical time. Perhaps a teacher helped you recognize your true ability for legal work, or a classmate showed you how to format a pleading, or the librarian showed you how to do legal research. The strength of the relationship may be such that these individuals have not become part of your inner circle, but it would have been very difficult to make it this far without their help. If you haven't adequately shown your appreciation to them, now is a good time. It's important to get into the habit of saying "thank you." You'd be surprised how something as simple as this increases the amount of help others are willing to give.

Although it may be fairly easy to determine who has helped you thus far, it may be more difficult to determine who can help you in the future, especially if you're new in the legal profession. The following list isn't intended to be exhaustive, but it does identify those who are most likely to help you achieve your career goals. Remember that if you take the attitude that *you* will help those in need, you are much more likely to come into contact with those who will do the same for you.

Coworkers

I have yet to be employed at a place where at least one coworker didn't go out of his or her way to help me be successful. My first legal job was working as a clerk in a private law firm. One of the legal secretaries there showed me the "forms files" after my supervising attorney gave me the assignment to prepare a motion to dismiss. I barely knew what a motion was, let alone what it was supposed to look like. When I dictated the motion (in those days, most attorneys did not use word processors), she would make helpful suggestions based on motions attorneys in the office had previously dictated. The result was an end product that didn't look nearly as poor as my level of expertise at the time may have warranted.

When I took my first job as an attorney, another young associate offered his help consistently. Although he was extremely busy and in theory was competing with me to advance in the firm, he never failed to

Part I > Setting Goals: What Should You Expect from a Paralegal Career?

48

take the time to answer a question. He was technically my senior—he had been with the firm for about a year before I came along—but never acted in a condescending manner toward me. He proofread several of my assignments and offered helpful comments without anyone else's knowledge. He readily shared his experiences in the firm and made my first year of law practice a much better time than it otherwise would have been.

There have been numerous other acts of kindness by fellow workers. I have learned several lessons from this experience. First, help can come from any level. Don't assume that someone with less formal education or training can't be helpful. The help I received from a secretary in my first law clerk position was invaluable because she knew much more about preparing motions than I did. Second, it's important to realize at the beginning of your legal career how much you have yet to learn. Although you have learned a lot already, the legal profession will require that you continue to learn the rest of your career. Don't assume that you couldn't benefit from help even when you think you know what you're doing. It's important to be humble. If you have a humble attitude, your coworkers will be much more likely to offer their assistance. Third, it is important to offer help to your coworkers when they need it. Don't assume that because you are new, you have nothing to offer in the way of assistance to your more experienced coworkers. Don't offer to help with only the more glamorous assignments. If the copier needs more paper and the secretary is in the middle of a rush job, offer to load the paper. The offer to help signals that you are a team player. Employees have been known to become suddenly too busy to help when they perceive a new employee is in the career game only for himself or herself.

Don't convey the attitude that you have enough time only to help someone whose help you may also need sometime. That kind of self-centeredness will invariably trickle down to those who are in a position to help, with adverse consequences. Also, your assumptions about who is in a position to help you may be incorrect. You cannot possibly foresee the problems you will have in the future and whose assistance would be helpful. In this regard, do not discount *anyone's* ability to help you in the future. I have befriended the janitor in my office building. When someone spilled a soft drink on my carpet, the carpet was given immediate attention, even though that kind of service doesn't usually occur quickly. If you'll simply be the kind of person who genuinely takes an interest in others, no matter who they are, you'll find people are always there to help you out of a bind.

Current and Former College Professors

Sometimes professors become part of your inner circle; often they do not. However, nearly all professors have the ability and inclination to help you substantially in your career. Most of these people chose their professions because they have a sincere belief in service to others. They find meaning and satisfaction in sharing what they know with any student who can benefit from their knowledge. It is part of their job duties to be current in both the law and the paralegal profession. In paralegal school, you have probably noticed that most of your professors have practical legal experience. They also maintain valuable contacts in the legal community. Especially early in your legal career, they will be among your most important career relationships. I strongly recommend that you get to know all the professors in your paralegal program, even those whose classes you have not yet taken. Students who have not yet taken a class of mine sometimes make a point of introducing themselves to me, often with a request for some kind of assistance, such as looking over a resumé or asking career advice. I have yet to turn such a student down and know that is the attitude almost every other professor takes. Don't hesitate to ask for help even if you don't know the professor well or even if you have already completed the paralegal program and are new to the job.

Although most professors are generous with their time, it would be a mistake to assume that this means their time isn't valuable to them. Professors have a lot of other things they could be doing and will appreciate it if you recognize this. The best approach is to make an appointment and let the professor know before you come in what it is you would like to discuss. This way the professor will be prepared to help you when you do meet, and it is less likely the meeting will be interrupted by a phone call or conflicting commitment.

Don't exclude any professor or ex-professor who is in a position to help. I have even received help from a professor I didn't even know. A long-term career goal of mine was to write a book that I thought could benefit others. Prior to beginning the book, I contacted a professor where I had attended law school. I did not know him, but I knew he had written several legal books. The information he gave me, freely and without condition, proved invaluable. He said he is "always happy to see our grads do well."

Court Personnel

Courthouses are interesting places. People from every walk of life pass through them, often hoping a legal problem they have will be resolved

Part I > Setting Goals: What Should You Expect from a Paralegal Career?

50

there. Besides the parties themselves, courthouses are filled with attorneys, paralegals, and legal administrative staff. Who is in the best position to know what these people are up to? Those who are employed by the courts. Clerks, bailiffs, and research assistants often can give you invaluable information that you can't come by anywhere else. Which firm just received a large verdict and may want to hire more staff? What judge needs to hire another employee? What computer software did a particular firm use in presenting its case that was especially effective? What does a particular judge like or dislike when preparing exhibits for trial? Does a judge like to receive a courtesy copy of motions filed in her department? How has the opposing attorney fared in this court or before this particular judge? Answers to these questions can be extremely valuable. The court's legal staff often has answers to these questions and many more. Contrary to popular belief, court legal staff are usually willing to help you when you ask. I recall several occasions when my secretary called the clerk's office, letting the clerk know we would be filing a brief just minutes before the court closed that day and received the assurance that the clerk would be there to accept our filing. Take every opportunity that presents itself to establish a relationship with court legal staff.

Incidental Legal Profession Members

Incidental legal profession members are people who have functions indirectly related to the legal profession, such as court reporters, private investigators, legal photocopiers, expert witnesses, insurance adjusters, law enforcement personnel, bar association employees, paralegal association employees, law library personnel, and law office administrators. These are not people who handle legal cases of the type you will have in a law office, but they are frequently an integral part of the handling of such cases. I know at least one person in each of the professions mentioned who can give assistance and advice when needed, usually limited to their own job functions. The great aspect of these relationships is that you often establish them in the course of your job in a law office. For example, if you work in a litigation law firm, you will come into contact with investigators, court reporters, and expert witnesses simply in the course of working on cases in your office. If you do legal research, you will likely come into contact with law library personnel at some point. Many law firms send their paralegals to continuing education, where you could come into contact with bar or paralegal association personnel. Where your job doesn't naturally bring you into contact with someone with a legally related job, make the effort to establish such a contact. Your inner circle members are excellent sources of information. Ask someone in your inner circle to introduce you to a county law librarian, for example. When your supervising attorney sends you to the law library to conduct research, it's nice to know someone on the staff who can give you assistance above and beyond the call of duty when necessary.

People Unrelated to the Legal Profession

It would be a mistake to assume the only people who can help you achieve your career goals are those who are in occupations at least indirectly related to the legal profession. Usually, those with at least some relationship to the legal profession are in the best position to help, but that is not necessarily always the case. For example, there have been occasions when a friend who works for a local elected leader has told me that certain agencies may be hiring paralegals—useful information for my students and available to anyone who asks. The fact that my friend knows I have a personal interest in this information has prompted her to volunteer it even when I don't ask. She would do the same for anyone else she knew had use for this information, but the fact is that hardly anyone makes these kinds of requests known to her.

When these contacts cannot directly help, they can often introduce you to someone who can. I know a local businessperson who knows absolutely nothing about the legal profession. If I didn't know better, I wouldn't think he could help someone in the legal profession. However, he has had an ongoing relationship with a midsized law firm for many years as his business has grown. Do you think his attorney might help me if my friend asked? Although I have yet to ask my friend for any assistance, our relationship is such that I could if the occasion arose.

> **ESTABLISHING PROFESSIONAL RELATIONSHIPS IS AN ONGOING PROCESS**

Your best relationships normally do not occur accidentally. If you want to become a paralegal manager, for example, you no doubt will want to know someone in that field. Although you could hope to meet a paralegal manager by accident, the chances of that occurring are slim. The chances increase exponentially if you join a paralegal manager association, volunteer to help with a paralegal manager association event, or call a

Part I > Setting Goals: What Should You Expect from a Paralegal Career?

52

paralegal manager and ask for some of that person's time to discuss career options.

CHAPTER SUMMARY

Although your goals must be your own, you cannot achieve them by yourself. Develop an inner circle of professional relationships. Your inner circle should be composed of people you can trust and whose members complement your weak areas. Begin forming your inner circle now, and remember that this is an ongoing process. Professional organizations offer abundant opportunities for involvement and may lead to relationships with people who can assist you both inside and outside your inner circle. These relationships must be reciprocal and genuine in order for them to last. In other words, form relationships and get involved in activities because of a true desire to help others.

> Web Research Exercise <

Go to www.quintcareers.com. At this Web page, you will find numerous articles that can assist you in your career. Search for articles related to networking. What information were you able to find? Be prepared to discuss your findings with classmates.

> Chapter Exercises <

1. Make a list of your inner circle members. For each person on your list, write the following on a sheet of paper:
   a. The knowledge or expertise that person possesses that can help you achieve your career goals.
   b. How you established this relationship. In other words, how did you meet this person? How did your relationship develop to the point where this person became an inner circle member?
   c. What have you done in the past six months to maintain this relationship?

2. With the list you made in exercise 1, ask yourself the following questions and write down your responses:
   a. Is my list complete? If not, what type of relationship is lacking?

    b. What was my most effective method of establishing a relationship for inclusion in my inner circle?

    c. Have I done enough in the past six months to maintain the relationships I have established? If not, what can I do now to ensure that each relationship is maintained, or strengthened if necessary? Make a timetable for completion of each action, and put it on your calendar.

3. If you determined from exercise 2a that your inner circle is lacking a certain type of relationship, ask yourself the following questions, and write down your responses:

    a. Who can help complete my inner circle? For each such person, what can I do now to begin to establish a relationship that will lead to inclusion of that person in my inner circle? Make a timetable for completion of each action, and put it on your calendar.

    b. After determining those you currently know who could fill any relationship lacking in your inner circle, is your list still lacking? If so, make a list of persons you do not yet know, with whom you could establish a relationship for eventual inclusion in your inner circle. (If you do not know the person's name, describe the type of person, such as "a graduate from my paralegal program with at least five years of experience.") For each such person, ask yourself what you can do now to begin to establish an inner circle relationship. Make a timetable for completion of each action, and put it on your calendar.

    c. Who do I know now (or who would I like to know) who can help me achieve my career objectives but is not likely to become a member of my inner circle? For each person, write down the name of the person and the nature of the assistance he or she might be able to render. What can you do now to enlist each person's assistance? Make a timetable for completion of each action and put it on your calendar.

4. Establishing professional relationships is an ongoing process. Write down the activities you are involved with now that will result in opportunities to meet those in a position to assist you in achieving your career goals. "Activity" refers to organizations to which you belong, volunteer work you may be doing, an internship, a job, or anything else of an ongoing nature that puts you into contact with those who are in a position to assist you in obtaining your career goals. Remember that not all relationships need result in inner circle membership. For each activity listed, write your responses to the following questions:

    a. Who have you met as a result of each activity that can assist you in achieving your career goals? For each such person, describe the type of assistance that person could render and what you can do now to

Part I > Setting Goals: What Should You Expect from a Paralegal Career?

54

      establish or strengthen a relationship with that person. Make a timetable for completion of each action, and put it on your calendar.

  b. Who would you like to meet in relation to each of your current activities? For each person listed, describe the type of assistance that person could render, the best way to meet that person, and what you can do now to establish a relationship with that person. Make a timetable for completion of each action, and put it on your calendar.

5. If your responses to exercise 4 do not put you into contact with a sufficient number of persons who could assist you in achieving your career goals, what activities could you become involved with now that would place you in such a position? Remember that it is far more effective to become involved with activities in which you have a sincere interest than to participate solely because you want to meet the "right" people. For each such activity listed, write your responses to the following questions:

  a. Do I have a genuine interest in this activity, or am I interested in it simply because I want to establish professional contacts? If your motives are the latter, strike the activity from your list.

  b. Is the activity one in which I will have the opportunity to come into contact with those who are able to assist me in achieving my career goals? If the answer is no, strike the activity from your list;

  c. For each remaining activity on your list, what specifically can you do now to become involved in the activity and, once involved, be in a position to establish professional relationships that will assist in achieving your career goals? Make a timetable for completion of each action, and put it on your calendar.

> Ethical Discussion <

Is it ever justified to compromise your ethical obligations as a paralegal in order to achieve your goals? How would you handle a situation in which your employer asked you to do something unethical but relatively inconsequential? How would you handle a situation in which your employer asked you to do something you consider a substantial ethical violation? Would it make a difference to you whether the ethical violation was inconsequential? Would you ever accept a paralegal position with an employer whose ethical standards are in doubt? Explain your responses.

≫ Suggested Reading ≪

Alan Gelb and Karen Levine, *A Survival Guide for Paralegals: Tips from the Trenches*, Delmar Learning, 2003.

Chapter 4
What Is Possible in the Paralegal Profession?

> ### Key Success Points
>
> > *Practicing financial discipline will give you more career options.*
> > *Compensation must be consistent with your personal and professional goals.*
> > *Careers advance both vertically and horizontally.*

> > > > > > > > >

"Worked herself to death.
What a great paralegal!"

HOW DO I EVALUATE SALARY AND BENEFITS?

A new career as a paralegal is an exciting prospect. Few other occupations have such enormous potential for challenge, variety, and personal satisfaction. The law is always changing, and the situations that clients find themselves in when they need legal assistance are interesting. It can be very gratifying to help those who have legal problems. Your coworkers and former classmates are a constant source of new ideas and great stories. Volunteering your time and expertise to professional and social service organizations offers an irreplaceable method of meeting those who share common ideas and ideals. When you're new to the profession, just setting foot in a law office or seeing your name on the firm's business letterhead is a thrill.

Nevertheless, there comes a time when the excitement of a new career must be tempered with practical decisions about the salary you must have in order to live the life you have chosen for yourself. Finding information about paralegal salary and benefits is relatively easy. The paralegal profession in particular has been extremely good at providing salary and benefit information to its members. Many paralegal programs conduct postgraduation surveys, which often provide information about salary and benefits. Employers increasingly disclose salary ranges in their job announcements in order to avoid receiving applications from those who have different salary expectations.

The real challenge with respect to salary is determining the appropriate amount for you. Although you can and should consult others about what is appropriate in terms of the salary you should seek, the final decision is one only you can make. This is a highly personal decision that speaks volumes about your own values; it is a reflection about what you consider important in your career and your life. This decision will necessarily preclude you from some jobs. It will have a drastic effect on your personal life; time spent at the office means time away from other pursuits. In determining the appropriate salary for you, there are a number of factors to consider: minimum salary requirements; the true price of a salary; salary structure versus starting salary; the whole package; lies, darn lies, and statistics; and the role money should play in decision making.

Minimum Salary Requirements

This is the most basic decision: It is the salary parameter below which you should not fall. Most of us have expenses that need to be paid. The

Part I > Setting Goals: What Should You Expect from a Paralegal Career?

58

total amount of your expenses tells you which jobs will not work for you regardless of your desire to have a particular job. You should consider the expense of a vacation and entertainment in the equation. Your career is a long-term prospect, and you must have time to recharge occasionally. It is also important to consider savings an expense—but one you pay yourself. Opinions vary, but in no event should you should have less than three months' expenses saved up for those inevitable rainy days. If you don't have a sufficient rainy day fund, you should budget to create one as soon as reasonably possible, preferably within a year and two years at the most. You should also try to project your future expenses. For example, will that car with 100,000 miles need to be replaced in the foreseeable future? Are there medical or dental expenses that will come due for yourself or a loved one? Do you have debts such as student loans to pay?

Take the time to add up all of your current expenses plus all of the future expenses you can reasonably expect, and then add 15 percent. Why add 15 percent? It is likely that in adding your current and future expenses, you left certain minor expenses out or minimized those expenses you included. Also, income taxes must be paid from the income you receive from any paralegal position. Since we're discussing your minimum salary requirements, there is little room for error. Keep in mind that individual financial situations vary. For example, your situation may be such that you pay more income taxes than the average new paralegal.

If your expenses are minimal you have more options. Therefore, if your current and projected expenses, plus 15 percent, are $25,000 annually, for example, you can at least consider a job with a starting salary of $25,000 a year. If your total expenses exceed $25,000, then you need not bother considering a job with that level of salary. Doing this calculation will allow you to eliminate consideration of some jobs that otherwise would be of interest. Lest you worry, the average paralegal salary far exceeds $25,000 and the figures in my example are for illustrative purposes only. Nevertheless, in every occupation there are some jobs that pay less than average for that profession but offer intangible rewards that make the job appealing to some. My point is that avoiding the "buy now, pay later" lifestyle will allow you to consider certain jobs that you otherwise could not. Furthermore, no matter how appealing you find a particular job, it is not a realistic option if you do not earn enough to pay your basic expenses.

Why, you might ask, would anyone even consider a job whose salary doesn't substantially exceed expenses? First of all, I am not necessarily referring to jobs that one would consider low paying. Your expenses may be at such a level that you have to eliminate jobs that pay fairly well to start. For example, in my law practice, I once hired a new associate starting at an average salary for a recent law school graduate at the time. After about two months, Allen came into my office and asked if he could close the door. He then told me that he and his wife were having a hard time financially: It turned out that they had student loans with a combined monthly payment of $3,000, each had a car payment and they had credit card debt, mostly from an expensive wedding and honeymoon trip to Europe. Allen's total debt expenses, along with his wife's, exceeded $5,000 monthly. This did not include the more routine bills that most people have, such as rent, food, and clothing. It is extremely important to refrain from spending a salary you expect to have later but may not materialize. This is true for every stage of your career. Practicing financial discipline will give you more career options.

Allen's situation is not unusual. I know several legal professionals, and many more clients, who have committed themselves to a lifestyle that makes it impossible to earn less than a hefty salary. It didn't occur to them that at some point in their career, it might be nice to have the option of spending less time at the office. Also, the option of one day using your training and experience in a position whose main reward is nonmonetary is something many people consider important, though they often do not contemplate this idea early in their career. Most of us go through fairly predictable stages in life where our career priorities change. When those priorities change, it will be difficult to allow a change in your career focus if financial commitments stand in the way. But notice that I said "difficult," not "impossible." Careful goal setting is the key. You can plan for the shifts in career focus that often occur through the stages in life.

About five years prior to leaving my law practice, I taught a night paralegal course in medical malpractice litigation at a local college. I thoroughly enjoyed the experience and began to think about a shift in my career focus to education. Although I enjoyed the practice of law, the desire to teach others about the law was beginning to take shape. I resolved to put myself in a position where I could afford to teach should that desire continue to grow. I paid off debt. I started to drive cars designed to provide transportation rather than to impress. I didn't buy the largest home I could afford. I put money aside for future use. By the time I was certain I wanted a career in education, I had placed myself in a position where that option was realistic. I had a plan, and I had followed through. There is no reason you could not develop a successful plan to shift your career focus if you have a strong enough desire. Note that I am talking about shifting your career focus, not giving up your paralegal

Part I > Setting Goals: What Should You Expect from a Paralegal Career?

60

career. Your paralegal training may be put to use in a number of ways. I want you to have the option to pursue alternative uses of your training at a later date if that is important to you. My shift from the practice of law to teaching law was simply an alternative use of my training and experience.

There are those who appear satisfied with a lifestyle of large debt and large income. Although I have not found that most people enjoy this kind of lifestyle throughout their careers, only you can decide the lifestyle that you want. However, it is difficult to anticipate everything you want in a career when you've just begun. You should seriously consider whether you would like the option of a career shift later in your career and provide for it in setting your goals.

Of course, some jobs are truly low paying by any reasonable definition, though desirable. One former student took a paralegal position in a legal services office, where she assists the economically disadvantaged. Another former student took a paralegal position for a nonprofit organization that advocates for battered and abused women. Both of these students felt fortunate to get paid for something they consider their calling in life. Neither could have afforded to take their position without a careful assessment of their minimum salary requirement. Before you consider a paralegal position, determine your minimum salary requirement.

The True Price of a Salary

We just discussed the minimum salary you should aspire to, but why would a high salary ever be a problem? Shouldn't we want to make as much as an employer is willing to pay? The answer is yes *provided* the salary is consistent with the personal and professional goals you have set for yourself. There are few employers who pay a salary and do not require something of at least equal value in return. Those who do not have this attitude are usually not in business for long. If you make more, more will be expected of you. This makes sense, and it is fair.

What someone new to a career often fails to recognize is the trade-off that occurs between more pay, with its corresponding job requirements, and lifestyle. Higher pay usually means more required production, such as billable hours, supervision over others, or other increases in workload. This translates to increased stress. I am not an advocate of taking lower pay when more is possible. Paralegals perform a vital function within the legal system, and their pay should reflect this. However, there is no free lunch. Positions with high pay and low responsibility rarely exist. When you are deciding whether to accept a paralegal position, whether it's your first or not, consider what will be expected of you in the position and how it will affect your lifestyle. I have found that a balance between career and lifestyle will be more satisfying in the long run.

Salary Structure Versus Starting Salary

When considering whether a paralegal position provides a reasonable salary, starting salary doesn't give a complete picture. Although starting salary is important, future increases in salary are at least as important. Often job applicants focus strictly on what a job pays now and ignore what it will pay later. In my experience as a legal employer, it was rare that a prospective employee asked what the job was likely to pay six months, a year, or five years later, even when discussing the topic of salary. When this question is asked, it should be coupled with an expression of understanding that future pay is related to superior performance. An employer will likely appreciate your looking at the big picture and will be impressed that you recognize that future increases in pay are tied to performance. The employer is also left with the impression that you view the position as a long-term proposition, something that is important to the employer, who will likely invest substantial time and money in your training.

It is shortsighted to overlook a particular job opportunity as paying too little without considering the prospects for future increases. This is especially the case with a smaller law firm. What is a "smaller" firm is necessarily both relative and subjective. The exact size of the firm is less important than understanding the relationship between size and starting pay. Starting salary is usually lower in smaller firms than in larger firms, primarily due to lower billing rates and fewer employees who can bill and increase the bottom line of the firm. However, since there are fewer employees, those who are productive are especially valued. You don't get lost in the shuffle as you might in a larger firm. Although larger firms generally pay more, the disparity is often narrowed to a great degree for paralegals who prove their value over time. In other words, if you look at the long term, working in a smaller firm is often not as disparate economically as starting salary might suggest. Regardless of the firm's size, you should consider salary structure as well as starting salary in determining your own salary requirements.

Part I > Setting Goals: What Should You Expect from a Paralegal Career?

62

The Whole Package

Salary is only one aspect of a broader term known as *compensation*.
Compensation includes what is commonly referred to as fringe benefits,
which includes anything of tangible value an employer offers an employee besides salary. Some of these fringe benefits may carry tax advantages that in effect increase your take-home pay. Employers usually
offer some combination of the following fringe benefits, with the
amount of employee-required contribution ranging anywhere from none
to the full cost of the benefit, depending on the employer:

> Health insurance

> Dental insurance

> Vision insurance

> Life insurance

> Accident and disability insurance

> Paid sick leave

> Leave without pay

> Paid maternity leave

> Paid paternity leave

> Retirement and profit-sharing plans

> Child care

> Paid vacation

> Paid personal days

> Professional association dues

> Paid or reimbursed continuing education

> Paid parking or public transportation

> Supplemental unemployment benefits

> Paid civic duty pay (for jury duty or military reserve activation)

> Health club membership

> Mileage reimbursement

> Meals when working late or out of town

Most employers do not offer all of these benefits, so the package of salary and benefits available for a particular paralegal position is important to assess. Certainly, at a minimum, any paralegal position worth its salt would offer health insurance and retirement benefits at reduced or no cost to the employee. I have seen paralegal positions that offer no benefits. Unless you are in dire need of a job or the position is temporary, you should avoid these positions. The lack of benefits is a red flag that the position is not going to exist for long or the employer has low regard for the value of employees, either of which is sufficient for you to look elsewhere.

Lies, Darn Lies, and Statistics

Salary and benefit surveys can be very useful. They often give information that is valuable in assessing whether a particular job offers fair compensation. These surveys can also provide an indication of the level of compensation you can expect in the future. However, every survey has its built-in limitations, and they are at best general indicators of what compensation is fair and at worst misleading. The surveys mentioned in this book are especially well done, but there are important considerations in determining the usefulness of *any* survey. The following considerations are not intended to be a lesson in statistics but an illustration of some limitations that are inherent in any statistical analysis of compensation.

How were the averages determined? Averages are computed in terms of *mean*, *median*, and *mode*. The *mean* is the most common method of calculating salary averages. In a salary survey, it is the total of all salaries divided by the number of salaries making up the total. For example, if three paralegals responded that they make $30,000, $50,000, and $70,000 annually, the total of the salaries is $150,000. Divide $150,000 by the three respondents, and the mean average is $50,000. Does this mean that the paralegal making $30,000 is underpaid? Is the paralegal making $70,000 overpaid? Not necessarily, since the lowest-paid paralegal may be new in the profession, and the highest-paid paralegal may have many years of experience.

Even when salary surveys evaluate results based on experience, specialty, or size of the firm, the numbers may not tell the whole story. There may be two paralegals with the same level of experience working at similarly sized law firms who make substantially different compensation. Is the lower compensation unfair? Not necessarily if there are other benefits that the survey failed to include, such as a liberal flextime or leave policy. The best surveys attempt to account for a wide array of factors that give a fuller picture of compensation, such as leave policies.

The *median* average is the middle figure: there are an equal number of salaries above and below the middle salary figure. In the previous example, the median is $50,000, which in this example is equal to the mean. What if the highest-paid paralegal in our example made $100,000, the middle paralegal still made $50,000, and the lowest paid made $20,000? The median would still be $50,000 because it is the middle figure. The *mean* in this example is slightly above $56,000. It is obvious that how the average is computed can make a difference in the final result.

The *mode* is the figure that shows up most often. If five paralegals reported salaries of $20,000, $35,000, $40,000, $40,000, and $75,000, the mode would be $40,000. The median would also be $40,000 but the mean would be $42,000.

Do you see how the method of calculating averages can change the results? Whenever you see a salary survey, consider how the averages were calculated. You might conclude that you are underpaid if average salaries are computed a certain way but not underpaid if the average is computed in a different manner.

You should also consider how the terms *paralegal* or *legal assistant* were defined. Some law firms are short on compensation but generous with awarding titles. If a respondent to a particular survey has the title of paralegal or legal assistant but lacks a skill level commensurate with those titles, the average salary may not be an accurate reflection of paralegal or legal assistant compensation.

The point here is not to discount the importance of salary surveys; it is to put the surveys in proper perspective. The information conveyed is very useful as a starting point in evaluating what paralegals make, but you must not overly rely on them. Survey results, along with demand for paralegals in your legal market, your productivity in the firm (how much you bill or how much you free up others to bill), the firm's reliance on you (how easily you could be replaced), traditional (such as health insurance) and nontraditional benefits (such as flextime), salary structure, your workload, intangible benefits such as promoting a worthy cause, and the quality of your work atmosphere should all be considered when determining whether your compensation is adequate.

The Role Money Should Play in Decision Making

While money (including substitutes for money such as fringe benefits) is the main reason most people work, it should not be the only reason.

I am surprised at the number of students who, when extended more than one job offer, automatically choose the offer with the highest starting pay. When comparing job opportunities, the choice that offers the most tangible benefits is not always the best choice for you. We previously discussed the price of higher compensation in terms of what is expected of you in return. You should also consider the purely intangible, though important, aspects of a job. Does the job give you enough personal fulfillment that you look forward to going to work every day? Do you enjoy the people you work with? Is your work space physically arranged so that you can do your work without undue interference or distraction? Do you find the work interesting and challenging? Are your supervisors accommodating when a health or other personal issue arises? Are you able to grow professionally in your job? Will the skills you develop make you marketable if you need to find another job? Does your job require you to compromise ethical rules or your own personal values? The answers to these and similar questions, along with compensation, are what determine whether you are making a correct decision about a particular job.

> Paralegal Perspective <

Even though I've been working for a family law attorney nearly two years, I am amazed at how much I have learned and how much I have yet to learn. The synergy of both the evening paralegal course work as I worked full time in a small law practice enhanced my experience of a law firm from a micro perspective. This was particularly helpful to me, mostly because it felt like a safe place to learn and grow.

HOW MUCH CAN I MAKE?

Generally, private sector jobs pay more than their counterparts in the public or nonprofit sectors. Paralegal salary surveys typically show a wide disparity in pay between the highest- and lowest-paid private sector respondents. This disparity is not as great in the public and nonprofit sectors. In the public sector, the government has a pay scale that determines the

Part I > Setting Goals: What Should You Expect from a Paralegal Career?

66

amount of compensation it pays its employees. Traditionally, the trade-off in working in the public sector has been lower pay than in the private sector in return for more job security, but that no longer seems to be the case. Government employees today find that their jobs are no more secure than those in the private sector.

The trade-off in the public sector for many employees now is lower pay for the opportunity to handle cases that advance a certain cause without regard to their economic value. In a private law firm, cases cannot be accepted unless they make the firm money, absent the limited pro bono cases many firms accept. This means that private law firms often must turn away cases that would otherwise be fulfilling in terms of the cause advanced or the issues presented. In the public sector, due to the nature of the governmental entity's function, cases are accepted without an analysis of whether the agency finds the cases economically profitable. For example, the public defender's office must accept the defense of certain individuals charged with crimes, but a private firm would have to determine whether it would be paid enough to warrant accepting the case. Today, nonprofit agencies afford a similar trade-off between lower pay and what are thought by those who work in that sector to be a greater degree of personal fulfillment in handling cases. But no sector—private, public, or nonprofit—has a monopoly on personally fulfilling cases since all of us have differing notions about what is fulfilling. However, it is also true that many legal professionals choose to accept lower pay in the public or nonprofit sectors because they support the employer's cause or find this work particularly interesting.

An excellent compensation survey is conducted by the National Association of Legal Assistants (NALA) annually. NALA's latest National Utilization and Compensation Survey can be found at www.nala .org.[1] It's survey for 2002 indicates the average paralegal salary plus bonus was $46,074. Further, since 1988, this average has steadily increased each year. NALA members make more on average than non-members. Those with the Certified Legal Assistant designation awarded by NALA make more than those without such a designation. As you might expect, those with more experience make more than those with less. For example, those with over 25 years of experience have an average salary plus bonus of $48,765; for those with one to five years of experience, the average is $31,993. Seven percent of respondents reported a salary in excess of $60,000 annually. The higher-paying specialties included intellectual property, securities, and telecommunications. The lower-paying specialties included family law, social security, and criminal law. As might be expected, those working in larger firms generally were better compensated than those working in smaller firms. For example, those in firms with six to ten attorneys received compensation averaging $42,858; those in firms with more than 100 attorneys received average annual compensation of $55,592.

Another good source of salary information is the *Bureau of Labor Statistics Occupational Outlook Handbook*, available on-line at http://www.bls.gov/oco.[2] This handbook provides salary data, expected job availability, and a description of paralegal job duties. It is general in nature but an excellent starting point to learn about the paralegal profession.

There are many exceptions to the compensation survey averages. For example, I recently met a paralegal with 18 years of experience who worked in the securities area for a law firm with several hundred attorneys. Her annual salary, excluding bonuses, was $80,000 and her fringe benefits were outstanding, including parking passes, tickets to sporting events, and meals when she worked late. I met a paralegal working for a small firm in San Francisco who made more than $100,000 in salary and bonus in the mid-1980s! This paralegal worked for a leading personal injury law firm that tended to handle very large cases. It did extremely well financially and paid the paralegal large bonuses at the end of each year. The point of these examples is to tell you what is possible, even though they do not conform to the averages.

Paralegals who manage or supervise other paralegals and staff do very well financially. A study conducted by the consulting firm of Altman Weil, Incorporated for the Legal Assistant Management Association (LAMA) in 2003 indicates that legal assistant managers in general earn an average salary of $91,335.[3] Legal assistant managers who worked in private law firms earned on average $85,406, while those employed by in-house corporation law departments earned $75,213 on average.[4]

HOW HIGH CAN I GO?

There are two types of career advancement: vertical and horizontal.

Vertical advancement refers to a progression of job advancement that builds incrementally on the last job. Public, private, and nonprofit sectors may give each of these increasing levels of responsibility a different job title. For example, a paralegal in a public defender's office might be known as a paralegal 1 when inexperienced and, with increasing experience, be promoted to paralegal 2. In a large, private law firm, the firm may have its own unique hierarchy of paralegal job titles such as paralegal assistant at the entry level, junior paralegal at the next level, then

Part I > Setting Goals: What Should You Expect from a Paralegal Career?

68

paralegal, then senior paralegal. Small law firms may have no job titles at all that signify a promotion but simply award more compensation and responsibility as a paralegal becomes more experienced.

Regardless of the progression of job titles for paralegals, vertical advancement can generally be described as passing through the following successive stages:

> Entry level

> Midlevel

> Senior level

> Paralegal manager

Entry-level paralegals can expect to perform the more routine duties associated with the paralegal profession, such as exhibit organization and preparation, summarization of documents, and searches of public records or other information. At this level, the paralegal is closely supervised. Direct contact with clients is usually limited. Legal research assignments are narrow in scope and very specific, such as finding the subsequent history of a case given to the paralegal by the supervising attorney. The paralegal here knows how to use basic legal software but may not know when or how to apply it to good use without substantial direction.

At the midlevel, paralegals are performing more complicated legal work. They prepare documents such as leases and partnership agreements for their supervising attorney's review. They draft pleadings. They research complicated legal issues with minimal direction. They have heavy client and witness contact. They are intimately involved in the discovery process by preparing discovery and responses to discovery. The paralegal at this level has a superior knowledge of legal software and understands its usefulness in meeting the firm's objectives.

At the senior level, paralegals become part of the planning arm of the law office. Supervising attorneys place great importance on the paralegal's opinion about a wide range of issues, both legal and nonlegal in nature. What does the paralegal think about the merits of a new case? How favorable a witness does the paralegal think the client makes? What does the paralegal think about the applicants for a position in the firm? The paralegal at this level is involved with complicated litigation tasks, such as preparation of evidentiary or discover motions, lists of questions for an expert deposition or trial examination, and preparing witnesses for deposition or trial, all under attorney supervision but with substantially less direction than was previously required. The paralegal is considered an ambassador for the firm and often attends business promotional meetings with clients or prospective clients. There is a public relations aspect to the job, with presentations to students or civic organizations on behalf of the firm. The paralegal often has achieved certification indicating superior ability, such as the Paralegal Advanced Competency Exam which allows the paralegal to use the RP (registered paralegal) designation.[5]

The paralegal manager supervises a team of paralegals and staff. The manager hires, trains, and evaluates employees under his or her supervision. A senior attorney delegates broad tasks, and the manager then assigns those under her supervision more specific tasks to ensure the senior attorney's tasks are met. The manager then reports to the senior attorney. The attorney supervises the manager, as is required by rules of ethics, but trusts the manager to delegate work as the manager deems appropriate.

As a paralegal's career advances through the stages described, there is almost always overlap between the stages. Paralegals probably have a wider range of job duties than anyone else in a typical law office. Even senior paralegals have to do more mundane duties at times. Managers may find themselves in the law library conducting research themselves when needed. There may be occasions when a midlevel paralegal is asked to supervise a new employee.

Further, a paralegal will not necessarily advance to senior paralegal or manager either by the paralegal's own choice or because of a decision made by the employer. The employer's decision may have nothing to do with his or her opinion of the paralegal. Some firms do not need, or cannot afford, a senior paralegal or manager. When the paralegal wishes to advance to the next stage but the employer is unable to offer that opportunity, the paralegal may want to consider a different employer. There are several factors to weigh when making a decision whether to change employers, and this is where your inner circle of advisers can be helpful.

What if you're content with your status as a midlevel or senior paralegal but want more challenge and compensation? You should first determine if your current employer can offer what you are looking for. If your current employer cannot, often the opportunities are available with a different employer. I call this *horizontal advancement* because your career stage does not change. There are paralegals who go from a midlevel position in a midsized firm to a midlevel position in a large firm, for example. Although these midlevel paralegals haven't advanced in the traditional form of passing to a higher career stage, they are now finding their work more interesting and more lucrative. Paralegals

Part I > Setting Goals: What Should You Expect from a Paralegal Career?

70

should be cautious not to change employers every time they'd like to be paid more (which for most of us is all the time), but there are occasions when horizontal advancement is necessary.

Before applying for a paralegal position, it is important to determine the appropriate salary and benefits you can accept. This will eliminate certain jobs from consideration. Consider the minimum salary for which you are able to work, the true cost of a salary, salary structure as well as starting salary, the whole benefits package, salary surveys, and the role money should play in your decision-making process. The minimum salary is what you need to pay your expenses at a minimum and should include provision for the kind of lifestyle you wish to have. The true cost of a salary is what an employer expects in return for a particular salary. Salary structure refers to what you can expect to make in the future. Too many new legal professionals looking at starting salary do not consider whether they will be content with their future pay. Salary surveys can be very helpful in determining whether a particular salary is reasonable, but surveys should not be overly relied on. The role of money in the decision-making process is important, but true career satisfaction is not achieved by making it the sole criterion. Paralegals can advance vertically, by incremental promotion, or horizontally, by having the same title in a different employment setting.

>Web Research Exercise<

Go to www.nala.org and review the latest National Utilization and Compensation Survey. How was the survey conducted? Did any of the results surprise you? How can you use the information contained in the survey to help you make decisions about your own paralegal career?

>Chapter Exercises<

1. Determine your minimum salary requirement by adding all of your expenses. Make sure you include the expense of a reasonable vacation, entertainment, and accumulating a rainy day fund within one to two years if you do

not already have a sufficient fund. The rainy day fund should total at least three months' expenses. Then add 15 percent to your total. What were your total expenses on both a monthly and an annual basis? Did the amount surprise you? How will your results affect your job search? If your expenses preclude you from considering certain paralegal positions you would otherwise desire to hold, what can you do now in terms of setting goals to make those positions possible in the future? Write those goals down.

2. Find three entry-level paralegal positions that are advertised on the Internet or in your campus placement office. One position should pay what you consider exceptionally well, one position should pay what you consider an average salary, and one should pay what you would consider below average. Each position should be one you would seriously consider. For each position, consider what will be expected of you in return for the salary offered, the tangible benefits such as health insurance that are offered (or likely to be offered due to the nature of the position), and the intangible benefits of the job (such as promoting a cause you consider worthy). After careful consideration of each of the three positions, which job is most appealing to you, and why? In a group of four to five students, discuss the details of each position you found, the expectations you believe would be required from the employer for each position, and why you found a particular position more appealing than the other two you found. Ask those in your group whether they agree or disagree with your assessment of each of the three positions, and why. To what extent did the opinions of others in your group reaffirm or cause you to reconsider your assessment of each of the three positions?

3. Draw a chart with three columns and four rows to assist you in determining whether a particular paralegal position meets your expectations. The chart should look like this:

Aspects of Job	Meets Requirements	Fails Requirements
Salary offered		
Tangible (fringe) benefits		
Intangible benefits		

For each position you found in exercise 2, place a check mark in the appropriate box. Unless a position allows you to check all three left side boxes ("meets requirements"), it is likely not a good position for you. Before you are able to accurately use this chart, you will need to determine what your requirements are in terms of salary, fringe benefits, and intangible benefits.

Part I > Setting Goals: What Should You Expect from a Paralegal Career?

72

Write those requirements on a separate sheet of paper, and refer to them in assessing each of the three positions.

> Ethical Discussion <

How are high ethical standards essential to success as a paralegal? How would the work environment and your job satisfaction differ in a law firm with high ethical standards as opposed to a law firm with questionable ethical standards? Explain your responses.

> Suggested Reading <

Andrea Wagner, *How to Land Your First Paralegal Job*, Prentice Hall, 2001.

> Notes <

1. 2002 National Utilization and Compensation Survey, permission to use granted by National Association of Legal Assistants (NALA). All rights reserved.

2. Bureau of Labor Statistics, U.S. Department of Labor, *Occupational Outlook Handbook, 2002–2003 Edition.* [2003] http://www.bls.gov/oco/.

3. Altman Weil Survey of Law Firm Economics, copyright 2003, Altman Weil, Inc., Newtown Square, PA. All rights reserved.

4. Altman Weil Survey of Law Firm Economics, copyright 2003, Altman Weil, Inc., Newtown Square, PA. All rights reserved.

5. See www.paralegals.org for more information about the Paralegal Advanced Competency Exam.

Part 2
Beyond Survival:
How to Thrive as a
Paralegal

Chapter 5
Getting Off to
a Good Start

Key Success Points

> *First impressions are formed at the job interview and carry over into the early days of employment.*

> *The keys to creating a positive first impression are anticipation and preparation.*

> *Negative first impressions can be very difficult to overcome.*

> *Knowing what to expect in your new paralegal job will increase your chances of success.*

> > > > > > > > >

"What did you expect me to do?
Call in dead?"

FIRST IMPRESSIONS ARE IMPORTANT

First impressions made at the job interview carry over into the very early days of employment, even to the first days or few weeks on the new job. There are plenty of employers who feel they know all they need to know about an applicant at the interview, at least to make a decision whether to hire a particular applicant. Usually, what is sufficient to form a conclusion about another is very limited information. Hence, first impressions are often unfair, but they are a fact of life; everyone forms them. They can be very difficult to overcome when they are negative. It is much easier to make a positive first impression than to overcome a negative one. The story that follows shows how early impressions can be formed.

Several years ago, I was interviewing applicants for an associate attorney position in the law firm where I was employed. I had interviewed applicants most of the day by the time I interviewed Dale. Dale was sitting in the waiting room reading a small book that I only caught a glimpse of; the one word I saw on the book's cover in large type was *winning*. He quickly put the book in his inside jacket pocket when I introduced myself. His outstretched hand revealed an oversized imitation gold watch and watchband. His grip nearly tore my arm off. He was dressed in a faded blue three-piece suit that had gone out of style at least a decade earlier.

In the interview room, Dale sat down before waiting to be asked— and in my chair. I asked him to sit in the chair across from my chair. I then asked him something to the effect of how he was today, and he replied, "I am going to hire me an employer today!" Are you forming any initial impressions about Dale? Near the conclusion of what seemed like a very long interview, I asked Dale if he had any questions, which I customarily asked of each applicant. Dale reached into his other inside suit pocket (the one not containing the book) and pulled out a folded piece of paper. He then unfolded the piece of paper and revealed at least twenty typewritten questions for me—some good ("How can I be successful here?"), some not so good ("How can I have your job someday?"). On his way out of my office, Dale opened the door to the closet instead of the common hallway and actually took one step into the closet before choosing the correct door!

I could not recall much about each of the applicants who preceded Dale that day without reviewing the notes I took while I interviewed each applicant. But I could recall everything about Dale without my notes. I had formed certain conclusions about him based on our initial interview: that he lacked the social skills necessary to interact with coworkers, clients, and court personnel. All of this was based on a 30-minute interview.

My experience with Dale was a lesson about the qualities of first impressions. First, they are often made on the basis of incomplete or inaccurate information, making their reliability suspect. For all I know, if I had hired Dale, he may have proved my initial impressions about him were incorrect. It may have been that Dale simply did not interview well but would have been a fine lawyer. Unfortunately, an employer who recognizes the lack of reliability of first impressions is rare. Most employers do not have the luxury of proceeding against their first impressions, even if they were inclined to do so. Hiring employees is simply too costly and time-consuming. Second, once a first impression is formed, it is difficult to overcome. Had Dale come to work for the firm, every misstep in his interactions with others would have been chalked up to my conclusion that he was lacking in social skills, when it might have been the normal type of misstep that any new employee could make. Third, you have control over the first impression someone forms about you. Preparation is the key. Even if Dale did not know how to interview successfully, there is an abundance of information available about this subject, including books, Web sites, and people on any college campus who are experts on how to interview for a job.

Steps to Creating a Positive First Impression

Since it is clear that first impressions are important, the issue becomes how to form a positive first impression. Even if the first impression of a job applicant is positive enough to result in a job offer, the impression that carried over from the interview continues to evolve during the early days or weeks of employment. Here is what you should do to create a positive first impression.

Step 1. *Anticipate what will be expected, and prepare for it.* This sounds like common sense, but my experience is that most applicants and new employees do not prepare nearly as much as they should. In a job interview, make sure you dress appropriately. Know what you are likely to be asked and have ready answers. Do research about the potential employer, and prepare thoughtful questions when asked whether you have questions. Know your weaknesses, and be ready to address them. Know how to play up to your strengths. Do dress rehearsals until the interview becomes second nature. Make it a point to consult members of your inner circle, instructors, campus placement personnel, and anyone else who can help, even if you are sure you know that you are adequately prepared. Remember, Dale probably thought he was prepared by reading his book about "winning." Once on the job, ask your supervising attorney or managing paralegal what you can do to make their job easier, and then do it. After all, isn't part of the reason you were hired to make their job easier? This kind of an attitude from the start will go a long way in others forming a positive first impression.

Step 2. *Be conservative in your approach to the new job.* I am not talking about politics here; I am referring to the discretion over how to conduct yourself within a law office. Mild humor is fine, even good. However, don't try to be the life of the party when you are new and first impressions are being formed. Dress conservatively even on the casual days many firms have these days. A new secretary of mine once wore a halter top and faded jeans with holes in the knees on "casual dress day." I had nothing against her clothes except that they were inappropriate in a law office. If you are unsure what to say in a social situation, it is better to say too little instead of too much. Saying too much often exposes the inadequacies that may be common to a new employee, but it serves no purpose to highlight them. Avoid controversial topics such as religion or politics. Never criticize anyone in the firm even when your co-employees are doing so.

Step 3. *Recognize the value of time.* New employees in a law office often do not recognize that time is the firm's most valuable commodity. The success of the firm depends on the efficient use of time. Billing is usually based on the amount of time spent on a task related to a particular case. Cases that are not billed by the hour require the time to be managed in such a way that the firm completes certain tasks and can then be paid. It is obvious that time should not be wasted. When first impressions are being formed, you should avoid even the appearance of wasting time. Once you have established yourself as a hard-working, productive employee, mere appearances become less important. Therefore, as a new employee, don't spend too much time in the break room, on a personal phone call, chatting with fellow employees, on the Internet, at lunch, or doing anything else that conveys the impression you do not value time. Complete your work assignments in such a way that your supervisor's time is spent more efficiently reviewing and possibly correcting them. For example, if a legal research was given to you verbally, restate the assignment in writing when turning it in instead of causing your supervisor to have to recall exactly what you were asked to do. Think of ways to save time, and discuss them with your supervisor.

Step 4. *Show that you understand that success depends on hard work.* Here, you are showing that the quantity of time matters. The prior section concerned the efficient use of time, or the quality of how time is used. When you are new to the paralegal profession, doing a task correctly takes longer than it will when you are more experienced. When you are new to the job, relatively small sacrifices on your part will go miles creating a positive first impression. Consider not using your entire lunch hour when you don't need to use it. Arrive ten minutes before your workday is supposed to begin so you can get your coffee, chat with coworkers, set up your desk, or do whatever else you normally do at the start of your day. That way, you can start working at precisely the time your workday is supposed to begin. Work right up to the time your day is supposed to end, and before leaving, check with your supervisor to find out if anything else is needed before heading out the door. One of my best paralegals regularly checked with me before she left for the day; it did wonders for my impression of her. If you complete your work early, ask for more work. I have seldom been asked by an employee for more work; I have not forgotten the times I was asked.

Step 5. *Convey professionalism in all of your communications.* The term *professionalism* here denotes knowledge, organization, reliability, industry, social skills, and high ethical standards. When you are new to the job, you want to convey either these qualities or the clear potential to attain these qualities. All of your communications, written and verbal, should be professional in nature. This does not mean you cannot have a sense of humor. Indeed, humor is a way to connect with others in a way that is difficult to recreate. What I am referring to is communication inappropriate for a professional paralegal. For example, a new legal secretary of mine was prone to using slang and even profanity. When she left for the day, she would announce she was "blowing this joint." Although she seemed careful to use profanity only on occasion and within her office, I was concerned because this type of conduct at best shows poor judgment, something legal professionals cannot have. Some would take the secretary's use of language as indicative of a lack of intelligence. Others would worry about coworkers or clients becoming offended. Of course, putting the poor use of language in writing compounds the problem. Using unusually colored paper, putting "smiley faces" on memorandums, even the use of an untraditional font size or style can convey the impression that you are not a professional and therefore are not to be taken seriously. You have worked too hard to let a few inappropriate gestures create the wrong impression. When you are new to the job, you will need to consciously ask yourself whether a communication conveys a lack of professionalism; later, acting like a professional should be second nature.

> Paralegal Perspective <

Be sure to review a firm's Web site to get an idea of what type of law is practiced, as well as the names of clients or landmark cases handled by the firm. If you are interviewing with a specific attorney, find out what cases he or she has worked on, and ask questions about them during the interview. Everyone wants to share their accomplishments, and this will not only flatter the interviewer but illustrate your foresight and ability to research.

How to Correct a Poor First Impression

What can you do if you have created the wrong first impression? Sometimes you will not have a second chance. If you create the wrong first impression at the job interview, you will likely not have the opportunity to rectify the situation. If you did well enough at the interview to obtain the position, but your initial efforts on the job created a poor first impression, you usually have the opportunity to overcome any negative conclusions made about you. Again, having to overcome a poor first impression is much more difficult than conveying a positive first impression, but it can be done. We can all recall times when we got off on the wrong foot with someone despite our best efforts.

First, make sure that what you perceive to be a poor first impression actually exists. It is normal to suffer from mild paranoia when new to a job. Sometimes it is obvious you made a poor first impression. When your car breaks down the first day on the job and you arrive an hour late, no one needs to tell you there is a problem. When you misunderstood a due date and handed in your assignment late, you know the first impression is not favorable. When it is less obvious what initial impression you have made, the comments of your supervisor can be revealing. Comments on a returned motion that ask you if you know the office keeps a copy of local rules or where the law library is may be purely helpful in nature, but could be a signal that your supervisor believes you should have done better work.

When in doubt about whether you have started off poorly, the best approach is to ask rather than drive yourself crazy with self-doubt that may have no basis. When asking, there is no need to be suggestive by questions like, "I'm doing poorly, aren't I?" You may plant a seed of doubt in your employer about you that previously did not exist. The better method is to approach your supervisor in a neutral manner such as, "Thank you for looking over my assignment. Please let me know if there is anything you would like to discuss about it."

If you determine you have made a negative first impression, the best approach is to confront the problem honestly and directly. Speak with your supervisor. Give the situation the attention it deserves, but do not needlessly magnify the problem. Therefore, do not ask to make an appointment with your supervisor, but do not discuss the situation in the hallway or the break room. Wait for the appropriate time and ask if your supervisor has a "few minutes" to meet in her office. Then calmly and rationally tell the supervisor that you want to assure the supervisor you are aware you have not started off exactly as you would have liked. Tell her that you are working hard to correct any doubts, and you are always open to suggestions. Keep the conversation professional, courteous, and brief. Do not overdo it. It is likely your supervisor will then pay added attention to whether you are working to correct the situation. This is what you want, since you want your efforts to be noticed. The alternative is not confronting the situation directly but letting your true good qualities overcome the negative first impression over a much longer period of time. The risk is that the initial impression you made will have become ingrained in your supervisor's mind; the longer a false impression lasts, the more likely your supervisor will believe in its truth.

WHAT TO DO BEFORE YOUR FIRST DAY ON THE JOB

There are a number of things you can do even before you begin your new paralegal job that will help make you successful. The time to start is now, not after you accept a job offer. Make sure you learn to research and write well. All employers place a high degree of importance on these skills. Approach each paralegal class as if the job starts next week and this is your last chance to learn about your life's work while still in the supportive confines of the classroom. Take the opportunity to learn as much as you can if you do an internship. I recommend you do more than one internship if possible because the practical skills you learn are invaluable. Get involved with projects while in school that help you understand what you will be doing as a paralegal. For example, help organize a paralegal job fair. You will meet legal employers and gain useful information about the profession. If you are unsure of projects availble on campus in which to become involved, ask one of your professors.

Getting Off to a Great Start

Once you have accepted a paralegal position, there are still things you can be doing that will improve your chances of thriving on the job. Never consider your time between accepting a new position and your first day "dead time." It is an opportunity to get off to a great start. Here is what I recommend you do.

> Ask your new employer if there is anything you could do to better prepare yourself. Your employer should be impressed with your initiative. If you were not told during the interview, ask what legal software you will be using, what on-line legal research databases are available, if any, and if there is a forms file on disk you could review. Then follow your employer's suggestions about how to get ready for the job. Review the software you will be using. Become familiar with any legal databases you will use in the firm so you are ready the first time a legal research assignment is given to you. Look at the forms file carefully. Make sure you have at least a general understanding of when each form is used, why, and how it is prepared. Chances are you will not be expected to know how to prepare everything you see in the forms file right away, but you will gain a sense of comfort that accompanies the preparation of a particular document when you have seen and at least generally understood it before. But be sure not to overdo it with requests of your new employer. Ask politely for the information suggested. Should the employer decline to provide it, say thank you and that you are looking forward to your first day of work. If your new employer does not provide a forms file for you to review, try to anticipate the types of forms you will be working with by talking with professors, classmates who may have worked in the same type of firm, and your inner circle members. If you will be using software you are unfamiliar with, try asking one of your computer instructors where you could find more information. Most software has a Web site that can provide information. Remember that as a new employee, you will not be expected to know everything—but the more you know, the more confident you will be when you begin your new job.

> Find out if your new employer will let you shadow another paralegal for at least a half-day prior to your first day. There is a tremendous amount you can learn from observing an experienced paralegal in action. Once the job begins, you will be hard-pressed to find an equally beneficial opportunity to simply watch and ask questions. If you are

not able to do this, consider asking a paralegal in another firm if you can shadow him or her. I recall shadowing an attorney while in law school. He was glad to accommodate me; my impression is that he enjoyed talking about what he did. If you do not know who to ask, your internship site is a good place to begin. Try to shadow a paralegal in the same type of firm you will be working in, such as estate planning, litigation, criminal, or some other specialty.

> Find out more about the firm that has employed you. (You may have done much of this before your interview.) Consult a legal directory, and find out where the attorneys went to law school, their practice specialties, dates of admission to the bar, and any other information that helps you understand the firm's makeup. The librarian at your school or at a local law library can likely direct you to a useful legal directory. Your paralegal instructors may know something about the firm or whether any graduates of the school's program are employed there. Knowing more about the people you work with will make you more comfortable, which can go a long way in helping you to think clearly and act appropriately. Further, you will have information that helps break the ice with fellow employees.

> If the commute from home to work is unfamiliar, drive it at the same time you will do so after the job begins. If you plan to take public transportation, take the same route at the same time you will take when you go to work. You do not want to show up late your first day. Similarly, if your sleep schedule does not match your work schedule, set the alarm clock to wake up at the same time you will need to once the job begins. You will have enough to be concerned about without the lack of sleep making your first few days more difficult.

> Attend to any medical, dental, or other appointments for you (and children, if applicable) so you do not have to ask for time off from work shortly after beginning your new position. Your new employer will take note if you need to attend routine medical or dental appointments shortly after beginning employment. Most good employers should understand when you have to attend unexpected appointments, so by all means attend them if necessary. Make sure the appointments truly are "unexpected" however.

If you do the foregoing, you will have done more than nearly any employer would have expected. Think about the positive first impression you are making. You will be well on the road to distinguishing yourself without even working your first day! Remember that your goal is to thrive, not just survive in your new paralegal position.

> Paralegal Perspective <

Leaving your employer good first impressions can definitely make your life in a challenging law office so much
easier than you could ever imagine. If you arrive ten minutes early and leave a half-hour later than you are supposed to in the first month, your diligence will be
remembered by your boss for a whole year. If you turn in a
high-quality first assignment, you created a presumption in
the supervising attorney's mind that all your future assignments of the same nature are excellent. Once the presumption is established, it is more difficult for it to be
rebutted.

WHAT TO EXPECT THE FIRST DAY, WEEK, MONTH, AND YEAR

Every new job situation is different. Some employers are more methodical in their approach to new employee orientation and training than others. Your own experience as a new paralegal will be unique to you because that experience is a function of both what your employer does and how you respond.

Your First Day

There will be quite a lot of anticipation on your part and on the part of your new employer. Even an employer used to hiring looks forward to your first day on the job. Anxiety on your part is perfectly normal. You will be shown your work area and introduced to those you will work directly with, if this was not done earlier. No one should mind if you write the names of those you will be working with on a notepad. Chances are your desk will be clean. Sitting at your desk for the first time and turning on your computer may feel a little awkward. Don't be surprised if everything you do or say the first day feels a bit awkward. You would not be normal if you didn't have this experience. If your computer needs a password to log on, make sure you write it down and place it in a secure area. Although you may feel that everyone else is staring at you, odds are they will be so busy that you will go relatively unnoticed. If employees pass by you without saying hello or making eye contact, they are probably preoccupied with the assignment of the moment.

Sometime shortly after your arrival, you will receive your first assignment. Some firms have in-boxes on your desk or close by where all new assignments are placed. Other firms just place new assignments on your desk. Although you will eventually have handled thousands of assignments in your career, you will remember the first one. My first assignment was to prepare a motion to dismiss on the basis of the plaintiff's not having brought the case to trial within five years from the date the complaint was filed. Later in this book, I discuss how to approach handling your assignments. For now, suffice it to say that you should make sure you understand the assignment and ask to see a sample of what the finished product should look like in terms of format at least, and in terms of substance if possible. For example, if you are preparing a motion to dismiss, ask to see a motion to dismiss made on the same basis as the motion you will be preparing. If such a motion is not available, ask to see a motion to dismiss made on another basis. If that is not possible, ask to see any motion recently prepared in the office, so you can use the example as a guideline for formatting purposes.

Start your own forms file from day one, both electronic and paper. Whenever you ask for a form to look at, get an electronic version so you can easily save it. Print out a copy also. Continually update your forms file. When you come across a useful form, ask if you can have a copy even if it does not pertain to a current assignment. Index the forms so you can easily refer to them when necessary. A good forms file is a lifesaver.

When you have finished your first assignment, chances are you will feel it took too long to complete, was not as well done as you are capable of, and only your mother could like your finished project. You will also have the impression there is a level of urgency and seriousness that you did not feel in school or in an internship. The adrenaline level is elevated. Relax! We all experience self-doubt at this stage of a job. The self-doubt you have means you care about doing a good job. If you did not care about doing a good job, you would not be concerned about the quality of the assignment you just completed.

Sometime during your first day, you will find yourself in a social setting—perhaps when you take a break, go to lunch, or are introduced to others in the firm. It can be intimidating to meet all of these people who you know must be smarter and more articulate than you. (Actually, you will later find that usually is not the case.) Keep your comments brief, humble, and positive. Now is not the time to tell everyone your life story, why you are so great, or why the break room seems a little on the small side. If you are invited to make a negative comment ("Don't you think the furniture is out of style?"), be noncommittal ("I haven't had a chance to think about that."). If invited to make other than a negative comment ("How are things going?"), reply positively ("Great!"). Don't overdo it, however ("I am the most fortunate person on planet earth to work with such bright, interesting, nice-looking, athletic people.") Once you have the reputation of being insincere, people will not believe you when you really intend a compliment.

You will likely be asked to fill out forms related to health insurance, retirement benefits, taxes, and other preliminaries. Certain passwords that allow you to log on to your computer, an on-line legal research database, and other secure sources may be given to you. Keys to the office will probably also be provided. Treat all of these items with the care they deserve. Leaving confidential information on your desk instead of inside it can be considered a sign of carelessness and poor judgment.

You will likely find by the end of your workday that time went by very quickly. Be sure to check with your supervisor before leaving the office. Organize your desk and the rest of your work area for the next day. I have learned that an organized work area is the sign of an organized person—the kind of employee I prefer. Congratulate yourself for having made it through the first day.

Do you see how following the suggestions in the prior section of this chapter would have made your first day easier? You would have experienced many of the first-day activities already. You would have arrived at work being more familiar with your workplace, your coworkers, and what is expected of you.

Your First Week

During your first week, you should learn the names of the people you work directly with and the names of a few other coworkers. Your work area should be organized in a way best suited to your preferences. Although you want to be judicious about requesting items for your work area, it is important that you have the materials and equipment you need to be productive. My first office had no window. It drove me crazy, but asking for a new office was not reasonable at the time. Asking for two calendars (one that went everywhere I went and one that stayed on my desk at all times) was not unreasonable.

By the end of the first week, you will begin to understand the flow of your workload. Every office has a certain pace or speed at which tasks are completed. This pace ebbs and flows depending on the circumstances. For example, when a trial approaches, the pace quickens. During the holiday season, the pace may slow. At all other times, there is a certain rhythm considered normal for that office.

You should have received and completed several assignments by week's end. It would not be unusual to have been assigned simple legal research assignments, such as finding the subsequent history of a particular case, checking legal citations for accuracy in a motion, or finding a form to prepare a particular kind of contract.

You will likely have been exposed to some cases currently being handled in the office. You may be asked to review and summarize discovery in a certain case, arrange a meeting with a client, or match subpoenas with records received to find out if any records are missing. You will feel that you are a "real" paralegal once you work on actual cases and get paid for this work.

You will also begin to feel more comfortable venturing beyond your immediate work area. By the end of the week, trips to the copy room, firm library, or break room will feel more natural. You will still feel awkward in social situations but much less so with those with whom you work directly.

It is likely that you will have received at least one returned assignment by week's end. Unless the assignment was very simple, corrections will need to be made. The corrections at times have more to do with a supervisor's personal preferences than with your legal ability. For example, someone may prefer you attach headnotes to case briefs rather than the full text of the case. These types of corrections are fairly easy to address.

When the corrections concern your legal ability, your tendency will be to overreact. When a senior paralegal or attorney questions the legal portion of your assignment, which is inevitable at some point when you are new to the profession, it is important to put the criticism in perspective. Working in the law is a vast undertaking. Mistakes are inevitable. You are not expected to know everything right away. You are expected to learn from your mistakes.

You will probably have the opportunity to discuss your corrected assignment with your supervisor before week's end. It is important not to be defensive. This first meeting will set a tone for future meetings of the same type, and your supervisor will draw certain conclusions about your attitude and aptitude based on your approach to these meetings. If possible, try to meet before you turn in the next completed assignment.

By the end of the first week, you will also begin to understand the firm personality. Every firm has a certain personality, which is usually a reflection of the people who run it. A personality can best be defined by a single word: *businesslike, relaxed, aggressive,* and *family oriented* are all examples.

Your First Month

By the end of your first month, you will have completed a variety of different assignments, some of them relatively easy but most of them a challenge. If you have had constructive criticism and a positive attitude and worked hard, you will have a very good idea of what is expected of you in terms of your assignments. The challenge is to put into practice what you know you should do. Early in my legal career, when I was still learning how to write effective legal memorandums, my memorandums were often returned with the comment to "weave the facts with the law." What my supervisor meant was that in explaining an appellate court's analysis (essentially how it reached a conclusion), I needed to show how the court applied the law to the facts rather than simply state the law in one paragraph and the facts in another. I knew what my supervisor wanted but had trouble initially in following his suggestion. This is often the situation you find yourself in after one month, but in fact, this is a continuing process. As you demonstrate your proficiency in a certain area, you will be trusted with more complex tasks. Once I learned how to weave facts and law, I found that the briefing assignments became more complicated.

By the end of one month, you should have had limited communication with those outside the law firm such as clients, court personnel, or those in opposing law firms. These contacts will likely be of a routine nature, such as asking a client to provide certain information designated by your supervisor, a court clerk if there is a particular way the trial judge like exhibits prepared, or a paralegal in an opposing law firm for an extension of time to respond to discovery. Make sure you understand the rules of ethics concerning unauthorized practice of law by nonattorneys when making these contacts: none of your statements should be interpreted as giving legal advice.

After one month, you should begin to feel comfortable with those who work directly with you. You don't feel as much apprehension when you approach your supervisor as you did a few weeks earlier. You have a better sense of what is appropriate in terms of when to interrupt your supervisor with questions and when not to. Although you still feel like a new employee, you have a sense that you know more about being a paralegal than you thought you did a few weeks earlier. You see the potential, if not the reality, of being successful. You feel more of a sense of camaraderie with your coworkers as you discuss cases you are handling, issues you are researching, and people you have contacted. In most of your discussions with coworkers, they will do most of the talking and you most of the listening (These discussions are more equal as time goes on.) Not only do you understand the flow of work at this point, you find yourself working at the same pace, usually without any conscious effort to do so. You simply work as fast as those around you.

Your First Year

After one year, you should sense that you belong with the firm. You no longer feel like a new employee. You understand what your employer expects from you and have met those expectations appropriate for your experience level, and are well on your way to meeting yet higher expectations. For example, your employer expects you to be able to write an excellent legal memorandum after one year of experience, and you have developed such a skill. Now your employer is challenging you with writing motions whose complexity is beyond your existing skill level, though you are working hard to attain that competency. Your confidence level is high because you have learned over the past year that you can do more than you initially thought you could. What you do not know now you are certain you can learn.

Conversations with fellow employees are on a more even basis, with you not always the primary listener. Other employees come to you occasionally for information or advice. Some of the coworkers you thought were all-knowing when you began your job actually don't know as much as you thought they did. Your supervisor feels more confident giving you assignments with less supervision. You are more comfortable working on your own without the constant desire to ask for more direction that you experienced a year earlier. The firm, with so much invested in your training, starts to view you as a contributor to its success. Chances are it will have paid for your attendance at a paralegal training course by this time.

You anticipate your first formal job review. Although some firms formally review a new employee's job performance after the first six months, certainly by the end of one year you should have received one. Provided you were diligent in choosing your employer, there is a good chance you received a positive job review and a raise in pay. You should feel after one year that you still have a lot to learn, but your success is inevitable.

CHAPTER SUMMARY

First impressions are formed at the initial job interview and carry over to the early days of employment. To make a positive first impression, anticipate what is expected of you and prepare before the job interview and before your first day on the job. Be conservative in your approach to both your conduct and dress. Let your employer know you understand the value of time by your words and your actions. Law firms are places where people work hard; make sure you convey this understanding by making the extra effort to turn in excellent (as opposed to average) work. All of your communications with others, both inside and outside the firm, must be professional; your employer wants to know you will not embarrass the firm by acting less than professional. Remember that a negative first impression can be overcome, but it is much easier to create a positive first impression. When your employer has a positive impression, you can expect greater responsibility with less supervision.

> Web Research Exercise <

Go to www.legalassistanttoday.com. There you will find a tremendous amount of useful information about the paralegal profession. I encourage you to subscribe to the magazine. You will find directions to join the LAT e-mail list. Join the list; it will help you keep track of issues being discussed by practicing paralegals.

> Chapter Exercises <

1. Find a paralegal position that has been advertised that you believe is a good match for you. Assume that you have been asked to interview for the position in two weeks. Make a plan of each step you will take in the next two weeks to prepare for the interview. Who will you speak with to prepare yourself? When will you meet with that person, and what will you discuss? What information will you need to prepare for the interview, and where will you obtain it? What will you do to rehearse for the interview? Is there anything else you should do to prepare for the interview? Then, in a group of

four or five students, discuss and critique each group member's plan. Revise your plan as necessary.

2. Assume that you were offered the paralegal position you interviewed for in exercise 1. You start your new job in two weeks and decide to make a specific plan to prepare for the new job. Who will you speak with, and what will you discuss with that person? What information will you request from your new employer? If your new employer does not provide the requested information, where will you obtain it? Is there anything else you should do to prepare for your new paralegal position? Put your plan in writing. Then in a group of four or five students, discuss and critique each group member's plan and revise your plan as necessary.

3. Start both a paper and electronic forms file. Organize the forms according to type. For example, you might have a pleadings folder, a discovery folder, a motions folder, and a correspondence folder. Within each of these folders, organize your forms. The pleadings folder should have subfolders for summons, complaints, and answers. The discovery folder should be broken down into the different types of discovery, such as interrogatories and requests for production. Obtain forms from classes in which you prepared legal documents, internships, and on-line research databases that may be available to you. Consider meeting with other students to exchange forms. Remember that you will be referring to these forms on your first job, so pay attention to their quality. You may not have a good form for each of your folders, but now that your folders are organized, you should add to your forms file each time you come across a good form.

> Ethical Discussion <

In attempting to make a positive first impression, is it ethical to let your employer believe something about you that you know is not true? For example, you are asked to research an issue that another paralegal in the office researched just a few weeks earlier. The other paralegal is glad to share her research with you. You submit a legal research memorandum containing much of the other paralegal's research without attributing any of the work to her. Your supervisor later compliments you on a "fine job," referring to your legal memorandum. How would you handle this and similar situations?

> Suggested Reading <

Linda L. Edwards, *Law Office Skills*, Delmar Learning, 2003.

Chapter 6
What Is Important to a Law Firm?

Key Success Points

> *Knowing what is important to a law firm will help you be successful.*

> *Law firms value clients, fees, time, status, prestige, and reputation.*

> *You are the most valuable asset in a law firm.*

> > > > > > > > >

"Even if you shoot him, that doesn't mean I'm giving you his paralegal."

KNOWING WHAT IS IMPORTANT . . . IS IMPORTANT

If you know what is important to a law firm, you will be in a better position to be successful. Why? When you focus your efforts on achieving tasks that advance the firm's important objectives, you become valuable as an employee. Ultimately, the value of any employee is measured by how he or she furthers the employer's objectives. Paralegals who can keep clients satisfied, bring in sufficient fees, increase the firm's favorable reputation, and respect the value of time are those who advance within a firm. Keep these important objectives in mind at all times. These objectives may make sense, but they can hardly be considered common sense to someone new to the law office environment. New employees, for understandable reasons, do not tend to focus on anything beyond their own individual responsibilities. There is a tendency to focus on the trees and ignore the forest. Employees who are most valuable understand the big picture. They know what their employer's objectives are and focus their efforts on achieving those objectives. These employees have a vision of advancing in their careers by becoming an essential component of the firm's success. You should constantly ask yourself what you are doing to make your employer more successful: That is the attitude that allows you to thrive. If you do not understand what is important to your employer, the best attitude in the world will amount to a wasted effort at best. Law firms are results oriented. A good attitude is important but will not sustain your success without concrete results. In other words, having the attitude that you want to make your employer successful is important, but that attitude must result in conduct that truly advances the firm's success. Make sure you understand what is most important to your employer. The information that follows in this chapter should give you guidance.

CLIENTS ARE IMPORTANT

New employees often do not realize the importance of clients. More experienced employees understand why clients are important, but sometimes take clients for granted. There is an unfounded assumption that law firms with plenty of business will automatically stay that way. Of course, without clients, there would be no law firm and no paralegal position for you. Even in the public and nonprofit sectors, whose fees are not directly paid by clients, there would be no work without someone for whom to produce the work. Law firm owners think about clients constantly because their futures are directly implicated. If you want to please your employer, understand the value of clients, and treat them accordingly. There is no better compliment that can be paid than one made by a client about you to your employer.

All clients are important. There is an ethical obligation for the firm to represent and advise every client competently regardless of financial gain. Failure to represent and advise a client competently can subject your employer to liability also. However, the reality of the legal environment is that some clients require more attention because of their importance to the firm's success.

For example, assume you are given a tax issue to research. You use the legal research sources contained in your office to resolve the issue for your supervising attorney. In most cases, you have done enough. But what if the client for whom the research is being conducted is of major importance to the firm because it is a constant source of business? What if you know the law school library twenty miles away has a tax section that may, but likely won't, have additional information concerning the issue you were asked to research? Due to the client's importance to the firm, you may be sent to the library by your supervising attorney. Why? Although the likelihood of finding anything helpful at the library is remote, the risk of failing to find the best information is too great for the firm.

Remember that you would be ethically obligated to make that trip to the library for any client if you lacked sufficient resources in your firm to address the issue presented. What I am referring to here is going beyond what is normally expected when a particularly important client is involved. It is a fact of law firm practice that unlimited amounts of time cannot be spent on each case. Most legal professionals will tell you they could always do more on case if they had more time. Knowing the firm's mentality when it comes to its most important clients will help you understand why you are driving to the library when you feel your assignment is done. It will also allow you to anticipate what your employer might want in the treatment of a client and, in the process, win over both the employer and the client.

This illustration is intended to show the law firm mentality when its most important clients are concerned. There are, of course, various situations in which going the extra mile for this type of client is applicable. The point is that all law firms have clients who are treated with extra attention and care because of their importance to the firm. This does not mean that one client's legal problem is more worthy than that of another client. It does mean that firms competing with many other firms for top clients in terms of the ability to generate fees must take the steps necessary to attract and retain those clients. If you understand and respond to this reality in how you approach your work, you will go a long way in gaining your employer's trust and confidence.

Clients that are a constant source of business are vital to a firm. These are usually institutional clients such as businesses, governmental agencies, or associations. The law firm in which I was employed for many years had both corporate and governmental clients who referred new cases to the firm on a regular basis. The firm made constant efforts to maintain the professional relationship that existed between the law firm and these clients. But clients typically have little loyalty to a particular firm, so the relationship must be continually nurtured. Paralegals often have more day-to-day contact with the client than anyone else in the firm. It is important for the paralegal to understand the value of the professional relationship between the client and the firm and make every contact with the client a reaffirmation of the relationship.

What does this mean in terms of how to approach your work? You need to treat the client as if your paycheck depended on it, because ultimately it does. If it's 5:00 P.M. and an important client leaves a message to call, the call is returned that day instead of waiting until the next morning. If a client of this stature needs to speak with an attorney who is in a meeting, you let your supervisor decide whether to interrupt the attorney instead of just taking a message. If the client would like someone to come to her office to go over interrogatories instead of coming to the law office, a trip to the client's office is made. If the client can meet only after normal business hours or on the weekends, those accommodations are made. If you have not heard from the client for a long period of time, you contact the client to make sure everything is going well. These are the types of things that a firm should do for all its clients when the need arises. For the firm's best clients, these types of efforts are made regularly.

Of course, the best approach is to treat all clients as "the most important." But there is not always time to spend what would normally be unnecessary effort on every client. When any client needs that extra effort in order to receive competent representation, that extra effort should be made. When it comes to the firm's most important clients, extra effort should always be made. If you are unsure about the clients who require the extra attention, make sure you ask your supervisor. Further, if you are unsure what extra effort is sufficient in a particular situation, consult with your supervisor. You do not want to make twenty-mile trips to the law library without your supervisor's approval until you have established yourself as someone who knows how to manage time efficiently.

Naturally, there will be situations in which the extra effort required is obvious. No one needs to tell you that you should return an important client's phone call before you leave the office that day. Similarly, no one needs to tell you to let your supervisor know immediately when an important client wants to discuss a new legal problem. You do not need anyone's permission to see such a client during your morning break if the client requests. (You can take your break afterward.) Be willing to do this for all clients as you are able, but be especially accommodating in this manner to the clients that your firm values most.

Note that firms also highly value clients who may not themselves generate legal business but are in a position to refer business to the firm. For example, a client of mine was a well-known and much admired philanthropist in the community. He did not have much need for legal services himself, but he went out of his way to let people know I was his attorney; many of these people came to me for their legal needs.

> Paralegal Perspective <

I remember my ethics instructor telling the class he doesn't like advertising his business because he doesn't like clients sent in by ads or from off the street. I found as a paralegal that being highly selective about clients may be a privilege that most firms do not experience. For many smaller firms, clients are really their gods; it doesn't matter whether the clients are calling you from heaven or hell. Be nice and professional to every single client or potential client that you see.

FEES ARE IMPORTANT

Fees generated from cases are the lifeblood of any private law firm. Without a sufficient amount of fees, law firms shut their doors. Where there is no law firm there are no jobs, including yours. It is not hard to understand the importance of fees. If you were able to go behind the closed doors of partner or shareholder meetings, the topic of fees is often on the agenda. Why do certain clients merit special treatment? Primarily because those clients are a steady source of fees, either directly by their own need for legal work or indirectly by being a source of case referrals from others. Fees are normally classified as hourly, flat, or transactional.

Hourly Fees

Hourly fees are calculated according to the amount of time spent on a particular task multiplied by the hourly rate. If you spend half an hour doing legal research, and your hourly rate is $100, then the client owes $50 for that task. Time is usually billed in tenths of hours, so spending 0.2 of an hour (12 minutes) on a task, at $100 per hour, would generate a fee of $20. Each person who works on a case keeps track of his or her time on a time sheet. On a periodic basis, usually monthly, all the fees and costs generated on a particular case are billed to the client.

If you are working on a case billed by the hour, there are some important considerations. First, pay attention to how much time you are billing for each task. Clients often ask that budgets be established for their legal work, and it is important not to go over budget without the client's prior approval. You normally would not have any control over your hourly rate which is set by the firm owners with approval of the client. Remember that your billing will be highly scrutinized by both your employer and the client. Make sure you can justify the amount of time you spend on each task. If you spent two hours on a task that on its face seems as if it should have taken less time, be prepared to show why it was necessary for you to spend more than the task would usually be expected to take. A red flag to the client would be a situation where a maximum of five hours were budgeted for legal research, and you used up four of those hours the first time you worked on the case, with the case far from complete. If you find yourself in this situation let your supervisor know as soon as you recognize it. Make sure you document your file well enough so you can explain weeks, even months, after completing the task how you spent your time. If you checked with your supervisor when you discovered that you may be taking more time than previously thought necessary, make sure that the conversation is documented in your file too. In most cases, clients understand that not everything you will need to do on a case is foreseeable at the outset, but they want to know as soon as you know that the situation has changed.

Second, when working on an hourly billing type of case, recognize that not all of the time spent on a case is going to be billable to the client. There are both ethical and practical reasons for this. It is unethical to bill the client for time spent that is not directly related to the case. If, for example, you have to make two trips to the law library instead of one because you left your notes there and had to go back, you cannot bill the second trip to the client. Also, when you are new to the paralegal profession, it takes longer to accomplish most of the tasks you will be asked to complete. With experience, you will become more efficient in the use of your time. However, the client cannot be expected to pay for multiple drafts of a routine document if they were necessary because you are still in the learning mode. Most firms want new employees to record all of the time spent on a task on their time sheets and let management decide how much of this time is fair to bill to the client. In the next chapter, we will discuss how to meet your hourly billing requirements without compromising your ethical standards.

Third, when billing by the hour, be sure to avoid bundling your tasks. In other words, each different type of task should have a separate entry. Instead of billing two hours for "legal research, meeting with client, and phone call with court," each of those tasks should have a separate entry. Each separate entry might read, "legal research on issue of liability, 1.0 hour; meeting with client, .6 hour; phone call with court regarding trial date, .4 hour." Notice that in addition to separating out the tasks, I also made each entry more descriptive. A client may question "legal research" on a bill but may not question "legal research on issue of liability" because the bill itself explains what the research was about. Get into the habit of itemizing and describing your billing. The client will appreciate it, and you will likely spend less of your time having to justify a billing entry long after the fact.

Flat Fees

A *flat fee* is a preset amount that will be charged for a task, regardless of the amount of time spent handling the task. When a firm agrees to charge $800 for a living trust or $1,500 to defend a drunken driving offense, it is charging a flat fee. Normally, the flat fee is charged for tasks that are considered routine. Based on experience, the firm has a fairly good idea of the amount of time it should take to complete the task. Clients like flat fees because they know ahead of time the most they will be charged. Clients assume the risk that the amount of time spent on the case may be less than anticipated in exchange for the predictability of a flat fee. Law firms assume the risk that they will spend more time on the case than anticipated in exchange for getting paid up front. Further, competition has required in many cases that law firms accept a flat fee when they would probably rather bill by the hour. Clients simply expect a flat fee on certain types of cases and can always find a competing law firm willing to comply.

Flat fees do not tend to work well on nonroutine cases. A large corporate client of mine once requested that a flat fee be charged on litigation matters. The company wanted to control what it described as "out-of-control" legal costs. The flat fee proposed amounted to the best-case scenario for the case: a cooperative opponent, reasonable amounts of discovery, and minimal trial preparation time. Do you see a problem applying a flat fee to a nonroutine matter? It is extremely difficult to know at the outset of a litigation case exactly how much time you will spend on it because much of what you do depends on what your opponent does. We usually do not know at the outset of the case whether the opponent will settle early, serve voluminous discovery requests, or take the case to trial. Setting a budget of hourly fees rather than a flat fee for nonroutine matters made the most sense. The budget is a road map of how the firm expects the case to play out but can be adjusted with prior approval of the client. There are also a few unscrupulous souls in law firms who are tempted not to do much on a case as they otherwise would when they have already been paid the full amount.

If you are working on a flat fee case, there are a few things to keep in mind. First, the client will not be receiving a bill as in an hourly situation. Some firms will still ask you to keep a time sheet and record the time you spend on the case for its own internal purposes. You want to be sure to ask whether you should keep a time sheet on nonhourly cases. Law firms like to know how employees—especially new employees— are spending their time. Also, knowing the amount of time it takes to handle flat fee cases helps the firm set the amount of the flat fee. If time after time the amount spent on a particular type of flat fee case is not financially worthwhile to the firm, it may decide to raise the fee or switch to an hourly fee on future cases.

Second, since flat fees are normally applicable to routine cases, you can develop your own routine to handle cases that maximizes your efficiency. For example, a paralegal may know that all living trusts require the client to complete a checklist of assets and that the format of the living trust will vary little from client to client. On that basis, the paralegal can use a standardized form checklist and form trust. In other words, the paralegal knows ahead of time what she will be doing on the case and can establish a system that applies to most situations.

Third, recognize that unlike an hourly case, the firm cannot go back to the client and ask for more fees when more time is spent on the flat fee case than anticipated, even when all of the extra time was necessary to assist the client. Since there is no budget, as you often find on an hourly case, it can be difficult for the new employee to know how much time is too much when working on a particular task. If your supervisor is not in the habit of telling you when the assignment is given the amount of time it should take you, make sure you ask about it. I am not referring to a deadline such as "you have until next Tuesday." I am referring to the total amount of time it should take you to accomplish a specific task—for example, preparing a summons and complaint should take you two hours. Some firms may not be as diligent about telling you how much time you should spend on a case when a flat fee is involved. Then when it looks as if you might have to spend more time than your supervisor recommended, discuss it with your supervisor *before* you go over the allotted time. Make sure you note when the recommended time to accomplish a task is adjusted by your supervisor. Also, make sure that the allotted amount of time to accomplish a task takes into account that there may need to be more than one draft.

Transactional and Contingency Fees

Transactional fees are those generated with a specific event or occurrence—for example, closing of escrow on real property or issuance of investment bonds. I also include in this definition *contingency fees*. The idea is that the firm does not get paid, and the client does not have to pay, until the legal work is essentially complete. Firms like this type of fee because there is the potential to be paid an above-average amount, as in the case of a contingency fee paid when a personal injury case is settled. Clients like this type of fee because the firm has a financial incentive to complete the work early so it can be paid. These cases differ from flat fee cases in that the transactional fee cases tend to take longer to complete, often involve nonroutine legal work, and the amount of the fee is often unascertainable until the transaction or event is completed. For example, a firm might charge a percentage of the eventual settlement in a personal injury case not knowing the amount of such a settlement at the outset.

Cases involving transactional fees generally require a measure of self-discipline that hourly fee cases do not. In the case of a transactional fee case, there is no monthly bill, and thus no periodic reminder, that causes those working on the case to keep track of the case's progress. I have seen some firms tend to put these types of cases on the back burner in favor of hourly cases, which generate more immediate payment of fees. However, my experience is that transactional cases generally result in higher fees for the firm when they eventually are paid.

What does this mean for you? Avoid the tendency to treat these kinds of cases as less urgent than hourly cases or even flat fee cases. Keep track of your time just as if you were working on an hourly fee case regardless of whether your employer asks you to record your time for transactional fee cases. This will help the firm determine whether the case was worthwhile by comparing the amount of time you spent on a transactional type case times the amount of fees you would have generated on an hourly case using the same amount of your time. Keeping track of your time also will allow you to show your employer how much time you are devoting to all of your cases, not just the hourly ones. This type of information could be important when asking for a raise or in computing your billable hours. You want to make sure your employer counts the amount of time spent on transactional fee cases toward any billable hour requirement that may exist, or at least is aware that you are keeping track of your time in the event that your billable hours become an issue. Finally, keeping track of your time will show your employer you have initiative since you are able to work on non-hourly cases with the same degree of urgency as hourly cases. This will show a level of understanding of how fees are generated in a firm that most new paralegals are likely unaware of.

Contingency fees are common in most law firms. They merit additional attention here because you are likely to work on this type of case as a paralegal. These types of fees are paid by plaintiffs in cases usually involving personal injury or wrongful-termination employment situations. There are ethical prohibitions against their payment in certain types of cases, such as marital dissolution or criminal cases, so your state's ethical codes should be consulted where there is doubt about the type of fee that may be charged. They are paid as a percentage of recovery by the law firm. The amount of recovery is normally the gross amount of the settlement, less any costs advanced by the firm on the client's behalf, and less any liens against settlement, to arrive at a "new settlement." The fee is a percentage of the net settlement. The percentage is agreed to by the firm and client at the beginning of the case and usually ranges from 20 to 33 percent. Some firms request a higher percentage as a fee for cases that go to trial because of the additional risk and work.

Therefore, if a contingency case settled for $12,000, the costs advanced by the firm were $2,000 and there was a medical care provider lien in the amount of $1,000, the firm's fee would be $3,000, assuming a 33 percent contingency. The $2,000 advanced by the firm would be reimbursed to the firm, but it is not part of the fee. This means the firm would receive a total of $4,000—$3,000 (fee) plus $1,000 (reimbursed costs.)

When the defendant (or its insurer) pays the $12,000 settlement, the check is made out to the firm and the client, both of whom must endorse the check for deposit into the firm's trust account. Only after the depository bank confirms the check has cleared, meaning the settlement funds were transferred from the defendant's (or insurer's) bank to the depository bank, may the funds be disbursed to the client and firm in the manner described in the prior paragraph. The client must agree to the disbursement by way of a signed itemization, or "recapitulation" statement.

> Paralegal Perspective <

Paralegals are moneymakers for law firms. Many firms employ paralegals instead of associates because paralegals can essentially perform the same tasks other than what is prohibited by law. Demonstrate that you can positively affect the firm's bottom line.

STATUS, PRESTIGE, AND REPUTATION ARE IMPORTANT

You will find that most lawyers care about what their colleagues in the legal community think about them. We all want the approval and acceptance of our fellow professionals to varying degrees, but lawyers seem to place a higher value on this than others. Part of this no doubt stems from the practical: when colleagues think highly of another lawyer or another law firm, they are more likely to refer clients to that firm. When a firm's reputation is good, professional life is easier. Opposing counsel tends to trust and cooperate with lawyers or firms deemed honest. Judges keep a special lookout for those who have reputations for dishonesty.

Another reason that lawyers value status, prestige, and reputation is less practical: they are competitive by nature and have a sometimes unhealthy need to "keep score." After all, you don't know who won unless scores are kept. That's why you will hear lawyers talk about a good many things like their won-loss trial record, the size of their firm compared with others in the community, or even the kind of cars they drive compared with other attorneys. While I am certainly not proficient in psychology, I do believe some of this behavior stems from insecurity.

While you as a new paralegal should not get caught up in this kind of a mentality, it is important to be aware of it because it affects your professional life. How? You will be in a position to advance the firm's status, prestige, and reputation. When you know something is important to your employer and you make efforts toward those ends, you become a more valuable employee.

An example is a paralegal who recently accompanied her supervising attorney to a class of mine. I had read in a local newspaper about a large settlement a local firm just made with a governmental entity in a civil rights case. I was teaching a class in civil rights, so I invited the attorney to come in and discuss this case (keeping certain information confidential as required by the terms of the settlement). To my surprise, the attorney said the paralegal who worked on the case with him also wanted to address my class. When the two showed up, they brought a slide presentation about how civil rights cases are handled, which the paralegal prepared just for my class. Both the attorney and the paralegal were a hit!

Speaking with my class probably did not result in new business for the firm, but it advanced the firm's status and reputation as a leading civil rights firm in the community. There were looks of admiration on the faces of my students, and they were told about all of the injustices this firm has attempted to correct. (The admiration was deserved, by the way.) The paralegal who accompanied her supervising attorney did much to advance her firm's cause that evening.

Any time you have an opportunity to make your employer look better to the public, take advantage of it. Your employer will appreciate and remember it. I recall the civil rights attorney who spoke to my class, saying several times that evening how much he appreciated the work his paralegal did on their recent settlement. The opportunities sometimes are as simple as pointing out to a client the firm's positive reputation. In other words, as a new paralegal, you may not have as many opportunities to speak with a class or other groups as you will later in your career, but even the minor efforts have a cumulative effect. The main thing is to have the attitude that you want to make your employer look good to clients, colleagues, court personnel, and the general public at every occasion.

YOUR TIME IS IMPORTANT

Time is the most important commodity a firm can offer. Once you recognize this and demonstrate an appreciation for its high value, you will advance in your career. Indeed, it is hard to imagine anyone in a legal career going very far who undervalues the importance of time. You need to treat your own time and the time of others as important.

Treating your own time as important means you treat every hour of your workday as if it were your last. What do I mean by this? Picture yourself with one hour to go before day's end. You work extra hard to finish up your work for the day. There is a sense of urgency. Not a moment is wasted. The urgency of the situation gives you extra energy you didn't know you had. You don't put anything off that you could do before you leave that day. You are thinking about what you need to do next even before you finish what you are working on now. It's amazing how much work you do in an hour. Now picture yourself with this rapidity and efficiency throughout your day. This is the high regard for time I am referring to; it is impossible for your efforts to go unnoticed. Being successful in large part means distinguishing yourself from the average employee. You want to stand out in a positive way. Managing your time for maximum production and efficiency will make it impossible for you to do anything but stand out from the rest of the pack. Being ahead of the pack is how you advance in your career.

I am not referring to throwing your life out of balance. An employer who values employees will not request unreasonable sacrifices. I am aware of employers who demand that employees work every weekend. Needless to say, those firms have more than their share of turnover. Remember that your career is a marathon and you don't want to tire early. This doesn't mean you should never come in early or stay late when circumstances require it, but you don't want to make it a way of life. When you give your employer the most efficient and productive effort every hour of every day, you are sending a clear message that you understand how valuable time is; you are not telling your employer that your job is your life. Besides, you may be surprised at how fast your day goes by when you are doing your best to squeeze in as much work before leaving the office.

Treating the time of others as important means recognition and appreciation that just about everything you do has an effect on the someone else. When you are writing a memorandum of law, the amount of time your supervising attorney spends reviewing it depends on how you write the memorandum. If it's written in a clear and concise manner, it will take less time to read. If the law referred to is attached, it will take less time for your supervising attorney to review than it would to either return it to you with a note to attach the cases or find the cases herself. If you make sure you understand a legal research assignment at the beginning, you will take less of your supervisor's time asking follow-up questions later. If a client calls and you answer the phone, it will take less of your supervisor's time if you, rather than your supervisor, can handle the client's request. If you can discuss several issues or cases in one meeting with your supervisor instead of multiple meetings, you will save your supervisor time. These are examples of how what you do affects the efficiency of others, especially your supervisor. There are few occasions more irritating to your supervisor than to take up needless time.

This does not mean you should always take the method that results in the least amount of time if it affects the quality of your work. If the work is subpar simply because you are trying to do it quickly, you will only have to do it again, thus using up more time. In the process, your employer will question your ability to do good work. What you should always do is consider the time usage implications for others of everything you do without compromising how well you do your work.

YOU ARE IMPORTANT

You and your coworkers are the most important assets in any law firm. You are more valuable than the expensive furniture some firms have, the computers, the office equipment, legal books, and on-line research accounts combined. The reason is that none of these assets is of any use without people to operate or use them. If people do not operate or use these assets, the work does not get done, the clients go elsewhere, and the firm shuts its doors forever. Although advances in technology will continue to make you and your coworkers more productive, there will always need to be someone like you to use the technology. Unlike some occupations (bank tellers come to mind), the work of paralegals will never be relegated to a machine. Your job is too complex and the need of clients to interact with legal professionals too great for your employer to fail to recognize your worth.

True, some employers are better at recognizing the worth of a paralegal than others, but your worth is the same regardless of your employer. By "worth" I am referring to your ability to help the firm meet its objectives: to retain and attract clients, produce high-quality legal work, and make a profit. The reason your worth does not change regardless of your employer is that you possess the same ability whether you work for one employer or another. An appreciation of your ability may change depending on the employer, but your ability does not.

How do I know you and your coworkers are your employer's most valuable asset? In pure dollar terms, labor is the firm's greatest cost. If the firm added up its expenses for rent, insurance, and all the other costs of running a business, it would be very likely that salaries and benefits would top the list. The firm's greatest expense is labor because its employees represent its greatest asset. The legal employer has invested thousands of dollars finding you, training you, and outfitting you with the tools to do your job. It will spend thousands more in the future keeping you.

Think about the cost of finding you. Members of the firm and their staff spent time deciding that they needed to hire someone, developing a plan to attract the best applicants, reviewing applications, interviewing applicants, checking references, in some cases asking you in for a follow-up interview, and making a final decision to extend an offer of employment. It would not be unusual at all for the firm to have invested the equivalent of days or weeks hiring one person. In my own legal practice, my partners and I often interviewed for a paralegal or attorney position at the placement office of the paralegal or law school we thought would likely yield the best applicants. Before you ever begin your new job as a paralegal, it is likely the firm has invested thousands of dollars in out-of-pocket expense and the opportunity cost of spending time in finding you that could have been spent generating legal fees.

Before you begin your job, you will also need a computer, printer, furniture, software, telephone, and office supplies. You will need an area to work; your employer pays rent based on the square footage of the office. Forms related to state and federal taxes, health insurance, and retirement plan will need to be prepared by staff.

The firm has already invested tens of thousands of dollars in you before you begin your first day on the job! Once you begin your job, the firm will spend thousands training you. Your training costs will consist of the opportunity cost of others' taking time to assign and review your work, sending you to classes, and the extra time any new person spends learning a profession that is not ethically chargeable to clients. For example, if you are asked to prepare a legal research memorandum, it may have to go through several drafts before the quality is such that your supervisor can rely on it. Each draft needs to be reviewed. It is not ethical to charge the client for multiple drafts of a legal memorandum prepared by someone still learning how to prepare them.

To be successful, you want to make sure your employer receives the highest possible return on the investment it has made in you. This means that you should not only listen to your supervisor when she tells you how to prepare the next assignment better, you should learn. If you do not understand why the supervisor wants you to prepare an assignment a certain way, ask. Make sure you take what you have learned in doing previous assignments and use that knowledge to make the next assignment better. If your employer sends you to a class, don't just attend the class; absorb the information. If your employer provides software for you to use, don't just use the functions that allow you to complete your work; use the functions that allow you to complete your work more efficiently and with higher quality.

All of this is much easier said than done. Yes, it does take extra effort to get the most out of the training your employer offers. Remember that the skills you develop go wherever you go; you do not leave them in a desk drawer when you change employers. These are the skills that are going to make you valued by other legal employers. All the extra effort you make benefits you, not just your employer. When the economy takes an inevitable downturn, which employees are likely to be out of work: the ones who showed up and did the minimum or the employees who excelled? When a great new position opens up in the firm or with another employer, who is more likely to obtain that position: the employee who went through the motions in his job, or the employee who constantly sought to improve? The answers are obvious.

Employees with the drive to excel enjoy their jobs more. A paralegal job is more interesting when you become better at it. The workday goes much faster when you get completely absorbed in what you are doing. Have you ever been in a job where you did not have enough to do? Time almost stands still. At the end of the day, you are more tired than you would have been if every minute was busy. Humans just are not built to go through the motions. Certainly, we could not have survived as a species if we were like that. Doing what is necessary to succeed is natural; attitudes resulting in failure are learned. That is why those from whom you seek advice about your career should be positive in outlook. You learn to fail from those with negative attitudes.

Doing what is necessary for success does not mean throwing your life out of balance. The difference between success and failure is relatively minimal in the paralegal profession as in other professions. For example, when you attend a class your employer sends you to, you are spending the same amount of time at the class whether you merely attend or whether you really listen and absorb the information. When your supervisor tells you how to do your next assignment better, you will be spending less time doing the assignment right the next time because you listened carefully than you would doing extra drafts because you were not paying attention. If you take the time to learn all of the features of the software provided to you, you will spend less time on future assignments because your knowledge has made you more productive. Success does not mean becoming a slave to your job; it means using your time wisely and productively. Knowing what is important to your employer will allow you to ensure your time is used in this manner.

CHAPTER SUMMARY

Knowing what is important to a law firm will help you as a new paralegal to focus on helping the firm achieve its objectives. A paralegal that has this focus will be valued by the law firm. Make sure you approach your job with the attitude that you want your employer to be successful. Law firms value clients. Without clients, there would not be a reason for the firm to exist. Fees are valuable because firms cannot continue to exist if they are not profitable. If the firm is not profitable, it cannot employ anyone. Firms also value status, prestige, and reputation because they affect their ability to attract clients and for less tangible reasons, such as the firm owners' need to be respected by its peers and competitors. Remember that the difference between success and failure for a new paralegal is relatively minimal. The extra effort it takes to help the firm achieve its objectives should not throw your personal and professional life out of balance.

>Web Research Exercise<

On the internet, go to http://www.paralegalgateway.com. You will find useful articles about paralegal careers as well as a considerable amount of other information useful to paralegals. Find what you consider a particularly good article that will assist you in becoming a successful paralegal. Share the article with your class. As your classmates share their articles, take note of any information that may be of use to you in your own career.

>Chapter Exercises<

1. Developing time efficiency habits is very important in your career. Ask yourself how efficiently you use your personal, school, and work time (if appropriate). Are there opportunities to use your time more efficiently? Write down every idea that comes to mind that would be likely to help you become more efficient. Put those ideas into practice. Place a daily reminder on

your calendar to follow these ideas until they become habit. Once a month, repeat the process of asking yourself how efficiently you are using your time, writing down new ideas, discussing them with fellow students, and implementing them. Discard any ideas that do not work after trying them for a month.

2. Assume you are starting a new paralegal job and you have been asked to prepare a legal research memorandum on an important issue your employer is handling for one of its clients. After working very hard on the assignment, you turn it in to your supervisor. A few days later, the assignment is returned with a hand-written note from your supervisor that says, "Needs work. Please see me." How can you best follow up to learn the most you can from the assignment? What should you ask your supervisor when you see him or her? What should you tell your supervisor when you meet? When should you see your supervisor? How much of your supervisor's time should you take? Is there anything you should do between the time you received the assignment with your supervisor's comments and the time you meet with him or her? What should be your attitude toward your supervisor's comments?

3. Recognizing the value of lost opportunities to improve on your career skills goes a long way in ensuring that you take advantage of those opportunities in the future. Are there occasions in the past month when you just went through the motions instead of getting the most out of your time? (There are for all of us.) For example, were you in class and not paying full attention? Did you have a question in class but never asked it or attempted to find the answer on your own? Were you at work and passed up an opportunity to learn more? For each such occasion, describe what happened in writing and what you did not learn even though you had the opportunity. Next, describe in writing what you will do in the future to avoid losing those opportunities to improve. For example, if you had a question in class that you did not ask, next time you will ask it in class, see your professor outside class, or find the answer yourself. If a coworker is using software you would like to know more about, you will ask if there is a time you could come by and learn more about how to use that software or if someone else in the firm could show you. If your employer invites employees to hear a presentation by a legal research database representative, you will make the time to attend and ask questions.

>Ethical Discussion<

Can a law firm place so much value on its most important clients that ethical issues are created? Under what circumstances? What can you do to assist your employer in meeting its obligations to the firm's most valued clients while also maintaining the firm's ethical obligations to all of its clients? Explain your response.

>Suggested Reading<

B. Eugene Griessman, *Time Tactics of Very Successful People*, McGraw-Hill, 1994.

Chapter 7
Handling the Dreaded Billable Hour

Key Success Points

> *Billable hours are the work hours that can be billed to a client, not the number of hours you work on a task.*

> *Meeting your employer's billable hours requirement calls for effort and organization.*

> *Never compromise ethical standards to achieve billable hours*

> > > > > > > > > >

"Well, well. If it isn't
Mr. Double Billing!"

WHAT ARE BILLABLE HOURS AND WHY ARE THEY IMPORTANT?

Billable hours are the hours, or portions of hours, a law firm charges its clients. For many law firms, billable hours determine its financial success. A law firm can stay in business in the long term only if its revenues are greater than expenses. Revenues are essentially legal fees. While the fees may be generated by fees from contingency or transactional cases, in a great number of firms, hourly fees supply most, if not all, the revenue. These hourly fees are deemed "billable hours" because only those hours that can be billed to a client result in revenue to the firm. Since these firms' survival, as well as the firm owners' lifestyle, is directly affected by the number of billable hours generated, they are very closely watched.

Here is how the concept of billable hours works in most firms. A firm expects each of its attorneys and paralegals to bill a certain minimum number of hours, usually expressed in terms of annual billing requirements. For example, a firm may require each attorney and paralegal to bill a minimum of 2,000 hours annually. (I use the figure of 2,000 for illustrative purposes only since the required billable hours vary from firm to firm.) In order to meet the 2,000-hour requirement, the attorneys and paralegal are given time sheets that they use to keep track of the tasks they perform on each case and the amount of time each task took. Usually the time spent on each task is expressed in tenths of hours, so if you spent 90 minutes preparing interrogatories, for example, the time indicated on your time sheet would be 1.5 hours.

You might be thinking billable hours should be easy to achieve. If you worked an eight-hour day, five days per week, 50 weeks per year (with two weeks set aside for vacation), the total is 2,000 hours. But remember that we are talking about hours that can be billed to the client, not the total number of hours you spend at work. Think about a typical workday. Is there time you spend doing tasks not specifically related to a particular case? You cannot bill a client for time spent turning on your computer, getting a cup of coffee, going to lunch, using the restroom, meeting with a vendor, small talk with a coworker, reloading the copier, or other tasks that may be important but are not directly related to legal work for a client.

A WORD ABOUT ETHICS

There are also situations in which your task is directly related to legal work for a client but is not billable. For example, most clients are not willing to pay for numerous drafts of a legal document that a trained paralegal could have done without all the drafts. Most clients are not willing to pay for you merely "thinking" about the case; you have to be doing something tangible, such as research or preparing a document or meeting with a witness.

Therefore, if you think about how best to handle a particular task for a client, the time spent thinking is usually not billable. The fact that your client normally will not pay for you to just "think" about the case is ironic because that is often where you come up with the ideas that help the client most. However, clients tend to want tangible results, such as a brief, meeting, or something else that makes sense to someone without legal training to have to pay for.

There are also ethical considerations that require fees to be reasonable, which usually does not include "just" thinking about a case. As a fee arbitrator (someone who arbitrates fee disputes between lawyers and clients), I have seen the client's trust violated by improper and unethical billing. One reason for this problem is there is a lot of room for abuse. Clients do not usually know how much work is involved with each task that is billed. If you spend less time rummaging through documents than you billed, the client may never know. It is tempting to pad the bill if you fall behind in your billable hour requirement. But *never* participate in any unethical behavior, whether it is billing or anything else. You will find that the legal community in which you work seems smaller the longer you are a part of it. Everyone has a reputation. I believe that there is no such thing as a neutral reputation; yours will be either positive or negative. *Make sure your reputation is positive.* Is any reputable firm going to want you to work there if they are not sure whether you can be trusted? Of course not. If your employer places you in a position where unethical behavior is supported or encouraged, change employers. There can also be criminal implications to unethical billing or other unethical practices. I cannot stress how easily a good career can be ruined by unethical behavior.

There are holidays, sick days, professional conferences, continuing education classes, and other days when you will be away from the office throughout the year, which could make meeting billable hour requirements more difficult to achieve.

Are you beginning to get the picture? Achieving the minimum billable hours your employer requires takes both effort and organization; it will not occur automatically just because you spend a lot of time at the office. New legal professionals are not nearly as efficient as they will be with more experience. This is normal and expected. With ethical considerations, nonbillable tasks, holidays, vacations, conferences, and many other distractions, how in the world will you bill the hours your employer requires?

HOW TO ACHIEVE BILLABLE HOUR SUCCESS

There is no getting around the fact that you cannot bill hours unless you spend a sufficient amount of time working. My rule of thumb was that I had to spend at least 25 percent more than the billable hour requirement to bill a sufficient number of hours. Therefore, if the billable hour requirement is 1,800 annually, I would have to spend 2,250 hours at the office each year. This works out to about 45 hours per week, assuming you work 50 weeks per year. Do you see why asking about billable hour requirements when deciding whether to accept a job offer is important? These requirements affect your personal life.

You should monitor closely the number of hours you spend at work compared with the number of hours you bill. This will tell you how many hours you must work to achieve a billable hour. For example, if you spend 50 hours at work to bill 35 hours, it takes about 1.4 hours of work to bill 1 hour. If you are required to bill 1,600 hours annually, it will take about 2,240 hours of work in one year to meet your billable hour requirement since 2,240 is about 1.4 times 1,600. If you work 50 weeks per year, that means you need to work about 45 hours per week, or 9 hours per day.

You will find that you become much more efficient as you gain experience. If it takes 1.4 hours of work to bill 1 hour when you begin your paralegal career, it may take 1.2 hours a year later. The reason is that you don't have to do numerous drafts of a document to get it right. You are able to find the cases that are on point by connecting the right terms and connectors using Lexis or Westlaw the first time. You are able to ask the right questions when interviewing a witness for the first time instead of having to call the witness back because you forgot to ask something important to your firm's case. In other words, you become more efficient because you know your job better. Therefore, it is important to constantly monitor the number of hours you work to achieve 1 billable hour since the ratio should be improving in your favor if you are learning your job. Then you will be able to adjust the number of hours you need to work accordingly. When you become a seasoned paralegal with years of experience, you will find that you settle into a more comfortable and predictable ratio of amount of hours worked versus hours billed.

> Paralegal Perspective <

Billing for my hours was one of the most difficult challenges in my new paralegal job. I have been on my job for
seven months now and still have to focus on incorporating
billing into my daily routine. Billing is now an extremely important part of my daily tasks not only for the firm, but for
the client as well. I sought out other paralegals in the firm
to see how and what they billed so I could find a billing
routine that worked for me. I regularly ask for feedback
from the attorney reviewing my bills and the legal administrator to ensure I am billing appropriately. Of course, I did
this over lunch so as not to impact billing hours!

Make sure you do not leave the office each day unless you have
billed the minimum number of hours required. If you get too far behind,
you will find it becomes very difficult to catch up. Anticipate whether
there are periods during the year when you will be able to bill more
hours or will not be able to bill as many hours, and then adjust accordingly. For example, I knew that in a litigation practice, there would be
several times a year when I would have to work longer hours to prepare
for trial. Since the nature of my practice was that there would almost always be trial preparation to do during the year, the minimum hours I
calculated I would need to bill each day seemed reasonable. If you work
in an office that specializes in tax law, there may be certain times a year
in which you know you will be working and billing more.

However, if you work in an office where you know there are not
fairly predictable times during the year to bill more, you should not be
content to bill the minimum each day. There may be lost time from work
due to illness, family responsibilities, an accident, or a host of other un-
predictable events. Further, you don't always know months or weeks in
advance that there is a professional course you may want to attend. Try
to build a "credit" by billing more than the minimum early in the annual billing cycle so you will have the comfort of knowing later in the
year that you will not have a problem meeting the billable hour requirements. How much of a credit you should build depends on your
situation. If you have no problem spending long hours at the office

when you need to, the credit you require may be minimal. If you are not so inclined or are not in a position to work extra hard in the event your billable hours become questionable (perhaps because you lack flexible child care), you will need to build up a larger credit.

Get into the habit of writing each billable event down the moment you do the work. If you do not write the time on your time sheet the moment you complete the work, you may forget to do it altogether. I once knew a new attorney who did not write his time down until the end of the day, and he often shortchanged himself. He felt he was too busy to write down his time during the day. Law firms are busy places: the phone seems to ring off the hook at times; clients sometimes walk in without appointments; your supervisor may ask you to stop what you're doing immediately because of an urgent matter. You will invariably not capture all of your billable time if you don't write it down immediately.

Identify aspects of your job where efficiency doesn't depend on experience. While some tasks take less time to do well only with experience (such as writing legal briefs), others do not. You need not be a seasoned paralegal to arrange files on your computer so that you can retrieve documents quickly. You already know that consolidating your trips to the courthouse or law library will save time. It is common sense that too much time spent socializing in the office is unproductive. Having your desk arranged at the end of the day so you can immediately start the next day without delay gets you off to a good start. Take a close look at your new job, ask others for their suggestions, and do those things more efficiently that do not depend on your having a lot of experience.

Make sure you truly understand the billable hour requirements. Is there an attorney billable hour requirement that differs from the requirement for paralegals? By "billable hours," is the firm referring to the amount of time you spend on a task or the amount of time the firm can ethically bill a client? The two amounts can often be different. Since paralegals often have a wide variety of skills, which means they can spend some of their time on nonbillable tasks, do they get to count the time for these tasks toward their billable requirements? If a paralegal works on a contingency or transactional fee case, should he or she record the time on a time sheet? Is the "requirement" just a preference, or is it firm? Conversely, is the requirement just a minimum to keep your job, and does the firm expect more from those who wish to advance?

DON'T BECOME OBSESSED

While nearly all firms whose income is derived from billable hours closely monitor them, some are obsessed. I know of a law firm that posts the billable hours of its attorneys and paralegals monthly, names and all! This creates a competitive, if not unreasonably stressful, atmosphere. You could imagine the temptation of employees to overstate their billable hours. It is certainly legitimate for firms to monitor billable hours closely, but this kind of fixation spells trouble. You would likely be better off staying away from firms like these. They tend to have a lot of turnover. In fact, I am convinced that many of them *depend* on turnover so that few employers ever command senior pay.

While you should avoid firms obsessed with billable hours, you should not become obsessed yourself. If you are working hard and as efficiently as reasonably possible, the billable hours usually take care of themselves. Although I was meticulous about keeping track of my hours early in my legal career, the problem wasn't too few billable hours; it was too much work. Find a firm in which the billable hour requirements match the balance you have decided you want between work and your personal life. This does not mean you shouldn't be willing to work extra hard to learn your new profession. It does mean that there should be light at the end of the proverbial tunnel. The firm's policy about billing should be one that you can reach without sacrificing your health or your personal life. The billable hour requirement shouldn't take the enjoyment out of working.

Although billable hours are important, they are not the sole criterion on which you will be evaluated by your employer. Your legal and interpersonal skills are also important. Your progress in your profession will make a difference. Are you getting better at what you do? Are you progressing at an acceptable pace? Can the firm trust you not to do anything unethical that would make it liable? Do you keep client confidences? Are you there to help when the firm finds itself in a crunch? Do you contribute to a positive working environment? Do you communicate well orally and in writing? These are all considerations that your employer considers important that have little to do with billable hours. This is not an excuse to discount the importance of meeting billable hour requirements; it is to place billable hours in proper perspective.

CHAPTER SUMMARY

Billing a certain minimum number of hours is a requirement in many law firms. This requirement is known as "billable hours." It is not always easy to meet billable hours requirements, especially for the new paralegal, because not all the time spent at work is billable to the client. Monitor the time spent at work and compare it to the hours billed. This will give you an estimate of the number of hours you must spend on the job to achieve the firm's billable hour requirement. Paralegals become more efficient at billing as they gain experience. In other words, the number of hours spent at work will more closely resemble the amount of hours billed as you become more experienced. Strategies for meeting billable hour requirements include not leaving work each day until the billable hours for that day are met, writing down the billable task immediately upon the task's conclusion, identifying aspects of your job where you can be more efficient without regard to your experience, and having a clear understanding of your employer's billable hour requirement. Firms are reasonable to place a high degree of importance in achieving billable hour goals, but those firms obsessed with billable hours may not be great places for a paralegal to work. Meeting billable hour requirements is a very important criterion for evaluation of the new paralegal, but not the sole one for evaluating the paralegal's worth to the firm.

>Web Research Exercise<

Go to www.nala.org and review the latest National Utilization and Compensation Survey. The survey will give information about billable hours requirements for paralegals nationwide. The data should assist you in determining whether a particular firm's billable hours requirements are reasonable.

>Chapter Exercises<

1. Assume you were recently hired as a paralegal with a law firm. You are aware that the firm requires 1,600 billable hours annually. Make a list of

everything you can do now that will make use of your time at work more efficient and result in achieving your firm's billable hour requirement. Examples would be to organize computer and paper files for documents you can expect to use, review both legal and nonlegal software functions for more efficient utilization, and practice using more advanced features of on-line legal research services. If you are already employed as a paralegal, immediately incorporate all ideas that would assist you in being more efficient. If you are not yet employed as a paralegal, save this information for use when you begin your first paralegal job. If you are unsure about an idea, ask someone whose opinion you respect whether a particular idea is likely to make you more efficient and achieve your firm's billable hour requirement.

2. Assume you are at your first day at work as a new paralegal. Your supervising attorney calls you into her office and wants to discuss your new job. She tells you the billable hour requirements of the firm. What questions would you ask her to assure yourself that you have a clear understanding of the billable hour requirements?

3. You just interviewed for a paralegal position that you think sounds ideal: the work is interesting, and the pay looks great. About a week later, you receive a telephone call from the firm offering you the position. During the course of the conversation, you learn that the firm's billable hour requirements are 2,200 per year. You tell the firm representative that you are happy with the offer and will let the firm know your decision the next day. You are concerned that the billable hour requirements seem high. How would these requirements affect your professional and personal lives? How would you go about making a decision whether to accept the position? What considerations are important to you in making your decision?

> Ethical Discussion <

Assume you are asked to prepare a motion for summary judgment for a large corporate client. You diligently record all the time you spent on the motion and clearly identify each task you completed on your billing time sheet. The motion is later granted, saving the client a substantial amount of legal fees since the matter does not have to proceed to trial. Your supervising attorney asks you to "revise" your time sheet so the entries are less specific. Further, you are asked to include all the time you "thought" about the case and label it either "legal research" or "motion preparation." Finally, since the client does not pay to have drafts of a motion reviewed and revised by your supervising attorney, some of the entries recorded on your time sheet are changed to reflect that the supervising attorney worked on the task. What ethical issues are presented by these facts? How should these issues be handled? Explain your responses.

≫ Suggested Reading ≪

Linda L. Edwards, *Law Office Skills*, Delmar Learning, 2003.

Chapter 8
How to Manage Your Workload

Key Success Points

> *You cannot successfully manage your workload without a proper approach.*

> *Prioritization of your work assignments by due date, assignor, and nature of assignment is critical.*

> *When you make a mistake, be the first to admit it. Learn from it, and then forget it.*

> > > > > > > > >

Maria is delayed at the office. On her behalf, I thank the Paralegal Association for this "Most Hours Billed" award.

HOW TO APPROACH YOUR WORKLOAD

Your approach to your workload throughout your career is important to success. In your first year as a paralegal, your approach is more than important. It is critical. The assignments you are given as a new paralegal will seem insurmountable without the correct approach. The good news is that you have it within your ability to do much more than you think you can. Even with your relative inexperience, you can survive and then thrive in your new work setting. Handling your workload with the correct attitude will make all the difference in the world. Here is how to approach your workload for success.

Treat Every Hour as If It Is the Last Hour of the Day

For most of us, the last hour of the day is a time when we are rushing to finish up for the day. There is no wasted energy. All of our focus is on the task at hand. When we complete that task, we immediately move to the next task without even the slightest pause. We know that we are trying to finish everything we need to do that day before the clock runs out on us. It is akin to the two-minute drill in football when the team marches down the field with single-minded determination to score. And when we approach each hour of the workday as if it were the last of the day, our tasks get done and the day is over before we realize it. It seems the more energy we need, the more we have.

Contrast this with a job in which there is too much time to do too little work. I took a job one summer as a grant writer. I was hired not because there was enough work for another full-time person but because the position was budgeted and would be eliminated in the next year's budget if it was not filled. It was the longest summer I ever spent working. Without enough to do I was exhausted at the end of the day. Had I been busy, I would have enjoyed myself more. Treating every hour of your workday as if it were your last of the day will not make you more tired; it will give you more energy!

Never Forget the Value of Time

Few other settings value time more than a law office does. Time is finite; when it is lost, it cannot be recovered and it is gone forever. Your time is valuable, and your coworkers' time is valuable.

Make sure each task you do is the most efficient way to accomplish it without sacrificing quality. For example, it is more efficient to carefully prepare one or two drafts of a legal document than to hurriedly do each draft but not have a high-quality product until six or seven drafts later. I have seen new legal professionals do as many as 10 drafts of a document when far less time would have been necessary had they used more care earlier in the process. Another example is the failure to combine trips to the library or courthouse. When you go to these places, make sure you bring along other work that needs to be done there instead of having to make two trips. Often it is a better use of time to take a phone call than to have someone else take a message and play phone tag for the next few days. It is a better use of time to make your lunch prior to arriving at work than to have to go somewhere and wait for someone to prepare it for you. Keeping a good record of exactly what you have done on a task and what you have left to do is far more efficient than jotting down a few scribbles and trying to figure out later exactly what you need to do to complete the task. I have seen people with dozens of tasks going on simultaneously not keep a single note of their progress on a task. You can imagine how much time they spend as they try to figure out what needs to be done on a task each time they go back to it. In every assignment you are given, think carefully about how you can best accomplish the task without wasting time.

You must value the time of your coworkers, especially that of your supervisor. This means saving all of your questions for one meeting instead of constantly knocking on your supervisor's door with a question. It means carrying a notepad with you everywhere, so if your supervisor asks you to do something, she does not have to repeat herself because you couldn't remember what you were asked to do. Valuing your coworkers' time means not asking someone to do something you can do yourself. Showing that you respect someone else's time is the same as showing that you respect that person. It will go a long way in others' perception of you as a professional rather than a novice. Although this seems like a common courtesy, it is not so common. I constantly see paralegal students who have not yet learned to value the time of others. Yet anyone can learn to value someone else's time; it just takes practice.

Do Every Assignment as If the Boss Were Watching

If your supervisor was present when you met with a client or called the court, wouldn't you make sure you did the absolute best you could with every part of the task? You would strive to say and do all the right things in order to impress the boss. You would be alert to any problems or potential problems that needed handling. Your energy and attention levels would be elevated. You would do your best to ensure that the client or court clerk (or anyone else you were dealing with) came away with a positive impression of you. You would act professionally but do so without unnecessarily using time. You would attentively listen to a client's concerns but not go on for twenty minutes about the ball game or a television show you watched last night.

In a sense, your boss *is* always present. There are very few secrets in any law office. When I was a partner in a law firm, I regularly asked clients, as well as others whom employees came into contact with, if they received adequate service. The best compliment you can have as a paralegal is that a client tells your supervisor what a wonderful job you are doing.

View Your Work in Segments

In most law offices, looking at all the tasks you have in the aggregate can seem overwhelming. Especially for a new paralegal, the prospect of having to complete *all that work* can be daunting. The reaction to all this work tends to be extreme: either you freeze and are unable to decide what to do first, or you rush through your work with little regard for quality. Either reaction yields poor results.

As you climb that mountain of work, set short-term goals and break those goals into smaller segments. For example, if you have to prepare a motion to dismiss, summarize deposition transcripts for a case going to trial, and meet with a client today, view each of these three tasks as a goal unto itself.

First, prioritize your tasks. Which tasks need to be done first? If the motion is due tomorrow, the client is coming in at 2:00 P.M., and the trial is next week, you would likely decide to work on the motion first. Then you would work on the deposition summaries but leave enough time before 2:00 P.M. to prepare for the client meeting. Always factor into your day the inevitable and unforeseen situations and tasks that are part of life in any law office. If you are asked to do something unanticipated (and that will happen often), reprioritize and reset your goals for the day. The term *multitasking* is relatively new, but the concept is quite old: you need the ability to do several tasks simultaneously. Obviously, you cannot physically work on two things at the same time, but you do need to be able to have multiple projects moving forward efficiently at any given time.

Since you have decided to work on the motion to dismiss first, break down the motion into logical components. You will work on the motion until 1:00 P.M. because you need an hour to prepare for the client meeting. If you are in the office at 9:00 A.M., you have two and a half hours to work on the motion (you have to factor in lunch and a cushion for unexpected tasks like a phone call you didn't anticipate or a rush assignment from your supervisor—for example: "Jon, could you Shepardize this case before I quote it in my brief that needs to be filed today?"). Since you have two and a half hours, you might break the task of writing the motion to dismiss down to one hour for legal research, one hour to write the motion, and a half-hour for any revisions that need to be done. At 1:00 P.M., you stop what you're doing and pull the client's file to review it in anticipation of meeting the client an hour later. At 2:00 P.M. you have met with the client and noted the file. You did not quite finish the motion and have three hours left in the day. You spend another hour finishing up the motion and then go straight into deposition summaries. When doing the summaries, you anticipate which ones the trial attorney will need first and start with those. At the end of the day, you assess what you accomplished and what you have yet to accomplish tomorrow. Then you once again start the process of breaking down your tasks and prioritizing.

Although every situation is unique, the process of breaking down tasks and prioritizing is applicable to all situations. Do you see what happened? Once the tasks are broken down into manageable components, they do not seem nearly as enormous. In the process of breaking down and prioritizing, you have also planned your workday. Your confidence level increases because you have planned how to accomplish your work. Even when the inevitable unforeseen task arises, you have a process by which to reassess, prioritize, and break down your work into manageable components.

> Paralegal Perspective <

Complete as many tasks as possible on a case without being asked, and present your work to your attorney for review. What a surprise it is for an attorney to find that the mediation package she has been dreading and postponing is sitting on her desk in draft form to review and finalize! It is a tremendous learning experience for you; it allows you to show your attorney what you are capable of and reminds the attorney of how valuable an asset you are to the practice.

Pressure Is a Motivator

Everyone has felt pressure sometimes, and many do not respond to it positively: they get angry, frustrated, confused, indecisive, or otherwise respond in a manner that makes them not perform to their potential, thus *increasing* the pressure. The cycle keeps getting worse until they bend or break under the increasing and seemingly insurmountable pressure. When this happens, their effectiveness decreases, their health may suffer, and their personal life is adversely affected.

The root of the response may be blamed on one overriding emotion: fear. It is not pressure itself that causes a negative response but fear derived from the pressure. Those who do not respond to pressure well fear not getting their work done, not doing their work well, not being respected by coworkers, not lasting in the job, not paying their bills, not providing for their family, and even worse fates. The fear is really apprehension of the unknown. As a paralegal, you have complicated legal work to do and important people telling you they needed it done yesterday. And largely because you are new to your profession, you don't know how you're going to do what is expected of you.

You overcome fear based on the unknown by lots of preparation. Reading this book and following through with its ideas and suggestions is part of the preparation. The more you prepare to succeed and the less you leave unknown, the less you will fear. And the less you fear, the more you will treat pressure as a partner.

Think for a moment about the positive aspects of pressure. When you are under pressure, you are extremely focused on the task at hand. You have incredible amounts of energy. You complete the task without any wasted effort. These, in fact, are all traits that an employer wants in an employee. Since pressure in a law office is always present at varying levels, you always have two choices (notice I said the choice was *yours*): let the pressure adversely affect you by the fear it engenders or view it as a constant ally that makes you sharper in everything you do at work. Keep in mind that simply calling pressure an ally or partner without adequate preparation will not work. However, anyone can prepare, including you. This means that anyone can overcome the adverse effects of pressure and view pressure as something positive.

Recognize How Much You Have Yet to Learn

The early stages of your career as a paralegal will be much easier if you recognize that the law is complicated and you won't know it all right out of school. This is not an excuse for not trying to learn as much about your profession as you can, but it does mean that you should expect to make mistakes despite your greatest efforts. Your goal early in your career should be to keep the mistakes to a minimum and do everything you can not to repeat the same mistakes. That is all any reasonable employer should ask of a new paralegal. If your employer expects you to be perfect, you may want to reassess whether you are working for the right firm for you. Knowing that you are going to make mistakes makes it less likely that you will be devastated when the mistakes occur.

What your employer is interested in is how you respond to the mistakes. Do you learn from them? Do you take the steps necessary to minimize the chances they will occur in the first place? Does your attitude reflect that you understand the importance of *not* making mistakes? Do you appreciate that your mistakes can have an adverse effect on others, such as the firm's client?

Before I became a full-time paralegal educator, I had a paralegal who had worked for me for many years. She was as diligent, honest, and hard-working as any employer could expect. I left the office for a couple of weeks one time for a vacation and when I returned learned that she had allowed a statute of limitations to run without filing a complaint, a serious mistake. I also learned that she went through every case we were working on that had a complaint yet to be filed and rechecked the filing period just to make sure the error did not happen again. When she explained what had happened, I could tell she felt awful. I did not need to tell her to be more careful in the future. The point is that my paralegal learned from her mistake, made her best efforts to ensure the mistake would not be repeated, and appreciated the magnitude of the situation. When a paralegal does all of these things, the employer is a lot more forgiving about a mistake.

It is important to be careful not to label something a mistake that is really a character flaw that your employer is not likely to forgive. Acting in an unethical or dishonest manner is not a "mistake" but reflective of work traits that will disqualify you from your job. Showing up late to work repeatedly is not a "mistake" but indicative of poor work habits. Gossiping about the boss is not a "mistake" but poor judgment. These types of errors cannot, and should not, be dismissed by you as a rookie mistake. They are errors that no employee should make regardless of experience.

When you make a mistake, be the first to admit it. The sting of a mistake is deflated considerably when your supervisor hears about it from you first. This is a tried-and-true way to minimize the negative perception your employer may have about a mistake. I first learned that my paralegal missed the statute of limitations from her, not from the client or by reviewing the file. Her admission contributed to my conclusion that she took the matter seriously, was trustworthy, and felt bad about the error.

When you recognize that you don't know it all and that mistakes will occur despite your best efforts, you can accept them and move on, determined not to let the same mistake occur again. The law is vast and complicated. You are a relatively new paralegal. You cannot always avoid a mistake, but you can always respond in a manner that will make you better for the experience.

> Paralegal Perspective <

> My definition of a paralegal is a person who is a problem solver. You are the one who is in the background getting the cases ready, whether for a simple hearing, settlement, or trial. You are the one who has to get all the details in order and make the attorney look good. Be as organized and detail oriented as possible.

Keep a Proper Perspective

If you are truly making an informed effort to do well in your new paralegal profession, you have a high probability of success. You did not come this far without having a great deal of ability. Paralegals are in demand because not everyone has the aptitude to do this work. If finishing paralegal school was easy, a lot more people would be doing it and the supply of paralegals would far exceed the demand. The point is that your workload is something you can handle because you wouldn't have come this far without having the requisite ability. The feelings of inadequacy, of being overwhelmed by how much you have to do and know, are perfectly normal. Many others of abilities comparable to yours have experienced the same feelings and gone on to do exceptionally well. Success may not be automatic, but it is definitely achievable. The road you are traveling is one that many others have traveled before, and many others will travel after you.

I had my first legal job in 1984 as a law clerk the summer after my first year of law school. I was intimidated even walking into the office the first time for a job interview. My first day on the job was humbling, to say the least. I didn't even know how to turn on the dictating machine for transcription by a legal secretary. I felt lost. However, I told myself that they would have to fire me before I'd leave. I was determined to make my first experience in the legal arena a successful one. I left a year later to take a clerk position with another law firm. By that time, I realized I could do a lot more than I thought I could a year earlier. I found out all those questions I had asked, which I thought sounded lame, were the same ones that other law clerks had asked. Although I would not have predicted this when the job began, I found out later the firm really liked my work and was sorry I decided to pursue another opportunity.

The point is that when you put your workload in perspective, you realize you can do more than you think you can. The questions and concerns you have are the same ones that others in your position have had. The mistakes are seldom, if ever, career threatening. Your employer is used to handling the misgivings of new employees even though you may not realize it right away. Tell yourself that the only way you won't succeed in the profession is if you don't apply yourself adequately, something you won't let happen.

PRIORITIZE BY DUE DATE, ASSIGNOR, AND NATURE OF ASSIGNMENT

As you no doubt know by now, law offices are typically busy places. There never seems to be enough time to complete all the work that is required. Many people thrive in this environment, yet others always seem to struggle with it. A proper approach to your work helps enormously. However, you cannot manage your workload successfully unless you also prioritize your tasks. The ability to prioritize your work is something you will need your entire career, so it is extremely important your first year that you develop that skill. Generally, you will prioritize by due date first, then by who assigned the task, then by the nature of the assignment. Sometimes, there are exceptions to this order of prioritization, but most of the time this is the order you will follow.

By Due Date

Law offices are deadline-driven places. Almost everything you do has a deadline. Some of the deadlines are statutory in nature; for example, local, state, and federal rules of procedure determine the amount of time you have to file various types of motions, to serve a party with summons and complaint, when to respond to discovery requests, and when pre-trial matters must be considered. Some of the deadlines are nonstatutory but from your employer's viewpoint still mandatory. For example, a client wants to purchase a large commercial property, and the seller has requested the final offer be in writing within 48 hours. Some deadlines are neither statutory nor client driven. Your supervising attorney may tell you to have a brief on her desk by Monday morning, the only time that the attorney will have next week to read it.

Deadlines are not a problem when you have enough time to complete all your work by the deadline for each assignment. Often you will not know if you will have enough time to do every assignment by deadline. Assignments can take more or less time than you originally anticipated. New assignments are given to you constantly. Controlling this situation means prioritizing by due date first. (Your employer's due date will often be earlier than the actual due date because there needs to be time for review and revision.)

Keep an electronic calendar of every due date. Electronic calendars have become essential because due dates often change and new dates are added as you receive assignments. I strongly recommend an electronic calendar that synchronizes with your office computer. Handheld computers contain useful software as well as manage your calendar. They allow you to carry your appointments and deadlines with you wherever you go. In the event you misplace or lose your handheld, there is a duplicate of everything on your office computer.

For each assignment, put at least three dates on your calendar. The first is the obvious date: when the assignment is due. Second, note the deadline by which you have estimated you will need to begin the assignment in order to have it done by the due date. This, of course, depends on the assignment. A motion for summary judgment may need to be placed on your calendar a week before it is due, while a letter to a client may need only a day or two notice. *Do not ever erase this date from your electronic calendar until the assignment is completed and handed in to your supervising attorney.* Your electronic calendar will keep giving you reminders to begin the task as long as you do not delete the reminder. Make sure your calendar reflects realistic amounts of time needed to complete a project, taking into consideration the nature of the assignment and the flow of work you will most likely have between the notice date and the due date. Finally, enter the date for the day before the assignment is due. You will always want to make sure an assignment did not slip through the cracks before it is due. You may not always have time to complete the assignment that somehow was omitted the day before due date, but you will at least have an opportunity to address the situation. If your motion is due tomorrow and for some reason you didn't do it, you could ask for an extension of time, get someone to help you, or work past the end of the workday to get it done. If you wait until the due date, it is too late.

If it is likely another assignment will arise out of the one you just completed, put that on the calendar too. For example, assume you are preparing a motion to dismiss that is due next Monday. If your supervisor wants the motion done by Thursday, so it can be reviewed in time to make any needed revisions and filed by the following Monday, it is a good idea to note it on your calendar for Friday to follow up with the supervising attorney. He will appreciate your being so organized. You will help avoid a situation where the supervising attorney recognizes on Friday at 5:00 P.M. that there isn't enough time to have the motion finalized by Monday without your working over the weekend. Once the motion is filed, put on your calendar the due date by which a response is due. You can then look for the response on the due date and anticipate what needs to be done. Note that I didn't say to *begin* working on the response; I said to *anticipate* working on it. Go to your supervisor and ask if she wants you to do anything with the response. You again have the opportunity to impress and will tend to avoid the last-minute rushes that plague so many law offices.

When you receive new assignments and place them on your calendar, you will be in a better position to determine whether you are able to complete all of the assignments by their due dates. If it looks as if too many assignments are bunching up, you can address the situation before it becomes a crisis. Let's say you are given an assignment to prepare a settlement demand letter within 10 days. You notice that on the same date, you are to have completed a trial brief and a letter to the client for your supervising attorney's review. Often assignments are due on the same day, and it's not a problem. In this case, you will need to determine what you expect in the way of workload in the next 10 days. If it appears you will be hard-pressed to complete all three assignments in the next 10 days, determine which of those dates are mandatory and which are simply desirable. Come up with a suggestion about how to address the situation. Maybe it would be a suggestion that the client letter be due several days later, the demand letter be due a day after the trial brief, and the trial brief still be due in 10 days.

You will need to go to your supervising attorney and inform her of the situation and your suggestions for addressing it. Not only have you shown that you are anticipating and addressing a potential problem, you are proposing a solution. If you have several people who give you new assignments, you usually will ask the most senior assignor first. Be cautious not to consider too many situations a "crisis." Law offices are places where anything viewed as whining are not met with much sympathy. Nevertheless, there are going to be times when a true deadline problem exists. Your employer wants to know about these situations with enough notice to deal with them.

By Assignor

Problems sometime arise when more than one superior wants his work given priority. In other words, more than one person wants his work done first. What do you do in this situation?

If your office is organized such that you receive all of your assignments through one person, perhaps a managing paralegal, you have an easier solution: ask your assigning supervisor how to prioritize among several attorneys who all want their assignment to be given priority. Make a note of what she tells you, and be specific as to when the conversation took place and what was said. If it turns out that you can complete the assignments in a timely manner, you don't have a problem. If you are unable to complete all of your assignments on the due date in question, let your assigning supervisor know as soon as you know so she will have time to solve the problem. Sometimes the solution will be to reassign certain tasks to others in the office. At times, the situation may warrant the assigning supervisor's readjusting the deadlines after a discussion with the attorneys involved. Your supervisor will appreciate the opportunity to address a true problem with enough time to resolve it. She will not appreciate your making a crisis out of the normal heavy workload that often exists in law offices. The point is to go to your supervisor *only* after you have determined that you cannot complete the work in the time given and, where possible, have some solutions to propose.

Some offices do not direct all of the paralegal's assignments through one person. Instead, you are assigned several attorneys, and any of them will give you assignments without much, if any, coordination of work flow among the others. This is a tougher situation for you than having your assignments flow through one person. What do you do after you have determined that you will not be able to complete every attorney's assignment by the requested due date? In the absence of a policy by your employer on how to handle a situation when more than one superior wants you to give priority to his own assignment, it is best to check with the most senior of the assignors first. Sometimes the most senior person will want his assignment given priority without much, if any, regard to the merits of the situation. Sometimes, the most senior person will take a back seat to someone less senior but more deserving under the circumstances. Either way, you have anticipated a problem before it became a crisis, which your employer should appreciate. Be careful not to create the impression that you are going over the head of the less senior assignors. Ask the most senior assignor if he will let the others know that your workload has been reprioritized instead of your bearing the news. Tell your other assignors that you will make every effort to meet their original deadlines if possible. Let everyone know that you care about all of your assignments and recognize their importance.

If the most senior assignor is unavailable, because he is too busy, unapproachable, or out of the office, go to the next most senior assignor and explain the situation. Ask that person to tell you how to reprioritize your workload. Continue to work down the hierarchical structure if the next most senior assignor is unavailable. Make a note of whom you spoke with and what you discussed. Also note your attempts to speak with the more senior person who was unavailable. These notes are useful in the event someone asks why you prioritized your work in the way you did.

One of my first legal jobs involved my working under the supervision of the firm's senior partner and one of the more senior associates, both of them extremely demanding. The senior partner almost always wanted his work done first regardless of the situation. The senior associate also would almost always want his work done first, though not in so many words. He would tell me his deadlines were reasonable even when they were not. Although I worked hard to meet both attorneys' deadlines, there were some rare occasions when I could not meet two deadlines at the same time. I found it effective to discuss these situations with the senior partner even though the junior associate was someone I had more contact with daily. In those conversations with the senior partner, not a negative comment or suggestion was ever made about anyone in the office, including the senior associate. In fact, I went out of my way to praise the senior associate for his hard work, attention to detail, and efforts to train me. I simply could not do all the work in the time allotted. The senior partner understood. I still ended up doing his work first nearly every time, but both attorneys tried to coordinate their assignments more. On rare occasions, they reassigned my work to others in the firm. The senior associate understood that when I did not do his work first, it was because it was unavoidable, not because it was undesirable.

> Paralegal Perspective <

My training as a paralegal has helped prepare me for my position at the U.S. Department of Labor by developing skills and knowledge in the area of legal understanding. Skills such as effectively communicating, interpreting, and understanding decisions of the court and federal acts have given me the advantage necessary to advance in the federal government arena. I enjoy reading decisions from the Office of Administrative Law Judges or the Benefits Review Board and discussing them with my district director. For example, I briefed a case one day, and she and I discussed how the court came to its decision. Without my paralegal training, I would not be able to understand anything.

By Nature of the Assignment

You have already prioritized by due date. Where the due dates conflict, you have prioritized according to your assignor's requests. Now you have several nonconflicting assignments you are working on simultaneously and have to decide which to do first. Where do you start?

It is usually best to get the short, easier assignments out of the way first. A simple phone call, a one-page letter, or short research assignment (e.g., cite checking a brief) are the types of tasks that will nag away at you if you don't get them accomplished early. Also, those short assignments have a way of building up, so get them done early.

Note that I didn't say do only the *pleasant* short assignments first. Some assignments are unpleasant yet short. For example, it may take only a few minutes to tell the opposing law firm that the attorney will not grant an extension of time to respond to discovery, but it may well be an unpleasant conversation, especially if you are dealing with a difficult person at the other end of the phone line. You especially want to get these types of short assignments done first. They nag away at you not just because they are incomplete, but because you know you will not like the experience. This creates stress that you do not want to have drag on any longer than necessary.

As for any remaining assignments, tackle the more difficult ones first. If you have never prepared a motion for summary judgment but you've summarized depositions many times, prepare the motion first. Even if both assignments may take roughly the same amount of time, the motion is more difficult. If you prepare the deposition summaries first, you will have the prospect of the motion lingering over you like a dark cloud. If you work on the motion first, the stress level is reduced because you are working on the problem instead of having to replay it over and over in your mind while you're looking at all those deposition transcripts. Your deposition summaries will be more accurate when you're not preoccupied with the motion that lies ahead.

A word of caution is in order. Make sure that when you work on the more difficult assignment first, you are not spinning your wheels. I have seen people take on the more difficult assignment without making any progress and leaving themselves with insufficient time to complete either of two competing assignments. Keep the difficult assignment on pace. Anticipate when you are not getting much done despite your best efforts. In our example concerning the motion for summary judgment, if you've spent two days doing the necessary legal research and have yet to find anything that is very helpful, it may be that you have been looking at the wrong legal sources, have confused the issues in the case, or are using the wrong search terms. Rather than continuing to eat up more time in the process, you should seek guidance from others who can help you. If you continue to do the research without the guidance, you may find that you do not have sufficient time to prepare both the motion and the deposition summaries.

You will find that as you work on the more difficult assignments, the shorter simple assignments keep coming up. While you are working on the motion for summary judgment, you are asked to call that client, summarize this appellate court decision, or write a letter. Keep on top of those simple assignments by doing them now rather than after the more difficult assignment you are currently engaged with. If possible, set aside time each day specifically to do these assignments. Don't let them build up.

Nevertheless, you will need to exercise good judgment here. If your motion for summary judgment is due tomorrow morning, you would normally want to get the motion done first. In these situations, you would put off the phone call, case summary, or letter until after the motion is filed. You would not want to risk filing the motion late so you could return a phone call that could wait for now. If the phone call, case summary, or letter could not wait for some reason, that is another matter altogether.

>Paralegal Perspective<

> **>Paralegal Perspective<**

> Intrinsic rewards and having hard work appreciated by my employer, give me more reason to give her my best in return. We are a team and try to give the clients the best we can. As you can tell, I love my job and am so happy to be a paralegal.

WHAT TO DO IF YOU ARE UNABLE TO FINISH YOUR WORK ON TIME

If you follow the foregoing principles, you will finish your work on time in most instances. Nevertheless, there will be occasions when you cannot finish your work on time even though you've approached your workload properly and prioritized correctly. To put it mildly, things happen in a law firm that are outside your control. You may be right on schedule with your assignments, even accounting for the normal unforeseen work that you have become used to, when something totally unforeseen presents itself. It may be that your coworker suddenly takes ill and now you have to drop everything to complete the brief that he was supposed to hand in yesterday. It may be that a good client is leaving for Europe tomorrow and just remembered that he needs someone to prepare a will. Perhaps you had no way of knowing your car would break down that day and you are several hours late for work. These disruptions mean you can't get an assignment done by its deadline. What do you do?

It really depends on whether the assignment can still be done on time but someone else may have to help, or whether the assignment cannot be done on time at all. The first situation is preferable, of course. When the work can still be done on time with someone else's help, *do not delay in seeking that help.* It is far better to ask for help than to hope the problem will somehow correct itself; it rarely does. Hopefully, you have already taken the opportunity to help others in the office in a similar situation. Your car breaks down, you are waiting for the tow truck, and an attorney needs a case briefed before he argues a motion that afternoon. Contact your supervisor or, in her absence, the attorney who will argue the motion, explain the situation, and suggest the person whom you've previously helped brief the case. While this may be annoying to the supervisor, the attorney, and maybe even the other paralegal, it is not a disaster. Not having the case briefed before the hearing on the motion *could* be a disaster, and one that is hard to forgive.

What if you miss a deadline completely? If it's a flexible deadline, it may be a matter of setting another deadline. An example would be when a client wants to meet this week because his schedule is less flexible next week. While it is important to meet the client's wishes where possible, this is the type of deadline that can be adjusted in most circumstances.

If the deadline is inflexible and you have missed it, you should *always* be the first one to bring it to your supervisor's attention and do so as soon as is reasonably possible. Don't let your supervisor find out from someone else or by her own efforts. When you are not the first to admit a mistake, you are compounding the problem. Not only has an important deadline been missed, but you are covering up the mistake. Your supervisor may now wonder what else you are covering up.

If you can do so without any delay that would exacerbate the problem, research possible solutions. Once when a new associate of mine was helping me prepare for trial, he came to me and said that he had missed a deadline to disclose expert witnesses prior to trial. He had simply gotten busy and overlooked the deadline. This usually means the nondisclosing party cannot call experts except to rebut the other party's experts, a severe limitation. However, before telling me about missing this deadline, the associate had researched the likelihood of the court's granting a motion allowing us to disclose experts, which caused me to be hopeful. I was still not pleased about the situation, but the associate's earnestness in regretting the situation, coupled with his efforts to find a solution, considerably softened the blow.

We later made the motion to supplement our expert witness list, which was denied. We called experts at trial for rebuttal only. Fortunately, we won the trial, and it was all moot. The moral of the story is that it is best to be the first to admit your mistakes and give your supervisor a possible solution. And it may not be as disastrous as you originally thought.

CHAPTER SUMMARY

Especially as a new paralegal, it is critical to have the right approach to handling a workload that may seem overwhelming. Treat every hour of the day with the same sense of urgency that most people treat the last hour of the day as they attempt to finish all their tasks that cannot wait. Never forget the value of time; protect it, and avoid squandering it. If you treat every assignment as if your supervisor was watching over you, you will be amazed at how your work is consistently good. Remember that even if your supervisor is not physically watching you, everything you do as a new paralegal is being scrutinized anyway. Divide your work into logical, manageable segments. Prioritize your work by due date, assignor, and nature of the assignment. Pressure is a reality of working in a law firm. The sooner you view pressure as an ally, the sooner you can take advantage of the positive aspects of being under pressure. Despite your best efforts, mistakes will occur—everyone makes them. The key is to do everything within reason to avoid mistakes and, when they are made, learn from them so you do not repeat them. If you cannot finish your work on time, do not delay in seeking help. Law firms are places in which both formal and informal deadlines are extremely important. Keep the job in proper perspective: the job is extremely important, but not everything in your life.

> Web Research Exercise <

> Go to a search engine on the Internet such as www.google.com. Enter the search terms "manage your workload." You will find many articles that give advice about how to manage your workload effectively. Find one that is particularly helpful, and be ready to share it with your classmates.

> Chapter Exercises <

1. Assume you are a paralegal in a litigation law firm. You have the following assignments to do, all assigned by your supervising attorney:
   a. A motion to dismiss a motor vehicle accident case that must be filed in 10 days
   b. A settlement demand letter in a wrongful termination case that needs to be finalized in the next 20 days
   c. Preparation of interrogatories in a patent infringement case that needs to be finalized in two days
   d. A meeting with a client tomorrow to go over requests for production of documents
   e. A telephone call to an insurance adjuster to find out what information the insurance company needs to evaluate a new products liability case your firm is working on

Describe how you would go about organizing and prioritizing these assignments, including what you would place on your calendar, how much time you would estimate to accomplish each task and why, and what allowance you would make for any currently unforeseen assignments.

2. Assume the same assignments as in exercise 1, including the same due dates. Now assume your supervising attorney gives you a rush assignment to check all of the cases cited in a motion to dismiss filed by an opposing party in a case your office is handling. You are to check all of the cases cited to see if they have been overruled and whether they stand for the proposition indicated in the opposing law firm's brief. You have to have the assignment completed in two days. How would you rearrange your workload to adjust for the rush assignment? What would you do if you could not complete all of the assignments you are currently working on? Be specific.

3. Go to a store that sells electronic calendars, handheld computers, and other electronic organization products. Talk with a salesperson about the features of each product and the price. Which product or products would be best suited for your needs? Why? How can such a product help you organize your work?

> Ethical Discussion <

Assume a summons and complaint are filed against a client of the firm where you are employed. You notice that the complaint has what appears to be a typographical error stating that the accident in question occurred earlier than a police report in your possession indicates. On the face of the complaint, due to the typographical error, it appears the statute of limitations has run, making the complaint subject to a motion that may result in the case's dismissal. Should you bring the motion even though it is likely, but not a certainty, that the court would recognize the typographical error and allow the plaintiff to file an amended complaint? Explain your response.

> Suggested Reading <

Zig Ziglar, *Over the Top*, Thomas Nelson, 1997.

Chapter 9
What Kinds of Assignments Can You Expect?

Key Success Points

> *Most legal work can be described as transactional or litigation in nature.*

> *Legal employers that emphasize transactional work have a different environment from those that emphasize litigation.*

> *There are steps a new paralegal can take to produce high-quality legal work.*

> *Law firms usually require a paralegal to perform nonlegal, as well as legal, assignments.*

> > > > > > > > >

Paralegals of the Wild

"I hate interviewing hostile witnesses."

TRANSACTIONAL VERSUS LITIGATION ASSIGNMENTS

Your legal assignments generally can be placed into one of two categories. *Transactional* work involves the creation of documents that result in creation of legal responsibilities or relationships. For example, preparation and execution of a written contract makes the signatories legally obliged to perform certain duties (known as "consideration") under the contract. Creation of a durable power of attorney for health care may result in legal obligations for someone acting on an incapacitated person's behalf. Preparation and filing of articles of incorporation creates obligations for the owners of the corporation.

As you can tell, transactional work is often about planning for the future. Clients want to create future legal obligations where they may not currently exist. In contrast, *litigation* involves the past. Something occurred in the past that created a dispute that is to be resolved by litigation, or at least the prospect of litigation. For example, the parties to a contract disagree on its terms. At least one of the parties to the contract believes there has been a breach of the contract and is either considering litigation or has initiated litigation to resolve the dispute. The medical care provider refuses to end life-saving treatment, so a lawsuit is filed to determine the medical care provider's obligation under a durable power of attorney executed by the patient before incapacitation. While I am primarily referring to civil litigation, many of the observations in this chapter are also applicable to offices that practice in the criminal litigation arena.

There is often overlap between the two types of legal work. Transactional work often leads to litigation arising out of that work. For example, parties disagree about the legal obligations under a document. When the parties cannot resolve the dispute on their own, litigation is often the result. While there are reasons not to litigate over disputes, one of the benefits is finality. Once a dispute finds its way to the court system, it will be resolved at some point, by either mutual agreement of the parties (settlement), trial, or an alternative to trial, commonly known as *alternative dispute resolution* (ADR). With respect to ADR, transactional documents often contain an ADR clause requiring some form of ADR, such as mediation or arbitration, should a dispute arise. With ADR so prevalent in the litigation field, any paralegal interested in litigation should learn as much about ADR as reasonably possible.

Differences Between Transactional and Litigation Work

Despite the overlap between transactional and litigation work, there are important differences that have an effect on your career as a paralegal. Firms that practice primarily transactional work often have more predictable work hours. The work seems to get done in a more orderly fashion than in a litigation office. Appointments are often set well in advance because clients view their legal needs as part of long-term planning. Usually a will or trust does not have to be prepared on a moment's notice and clients forming a business partnership understand that it takes time to iron out the particulars of an agreement, for example. This is not to say this type of work is not capable of being as hectic and fast-paced as work at a litigation firm. Sometimes clients really do need a document created on a moment's notice. Firms seldom turn away business, so even if a particular transactional assignment is not due for a few weeks, there are many competing assignments that must be completed in the interim period. However, generally there is more control over the schedule than in a litigation office. Deadlines are not court or statutorily imposed as in litigation work. There is usually more flexibility.

Firms that do primarily transactional work tend to have a calmer atmosphere than litigation firms. The people attracted to this type of work tend to be more introspective and introverted in nature. They would rather spend time reading a document, researching, and writing, and in their office, than talking with people, visiting accident scenes, and rushing off to the courthouse. If given a choice between sitting at the computer and doing research, or interviewing and preparing witnesses for trial, they would choose the former.

Firms that practice primarily litigation tend to have a different atmosphere entirely. There is a sense of urgency and briskness. Preparing for trial is both exciting and labor intensive. In the days before trial, the hours are long and intense. Although most civil lawsuits do not ultimately proceed to trial, litigation firms are always preparing for an upcoming trial if not actually in trial. There are mandatory deadlines that must be complied with or the client's interests may be compromised. There is also the prospect of not knowing the outcome of a case when the firm first accepts it.

Those who work in litigation tend to be people oriented: they find people and their situations interesting. Litigation firms tend to attract those who believe in a cause. I have seen my own paralegal students go to work for family law or employment law firms because of their own personal experiences. Some of my students have gone to work for organizations advocating for the civil rights of others because their own civil rights were denied in the past.

Although the emphasis in a firm may be either litigation or transactional in nature, many firms that hire paralegals can provide opportunities to work in both areas. In my own law firm, one of my paralegals worked primarily in transactional work, but if litigation arose from the transactional work, she was usually involved in the case. One of my other paralegals did primarily civil litigation work, but if a client needed something of a relatively straight-forward nature, such as a durable power of attorney, she would assist. My observation is that paralegals who generally do transactional work have more opportunities to do litigation than paralegals who do litigation will have to do transactional work. The reason is likely that transactional work has a greater prospect of litigation arising out of that kind of work than litigation has of resulting in transactional work.

In large firms, the demarcation between litigation and transactional work is clearer. Large firms have a greater division of labor, which results in paralegals' not straying from their primary duties much. Thus, there is less opportunity to learn both litigation and transactional work. The benefit of this is that some people do not want to do both types of work. Further, in theory, if you concentrate in one area, you will become better at it than if you delved into other types of law. The cross-over between the two types of legal work seems to increase as the size of the firm decreases.

Unless you are sure you prefer either litigation or transactional work over the other, the best course is to try them both early in your paralegal career. It is best to avoid being pigeon-holed until you have the chance to experience the two types of legal work. Go to work for a firm that allows you the opportunity to work in both areas. If possible, do an internship while you are still in school that will allow you to explore both types of legal work. You will probably find that you prefer one type of work over the other or that you prefer the variety of doing both types of work.

Keep an open mind. You may think of yourself as a quiet person but find you enjoy litigation. You may have thought of yourself as an average writer but find the experience invigorating. Stereotypes are meant to be broken!

What types of assignments can you expect? The list in the next section is for illustrative purposes but will give you a better idea of what you may do in either a transactional or a litigation setting.

Typical Transactional and Litigation Assignments

In a firm that does transactional legal work you could find yourself assigned to draft or review the following types of legal documents:

> Real estate purchase agreements and escrow instructions

> Wills, trusts, and other estate planning documents

> Loan applications and supporting material

> Articles of incorporation, limited liability company applications, and partnership agreements

> Zoning ordinances, subdivision maps, and land surveys

> UCC filings

> Insurance policies

In addition, you would have the following sorts of work:

> Conducting or reviewing title searches

> Completing applications for government benefits, such as Social Security

> Compiling or maintaining the financial records of an estate

> Drafting gift tax returns for attorney's review

In a litigation practice, you might be assigned one of the following tasks:

> Meeting with clients, lay witnesses, and experts to gather facts and opinions

> Preparing summons, complaints, answers, and other responses to pleadings

> Preparing and responding to discovery such as interrogatories, requests to produce documents, and inspections of tangible items

> Helping your supervising attorney prepare for an upcoming deposition

> Drafting motions related to litigation, including points and authorities

> Drafting trial, arbitration, or mediation briefs

> Summarizing evidence for use at deposition or trial or arbitration, such as deposition transcripts, medical and other business records, or court transcripts

> Viewing accident scenes

> Attending any or all portions of a trial or arbitration

> Preparing slide presentations of evidence for trial

NONLEGAL ASSIGNMENTS

Being trained as a paralegal can be both good and bad. It is good because your training affords you the opportunity to work in an interesting, challenging, and rewarding career. It is bad because your skills are more diverse than those of anyone else in the office. Paralegals are capable of performing anything, from the most rudimentary tasks to those that many unfamiliar with the legal field would assume an attorney would perform. Of course, the good far outweighs the bad, but you should be aware that employers may ask you to perform a wide variety of tasks, some of them not strictly involving legal work.

I have personally observed paralegals working as little more than file clerks and others doing more complex work than attorneys. Only you can decide whether your skills are being used in such a way that brings you career satisfaction. Most paralegals want their employers to recognize that they are highly trained legal professionals and want to be treated as such. They did not train to be legal secretaries, as vitally important as those positions are. As I stated early in this book, you should never consider a job that does not bring you the satisfaction you have earned. Your work should be something you enjoy, not something you dread.

Nevertheless, there are times in any law office setting when you need to pitch in and do your part for the good of the team. Here, the "team" is the law office where you are employed. If a document needs to go out today and the secretaries are short-handed, you may need to finalize it yourself. If important clients come in for a meeting and they need refreshments, you may have to get them. If the court runner calls in sick and a motion needs to be filed, you may have to take the motion over to the courthouse yourself. One of my first tasks as a new attorney was to meet with the senior partner, discuss the wine selection for the firm party that night, and purchase the wine on the firm's account. I was initially put off by that request but later realized that the other lawyers were extremely busy preparing for trial. Further, selection of the wine in this particular law firm was considered an important, though non-legal, task that couldn't be trusted to just anyone. In fact, the senior partner usually did it himself because important clients attended these social gatherings. After I learned the importance of the assignment, my ego was restored, and I volunteered to do the same task again.

Law firms want team players. They want employees who sacrifice personal egos for the success of the firm. You will find that when you're a team player, others in the firm will sacrifice for you when you need the extra help. Make sure to keep track of all the tasks you perform in this regard, and don't be afraid to toot your own horn when a job review takes place.

While you should be a team player and do tasks that are below your level of training when the need requires, those instances should not become routine. Yes, you may have to make the coffee, file the motion, or answer the telephones in a crunch, but when the exception becomes the rule, you are probably working for someone who does not value you or your skills as much as he or she should. If you or your skills are not sufficiently valued, do you think your career prospects look good?

There are situations when you may be willing to do anything to get hired. For example, there may be a particular employer you have a strong desire to work for but is not hiring paralegals right now. Or perhaps the employer has a policy of hiring only experienced paralegals or from within. In this situation, you may accept a position below your level of training as long as the prospects are positive.

> Paralegal Perspective <

There is a lot of calendaring in my new paralegal job. Calendaring is essential to getting motions and trial work. It is something that isn't covered sufficiently in school for the extreme importance of it.

I know a paralegal who wanted to work for a particular corporation in its legal office. This corporation was consistently chosen as one of the best to work for in various employee satisfaction surveys. She was willing to take any job in order to prove her ability as a paralegal and so accepted a secretarial position in the legal department. Although it took a couple of years before she rose to the level of paralegal, for her it was well worth the wait. She now works for one of the top companies in America, and her skills are being used in positive ways she never imagined. Others may not have wanted to wait a couple of years. It is a personal choice based on your own career goals. However, when the long-term prospects for utilization of your training do not look positive, you will not likely find the job something you will want to make a career. Further, if you are underemployed for too long, prospective employers begin to wonder whether you are capable of handling true paralegal work.

HOW TO TURN IN HIGH-QUALITY WORK

We have already discussed how to approach and prioritize your work. The right approach and careful prioritization will no doubt contribute to the quality of your work, but those ideas primarily were concerned with managing your work. Here, the discussion is focused on how to make sure what you turn in is of high quality. Your work, after all, is a reflection of you as far as your employer is concerned. Poor-quality work means you have poor skills in your employer's eyes. Average-quality work means you have average skills. Superior quality work means you have the superior skills your employer desires. Remember that your goal is to thrive as a paralegal, not just survive. Here are some tips that will help.

Understand the Assignment

Don't assume you know what your supervising attorney wants when it isn't completely clear. There is a lot more tolerance for questions about the assignment when it is given than at any other time. Ask questions to clarify the assignment when you receive it, and take notes.

Don't Reinvent the Wheel

Chances are that someone in the office has already done an assignment very much like the one you have just been given. When you're given the assignment, ask the supervising attorney if there is something similar a co-employee did that you can look at as a point of reference. Most employers welcome questions like this because your employer doesn't want you wasting time doing something someone else has substantially already done.

Do It Right the First Time

You have no doubt heard the adage that there is never enough time to do a job right the first time but always time to do it again. I have seen employees frantically throw together something in order to complete an assignment rather than take the time to do it right the first time. This wastes the employee's time and the supervisor's time as well. It creates an impression that you don't know what you're doing or are not organized, or both. Make sure you do any assignment right the first time. It may still come back from your supervisor with corrections, but the corrections will tend to be minimal.

Use the English Language Correctly

You may be the greatest paralegal ever to step foot in the office, but if you cannot communicate what you know with proper English, no one will know how great you are. Use the best word available. Use that word correctly. Make sure subject and verb agree. Use paragraphs correctly, and make correct transitions between paragraphs. Make sure your grammar, spelling, and punctuation are correct. Effective communication, especially in writing, includes both *what* you communicate and *how* you communicate it.

Proofread Your Work Carefully

Due to the multitasking nature of a paralegal's job, it is easy to overlook an error in your assignment, even an obvious error. You are about to complete a sentence and the phone rings—and you forget to complete the sentence. Proper proofreading takes discipline. *You have to read every word.* I recommend you cut a small hole in a piece of paper and run that hole over every word in your document. This is tedious but effective. Another idea is to ask a coworker to proofread an assignment of yours in exchange for your proofreading one of the coworker's assignments. Fresh eyes make a big difference.

Cite to the Law Correctly

Most of the time, you will know how to cite to cases and statutes within your jurisdiction since you will cite to them frequently. Take the time to look up the proper citation format for any legal sources you are not familiar with. Improper citation is at best an annoyance and at worst undermines the integrity of your work because the reader loses confidence in your ability.

Use the Best Secondary Legal Resources Available

A researcher is only as good as her library. You can probably find a case on point by going to a legal treatise, but there is likely a practice manual or other resource tailored for someone who wants to do exactly what you've been assigned. Know what resources are available to you for the type of assignment you are doing, and use them. When you are in the law library, find out what secondary resources are available that may assist you the most. Don't use just the first resource you find unless it is the best.

Consider Your Audience

If you are writing for your supervising attorney, you will write differently than you would for a client or the court. For example, you will not have to tell your attorney what a tort is, but the firm's client may think it's a type of pastry if you don't explain it. The court shouldn't hear your personal opinions about a witness, but your supervising attorney may find them helpful. Although all of your assignments will be reviewed by your supervising attorney, you should write them for their ultimate audience.

Anticipate Your Future Needs

Anticipate what you will need to know. It is not likely that your employer will ask you to do a motion for summary judgment (or something equally complex) your first week on the job, but you know that in the not-too-distant future, you may be asked to prepare one. Why wait until that day to learn what to do? The next time you are at the law library, find out what resources are available to help you prepare for an assignment you know is sure to come. The next time you are looking for a form from a co-employee, ask if he also has a summary judgment you could look at. You will impress your employer by demonstrating knowledge about the assignment when it is given, and you will increase your confidence in your own ability to do the assignment correctly.

CHAPTER SUMMARY

Most legal work can be described as either transactional or litigation. Firms that emphasize transactional work usually have more predictable work hours. Those who work in transactional firms tend to like reading, writing, and researching. Firms that do primarily litigation work tend to have less regular work hours, and a sense of urgency is often present. People who work in litigation usually enjoy interacting with others, such as witnesses, clients, court staff, and experts. Many firms practice in both the litigation and the transactional areas, giving you an opportunity to experience variety in terms of work. Large law firms tend to require more specialized work. Due to the wide variety of skills they typically possess, paralegals perform many nonlegal tasks in addition to their legal work.

Turning in high-quality work is different from managing a workload. The latter concerns how to complete the work on time, the former how to make sure what you turn in is the best possible final product. High-quality work is achieved by understanding the assignment before getting started. Chances are someone else in the office has already done a similar assignment, so usually there is no need to reinvent the wheel. Take time to do the assignment right the first time instead of handing in an assignment for the sake of getting it done. Use clear and concise English when writing an assignment; the purpose is to communicate, not confuse. Carefully proofread everything you turn in because your supervisor does not want to take the time to correct mistakes you should have caught. Use proper legal citation. Find out the best secondary legal resource available to complete the assignment, and use it. There are many high-quality secondary legal resources that will help improve the quality of your work. When writing, always consider your audience, and adjust accordingly. Do not wait to learn a task that you know you will be asked to do in the future; anticipate what you will need to know and learn it now.

> Web Research Exercise <

Go to http://www.sfpa.com/, the link to the San Francisco Paralegal Association. Click on "links." You will find information and further links to numerous transactional and litigation-oriented information. Use this information to help you decide whether you would prefer doing primarily transactional legal work or litigation-based legal work.

> Chapter Exercises <

1. Make a list of all of the positive and negative aspects of working in a law office that (a) practices primarily transactional legal work, (b) practices primarily litigation, and (c) provides for a combination of transactional and litigation work. After completing your list of pros and cons, are you leaning in one direction? Why? How does your conclusion figure into your career goals?

2. Assume you were just given the assignment to prepare a motion to dismiss a tort case due to a lack of the duty of care on the part of the firm's client. Write down the exact steps you would take to ensure you prepare the highest-quality motion you are capable of completing. Be very specific. What would you ask when given the assignment? What legal resources would you use? What measures would you take to make sure there were no errors? What else would you do?

3. Determine what resources are available at your school to help you improve your English skills. See if someone on campus such as the tutoring center or English Department (or other resources you discover) will critique your English skills. What areas do you need to improve, if any? Who on campus can assist you in improving those areas? What can you do on your own to improve your English skills?

> Ethical Discussion <

Assume you are a paralegal working on both transactional and litigation cases. Your supervising attorney asks you to keep track of your hours on both types of cases, even though your work on transactional cases is not directly billable to the client (the firm receives a set fee when the transaction takes place). It is near the end of the month, and you are short a few billable hours toward the minimum monthly requirement of your firm. Assume that you have been very efficient on both types of cases, often completing the work in less time than most other paralegals with your experience would take. Is it ethical to pad the transactional cases with more billable hours to make your minimum since the client is unaffected? Why or why not?

> Suggested Reading <

Teresa Ferster Glazier, *The Least You Should Know About English Writing Skills,* 7th ed., Thomson Learning, 2002.

Chapter 10
Where Do You Go for Help?

Key Success Points

> *Generally it is best to approach other paralegals in the office, legal secretaries, and attorneys with requests for assistance particularly suited for that person.*

> *Know which people in your office you should not expect to receive assistance from.*

> *Make sure you reciprocate in assisting others in your office when they need your help.*

> *Be aware that there are resources other than your coworkers that can assist in completing a task or assignment.*

> > > > > > > > >

WHOM TO SEEK OUT
AND WHOM TO STAY
AWAY FROM

Here, I am referring to those who can help you with a specific task or assignment at work. Earlier, we discussed an inner circle and other advisers outside the inner circle who can give you longer-term, strategic advice about your career. Every new legal professional finds herself or himself in a crunch from time to time. This typically occurs when the new paralegal is given a difficult assignment or one that is baffling. Sometimes the crunch occurs when the new paralegal feels overwhelmed with a particular task. "I don't know where to start!" To whom do you go for help in these situations? There are some people within your office who can be helpful and others it would be best to stay away from.

Other Paralegals in the Office

I have noticed a camaraderie among paralegals that is unlike any other classification of professionals in the legal profession. Paralegals tend to look out for one another and pitch in to help each other. This may have something to do with the fact that they are not usually competing within an office in the way new associates on the partnership track are prone to do. The spirit of cooperation may also be a reflection of the maturity many paralegals bring to the profession. Many have chosen to be paralegals after having a prior nonlegal career. Some believe they are in a battle for respect, and to the extent that paralegals in general succeed, the profession is enhanced. Those who enter the profession tend to want to help others. I am constantly amazed at the amount of time paralegals donate to professional organizations and educational institutions.

Whatever the exact reasons, the fact is that other paralegals in your office are the first resource to look to in a crunch. They understand what you are going through in a way that no one else in the office does; they have been there. Your questions will not seem stupid because they are the same ones all paralegals have when new to the profession.

If possible, find an experienced paralegal in the office to serve as a mentor. This person will be someone who can serve as a role model. I am talking about a *professional* role model. Your lifestyles and views outside the office do not need to match as long as the mentor is someone whose conduct as a paralegal is worth emulating.

A word of caution is in order. Having other paralegals available to assist you with your work questions does not mean you should feel free to ask questions or make comments about everything. Chances are you do not know your coworkers, including the paralegals, well enough to ask about subjects not specifically related to an assignment or task. You should not feel free to comment about anything not specifically related to the job at hand. You don't know when you are new to an office who is talking to each other. Play it safe, and stick to questions and comments strictly about your task or assignment. Avoid anything that gives even the appearance of being controversial. If you stay with the same firm long enough, you will have a much better sense of what is appropriate for discussion and with whom you can share it, but the best policy is to steer clear of controversy at all times.

Attorneys in the Office

The new attorneys in the office can be very helpful. They often do not have a lot of practical experience. Indeed, most paralegal school graduates who have completed an internship probably have more legal experience than the average law school graduate. However, new attorneys tend to be hard-working and intelligent and are usually quick learners. The attorneys in the office can be helpful when you are in a crunch, especially when there is an area of the law you are having trouble grasping. Law schools spend a lot of time on developing the skill of understanding the law. What does the appellate court case really say? What are the legal issues our client is facing? What is the best way to attack the opposing firm's legal arguments? Questions like these are well suited for new attorneys.

The new attorneys in the office are not as well suited for other types of questions. If you want to know the legal basis of a complaint, ask the new attorney, but if you want to know how to prepare the complaint, the experienced paralegal may be a better resource. Questions about strategy are best left to more experienced attorneys. Therefore, if the question is what types of experts to retain, how much discovery we should propound prior to the settlement conference, or whether to take a hard-line posture, the new attorney is not usually a good source.

More experienced attorneys—those who are not yet partners but have at least five years' experience—are a very good source of assistance. Chances are they have made it this far because they are doing something right. This does not mean they will all eventually become partners in the firm, but their longevity signals solid competence to do legal work. Assistance with strategic issues like those mentioned in this chapter already is very appropriate for these experienced attorneys. Nonroutine, complex legal issues are those that these attorneys will likely be knowledgeable about. For example, whereas a new attorney may be able to explain the legal basis of a complaint against an employer for wrongful termination, a more experienced attorney should be able to explain why some legal theories that are technically available may not be best to pursue given the client's situation.

When should you approach a partner or shareholder in the firm? There is a distinction to be made between your supervising attorney who happens to be a partner or shareholder, and the other partners or shareholders in the firm. Your supervising attorney expects questions. Always be careful not to ask questions that you could resolve yourself by finding the solution or talking with someone else in the office who can help you find the solution. Also make sure you ask the questions at the right time. Timing is everything. The same question will be met with a completely different reaction depending on when it is asked. As you work with your supervising attorney, you will discover when not to approach this person for a question, as well as the most opportune time to ask a question. It is always best to ask all the questions you may have at the same time if possible. Legal employers don't appreciate numerous interruptions.

What if the partner or shareholder is not your supervising attorney? As a new paralegal, it is generally best not to approach this person at all if possible. These attorneys have their own sphere of responsibility, which doesn't include you right now. Once you are with the firm long enough to get a sense of the rigidity of the firm's management structure, you may find one of these attorneys perfectly approachable. However, as a new paralegal, it is best not to assume this is the case. I know supervising attorneys who would take offense if an employee they are supposed to supervise and train asks a colleague in the office for assistance. Initially, approach the nonsupervising partners and shareholders only when you are unable to resolve the issue yourself or with the assistance of someone else in the office, your supervising attorney is unavailable, and the issue must be resolved before the supervising attorney will become available. Unless all three of these conditions are present, it is best to avoid asking the nonsupervisory attorney for assistance.

> Paralegal Perspective <

Ask many questions, and learn as much as you can about the job and the people you work with. Do not assume that you know better than the attorneys—although you quite often have more common sense—because a cocky attitude will hurt you in the legal community.

Legal Secretaries

In many ways, the secretaries in a law office are the least appreciated of the employees. They are typically working at an almost frantic pace from the beginning of the day to the end. They do the things that paralegals and attorneys prefer not to do. The question is how a legal secretary can help you with an assignment.

The days are long gone when all a secretary did was type. Today, legal secretaries must know how to use an array of computer software, be able to read and understand rules pertaining to pleading and motion formatting and filing requirements, understand the differences between the letter of court rules and how they are actually applied at the courthouse, and serve as a filter between the boss and all those who want his or her time. And this just scratches the surface.

Are you getting a clearer picture of how the legal secretary can be helpful? Your assignment may require you to prepare a table of contents; the secretary may be able to show you some software features that make that task easier. When the local court rules state something like, "The clerk, under the supervision of the presiding judge, may reject any documents that do not conform to these rules," what does this mean? What would be the best time today to see the partner to discuss a particular assignment? The legal secretary often knows where to look to find an example of the type of assignment you are working on, which has immeasurable use to a new paralegal. Further, legal secretaries usually have the confidence of the attorneys and paralegals to which they are assigned. If the legal secretary is on your side, it can make life in the firm easier. He or she is often the eyes and ears of the supervising attorney, who may at times be too busy to notice things like how early you arrive in the office, how late you stay, and generally how well you are doing in the job. Never take the legal secretary for granted.

Try to limit most of your requests for assistance to the legal secretary assigned to your supervising attorney. There is a natural sense of responsibility the secretary will have toward an assignment you are working on for a common supervisor. This is not to say that other secretaries will not want to help, but there is a tendency to view your requests as extra work instead of part of the normal work flow.

There are a few things to keep in mind. As with any other advice you receive, there will be exceptions. For example, your employer may well have a formal policy about whom to approach for assistance within the office. If such a policy exists, you should follow it. In some firms, it may be perfectly acceptable to approach anyone for assistance whenever you need it. Regardless of the firm in which you are employed, requesting too much assistance is something you must avoid. What is "too much" varies from employer to employer, but certainly includes requests that you could have resolved yourself. Always be respectful of others' time; chances are they are at least as busy as you are. Finally, remember that assistance is a two-way street: go out of your way to assist others in the office. You will feel more comfortable in asking others for assistance if you have been free in giving assistance.

OTHER RESOURCES THAT MAY HELP

There are handbooks for paralegals, usually in looseleaf binders, that are intended for use within a law office. These are essentially how-to manuals that explain the nuts and bolts of paralegal practice, with helpful tips and examples. Some of these handbooks are specific to a particular area of practice, such as estate planning. Others are of a more general nature. Some are state specific and others intended for a national audience. The best way to learn about handbooks that may be of particular use to you is to ask your coworkers or, in the unlikely event they cannot direct you to anything specific, to contact your local or state paralegal association.

One often overlooked resource is vendors. Most people try to avoid talking with a salesperson. However, legal vendors are often a great source of knowledge. The salesperson who sold your employer software will often be available to train you to use it efficiently. The company that supplies the on-line legal research service probably has a customer rep assigned to your firm. The publisher that supplies your employer's legal practice materials may be able to suggest where to find a particular form that you need. Just about anything you use in the way of a resource in completing your assignment was sold or rented by a company that has an interest in repeat business. It wants you to be a happy user. Just make sure that you determine whether there is a charge for the service. Most vendors do not charge to service existing accounts, but some do.

CHAPTER SUMMARY

Everyone who works in a law office, especially those new to the job, needs the assistance of coworkers from time to time. Seek the assistance of other paralegals when necessary. If possible, find an experienced paralegal where you work to be a mentor. Attorneys are also a good source of assistance, though the inclination to assist varies greatly. New, midlevel, and senior attorneys can all be helpful, but in different ways. Usually it is not a good idea to ask a senior attorney who is not your supervising attorney to assist you. These are, of course, generalizations; office customs and procedures in this area vary widely. Make sure you do not ask for anyone's assistance until you first try to resolve the problem yourself. Always keep in mind that assistance is a two-way street: be willing to help your coworkers even when it is inconvenient for you. There are paralegal how-to handbooks that are often very helpful to new paralegals. Make sure you have one of these guides to refer to when needed.

> Web Research Exercise <

Go to www.paralegals.org. There is a link to the "National Paralegal Reporter" magazine on the Web page of the National Federation of Paralegal Associations, an excellent source of career information. At this link, search for articles that contain information about how to succeed as a paralegal. Share the article with your classmates.

> Chapter Exercises <

1. Go to a local law library. Find out if the library has any practical, how-to handbooks. The handbooks should contain at a minimum an explanation of the law, useful forms, and advice about when and how to use each form. Preferably the handbooks will be written for paralegals but may be written for use by attorneys. Make a list of the handbooks you find particularly useful and a brief description of the information contained in the handbook. Keep the list for future reference.

2. Assume you were just given the assignment to prepare all of the forms necessary to create a limited liability company (LLC). You have heard of LLCs but do not have any idea how to go about forming one. Describe the steps you would take to complete the assignment. What would you ask your supervising attorney when given the assignment? To whom would you go if you needed any assistance, and what would you ask each person? What are you able to do yourself without the assistance of others? Write or type each step, and be as specific as possible.

3. Practice using a practical how-to handbook by consulting at least one to complete a current school or work assignment. If using the handbook for a

school assignment, check with your professor first to make sure use of the handbook is allowable. An example is to use a handbook on civil litigation to assist in preparing a summons and complaint. Assess the usefulness of the handbook. What did you like about using the handbook? What did you dislike? How useful was the sample form you used? How easy were the handbook's instructions to follow?

> Ethical Discussion <

Assume you are a new paralegal working in a civil litigation firm and have been asked to prepare a motion that you have not prepared before. No one in the office is able to assist you with the motion. Your friend from paralegal school works at another firm across town. Your employer has several ongoing files with the firm where your friend works. The friend offers to send you a copy of the motion he prepared that is similar to the motion you have been asked to prepare. If the motion you are preparing is not against a client of the firm where your friend works, is it ethical for you to receive the help described from your paralegal friend? Why or why not?

> Suggested Reading <

Robert R. Cummins, *Basics of Legal Document Preparation*, Delmar Learning, 1996.

Chapter 11
Communication: Coworkers, Clients, the Court, and Other Firms

Key Success Points

> *Follow the rules when communicating with coworkers.*

> *It is dangerous to assume anything about clients.*

> *When communicating with court personnel, always be helpful and courteous.*

> *When communicating with other law firms, keep your guard up at all times.*

> > > > > > > > >

<table>
<tr><td>

COWORKERS: WHAT
THEY LIKE AND
DON'T LIKE

</td></tr>
</table>

Communication with coworkers is essential. For our purposes, "communication" is the exchange of information between you and those you work with, both inside and outside the law firm in which you are employed. There are rules that apply; sometimes they are written, but more often they are unwritten. If you know what the rules are, you will be less likely to break them and cause embarrassment. At times, the consequences of breaking the rules of communication are more serious than mere embarrassment and can adversely affect your career and the client's interests.

Communicate in Direct, Plain Language

Don't beat around the bush. Whether in writing or orally, let the coworker know exactly what you are communicating right away. Instead of saying, "If you have time and your schedule allows, I was wondering if you could maybe show me some kind of example of this motion I am working on," say, "Would you please show me an example of a motion to dismiss?" By following this technique, you are showing that you're confident enough to be direct, courteous yet firm, and respectful of the coworker's time. Those are all attributes that are admired in a paralegal.

I once hired a new associate attorney who could never get to the point until about midway into the conversation. Sometimes the point would not come until the end. Initially it was just annoying. After a while, it affected our professional relationship. I found myself wanting to finish Corey's sentences. Later, I found myself not really wanting to listen. It was not surprising that Corey wrote much the way he talked. If *I* had trouble listening to an employee, you could imagine a judge having trouble reading one of Corey's briefs. Corey was intelligent and hard working. However, all the intelligence and hard work in the world won't impress your supervisor if you lack poor communication skills.

Never Forget to Be Courteous

Being direct does not mean being discourteous. Regardless of how comfortable you become with a coworker, never forget to say "please" and "thank you." Get into the habit of sending thank-you cards when a coworker goes especially out of his or her way on your behalf. The messages in the cards should be direct also: "Thank you for helping me with the motion to dismiss last week. I truly appreciated it." A message like this conveys your appreciation without reducing your professionalism. Make sure your courtesies are sincere, not merely perfunctory.

After weeks, perhaps months, of enduring Corey's attempts to communicate with me, I finally had a talk with him. I asked him to be more direct with me. I told him I didn't always have the time to indulge in his well-meaning but imprecise oral and written communications. He gladly complied. But it wasn't long before I heard from other employees that Corey was rude and demanding. A secretary came to me and told me Corey wanted something typed before the end of the day. When she questioned whether the typing had to be done by the end of the day (the motion wasn't due for several days), Corey responded with something to the effect that "you're the secretary. I'm the attorney. Your job is to type for me." Can you see that being direct without exercising common courtesy is unproductive? I had to have another talk with Corey. Corey worked at his communication skills, and they eventually improved considerably.

Being courteous is about showing respect for others. We all need respect. It is amazing how the seemingly inconsequential niceties of showing respect cause that person to want to listen and help. It is human nature to respond in this manner, and it is effective.

Tell the Truth

It takes months or years to build a reputation for being ethical but a single incident to tear it down. Working in a law office is a team effort. If you cannot trust your teammate, you are less likely to want that person on your team. If the copier jammed while you were using it, admit it instead of denying you used it or keeping quiet about it. Your coworkers will respect your willingness to be honest. If you're honest about the little things like jamming the copier, others will assume you're honest about the big things, like really being sick when you called in sick yesterday.

Usually the problem isn't a direct lie but one of exaggeration that gets the employee in trouble. Here is an example that I haven't forgotten even though it took place in the mid-1980s. I was a new associate in a law firm. One of the more senior associates one day came to me, frantic. He said that Sherry, one of the partners, absolutely had to have a demand-to-settle letter on her desk by the next morning. The case was complex, with many issues to address. The other associate also told me that Sherry had requested that I help out. It was late in the afternoon, so I was mildly annoyed, but I did not question the urgency of the situation and the need for my assistance. I left the office to get take-out Chinese food, brought my dinner back to my desk, and worked on the demand letter until around 9:00 P.M.

About a week later, Sherry asked why I had prepared the demand letter before a key deposition that was to take place next week. I told her I thought she wanted it sooner. She gave me a puzzled look as if she had no idea why I would have said that. What would you do in this situation?

I did not let Sherry in on the other associate's exaggerated claim that the demand letter had to be done by the next morning. I did speak with the associate, who insisted he was correct. Later, it occurred to me that the upcoming deposition would be important and it didn't make sense that a demand to settle would need to be completed prior to the deposition. That is not the situation in every case, but it made sense here to wait until after the deposition. I later learned from Sherry that she did in fact tell the other associate that I "might" be able to assist, but there was plenty of time before the demand letter had to be completed. I chalked the whole experience up to part of my training as a new legal professional. Do you think I had much confidence in the other associate from then on? Would you? Once you cannot be trusted by your co-employees, you have an uphill battle to restore the trust.

Without trust, your employer will be reluctant to let you meet with clients, speak with court, prepare briefs in which you represent the law you cited is correct, and generally do many other tasks that are critical to your success in a law office. Always tell the truth, without exaggeration, even when it hurts. Beyond that, be the first person to disclose the truth; it softens the blow. There is a reason that the time-tested technique of disclosing the problems in your case to a jury on opening statement is effective. It lets the wind out of the opposition's sails. You come across as honest and trustworthy. Further communication with the jury tends to be more credible because you were upfront about the weaker aspects of your case. The same goes for your communications with coworkers: they will think more of you if you tell them the bad news instead of their learning about it from another source.

Be a Good Listener

Early in my career, I read that listening is a difficult skill to learn. It sounded silly at the time; I thought listening was easy because you don't have to do anything when you're listening. I have since concluded that really listening is a very difficult and important skill. It is hard work!

Think about all of the situations in a law office when listening is necessary. Your supervising attorney is describing a new assignment. In fact, attorneys don't always give you written assignments. They might see you by chance in the hallway and ask you on the spot to do something. Often they simply ask you to come into their office with a notepad so you can write down your new assignment. A coworker may tell you that a client just called and wants you to arrange a meeting with you, your attorney, and the client to discuss a new legal situation. A clerk from the court may call and tell you the judge would like the motion that your office is filing today in triplicate, the third copy delivered to his chambers, and the attorneys to appear 15 minutes early for the hearing on the motion to take up "housekeeping" matters. The possibilities of situations where listening is important are endless. One thing all of the possibilities have in common is their importance: *there are no communications directly related to your job that are inconsequential.*

Although it sometimes seems that there are a hundred thoughts going through your mind simultaneously, you need to momentarily drop all of the other thoughts and concentrate only on the coworker who is attempting to communicate with you at that moment. You can assume that the coworker is at least as busy as you and would not take the time to give you information unless it was important. Further, any coworker, from the senior partner or shareholder to the new file clerk, detests having to repeat something. This is not just an issue of time; it is an issue of respect. When you fail to give a coworker your full attention, you are implying that the message and the messenger are not important to you. The messenger may not be enthusiastic when you find yourself needing that person's assistance if you have failed to give your full attention to him or her.

There are techniques you can use to become a good listener. First, *eliminate distractions.* When a coworker wants to tell me something, I put the phone on hold and shut the door. I look away from the computer so a new e-mail doesn't divert my attention. If possible, when a coworker says she wants to speak with me, I ask if we can set an appointment, even if it is only 10 minutes from now. This helps assure the coworker that I am setting aside time just for her and allows me to take care of last-minute items and devote my full attention to the coworker. Sometimes I ask to meet in a conference room or other location if I believe my office will not be free from distractions.

Another useful technique when listening is to *make eye contact.* You have no doubt heard the expression that the eyes are the window to one's soul. What this means is that a person's eyes communicate messages that may be important. You can gauge the feelings of the messenger about the message when you keep eye contact. Further, maintaining eye contact makes it less likely that you will be distracted by something else coming into focus. It takes practice and may make you uncomfortable initially. However, when the eyes are focused on the messenger, the ears seem to focus automatically on the message.

Repeating the message back helps the listening process. When someone tells you something, repeat back the key points, but rephrasing them in your own words. This causes you to listen for the key points. It also gives the messenger confidence that you heard the message and understand it.

For example, assume your supervising attorney came to you and stated he recently met with the Smiths, who are long-time clients of the firm and own a retail business. Someone slipped and fell a month ago at their business and has recently contacted the Smiths through an attorney, Jones. Jones wants to see the "sweep logs" of the Smith's store to determine if reasonable care was used in keeping the store safe from potential injury. Your attorney wants to know if Jones has properly stated the law and, if so, whether the Smiths have to turn over the requested information prior to litigation. Finally, even if the Smiths are not legally obligated to turn over the sweep log prior to litigation, is it in their best interest to do so anyway? If the sweep logs are turned over without any legal obligation to do so, should our firm attempt to limit the use of the sweep logs? Your attorney asks that you prepare a legal memorandum addressing these issues within three days.

If you were repeating the key points of this assignment, what would you say? You might say something to the effect that as you understand it, there are four issues here. First, can a retail store owner be held liable for failing to maintain sweep logs when someone slips and falls? Second, if the answer to the first issue is yes, does the store owner have to turn over the sweep logs prior to the filing of a lawsuit? Third, even if the store owner does not legally have to turn over the sweep logs, is it in the owner's best interest to do so anyway? Fourth, if the sweep logs are turned over, can their use be legally restricted in a way that is in our clients' best interest? By repeating the key information, you have forced yourself to listen carefully because you can't pick out what is key unless you listen to everything. You have demonstrated to the supervising attorney that you were listening carefully. Finally, you have made the assignment clear, so that you know exactly what the supervising attorney wants.

Remember to repeat only the key information, not everything. Repeating everything back to the messenger is annoying. Further, it takes less skill to repeat everything since you do not have to evaluate the information and choose what is most important.

Good listening skills require a conscious effort. Just as there are gifted speakers, there are gifted listeners. Some people seem to be born with the ability for listening. For most of us, though, it takes a conscious effort. Even after years of practice, I still have to tell myself from time to time to listen. Listening isn't always automatic. When a coworker indicates she wants to tell you something, tell yourself that you are going to eliminate distractions, maintain eye contact, repeat in your own words the key information, and expend real effort to hear and understand what is communicated. When you truly listen, you will find yourself expending as much energy as when you talk, and maybe even more energy.

Finally, to be a good listener you need to practice, practice, and practice some more! Although I still have to consciously tell myself at times to listen, those times are much fewer than when I began my legal career. You will find that the more you listen correctly, the more it becomes second nature. When you are away from the office, try using proper listening techniques in nonwork situations. You would be amazed at how people outside of the office, especially family and friends, appreciate a good listener. You will also be developing the listening skills you need in the office.

Think Before You Respond

Your coworkers do not want *any* response from you; they want a *thoughtful* response. Here, I am not talking about small talk at the water cooler. I am referring to communications related to your job as a paralegal. There is a tendency to want to respond immediately, but often an immediate response is an ill-considered one. There are situations that demand an immediate response, but most do not. If the situation does not demand an immediate response, it is perfectly acceptable to say you appreciate the message and will get back to the messenger shortly. Then make sure you do get back to the messenger in a short period of time and in the interim give careful consideration to your response. In the example about the Smiths' potential liability for a slip and fall in their store, there is no immediate need to say, "I think the Smiths will need to turn over the sweep log." The supervising attorney wasn't asking you to respond right away. You are better off withholding a response until you consider it first.

Limit Your Response

When you are new to a law office, you understandably want to show your coworkers you are worthy of your new position. One way new employees try to prove their worth is by offering advice, opinions, or information where none is needed. If you are listening carefully, you should make a determination of exactly what response the messenger wants: your advice, your opinion, or something else? Limit your response to what is requested. It is usually not helpful to volunteer additional information early on in your paralegal career unless you have made a careful determination that even though you are not required to give the additional information, it is likely to be helpful. Those instances will be few when you are new to the job.

This is not to say that *initiative* on your part should be avoided. You should always be searching for ways to assist your employer even when you have not been asked. However, misguided initiative will harm your career even though you had the best of intentions. In the example involving the Smiths, who own a retail store, your initiative would be demonstrated by asking your supervising attorney if he would like you to research jury verdicts in similar cases so the Smiths can factor that information into whether to turn over the sweep logs even if that is not legally required. Your initiative would be misguided if your research included the historical foundations of premises liability.

Know Your Purpose

Always be able to answer the question, "Why am I telling my coworker this?" or "Why is my coworker telling me this?" If you cannot answer the question in the former situation, your communication is not well thought out and may not be necessary. In the latter situation, find a diplomatic way in which to get the messenger to tell you why you are being told this. Often the purpose of the communication is obvious: "My supervising attorney is telling me about the Smiths because they need to know whether to turn over requested items of evidence." "I am telling a coworker about a new local court rule because it affects how she should prepare pleadings for filing in that court."

Sometimes, though, the purpose of the communication is not so obvious. Is the supervising attorney telling me about a new case because she wants me to do something on it, or just telling me because the facts are interesting? You could respond by saying "That sounds like an interesting case. Would you like me to do anything on it right now?"

When you know the purpose of your communication to a coworker, you will communicate more effectively. Suppose you tell a legal secretary in the office about a particularly difficult client in the office. If you're telling her because she will have contact with the client sometime soon, you should also tell her the client likes to be addressed as "Mr." and not by his first name, he doesn't like to be kept on hold, and anything else that will be useful to the secretary when the client calls. Knowing the purpose of your communication allowed you to determine exactly what the secretary needed to know. The secretary will appreciate knowing this information. If you simply told the secretary that the client was "difficult" without specifying the purpose of your communication, you might have omitted information that would be useful to the secretary.

Have a Sense of Humor

There is nothing like mild, well-placed humor to take the tension out of a situation. I am not talking about telling jokes and having people roll in the aisles with laughter. That kind of effort would backfire. I am talking about seeing the humor in a situation where it is appropriate. When you communicate with your coworkers, whether it is with a supervising attorney, paralegal, secretary, file clerk, or anyone else, humor is appreciated. Law offices tend to be tense. Breaking up the tension is healthy.

I once handled a personal injury where the defendant had the misfortune of getting into an automobile accident with a young lady named Rita. As a result of the accident, Rita claimed to have injured her neck and back. After the lawsuit was filed against my client, I learned that Rita had quite a history. She had been the star of a series of "adult" movies, the kind with XXX all over the video jacket. Furthermore, she had appeared in at least one film since the accident where her "acting" seemed inconsistent with a neck and back injury!

Although we took our responsibilities in this case seriously, the obvious humor in a situation like this made the case fun to work on. I took plenty of ribbing about exactly how I was going to depose Rita about her film career. Rita's case provides an example of how humor makes the work more enjoyable and how to keep the humor professional. The potential of gutter-level humor exists in a case like this; that would have been unprofessional. Keep the communications professional above all else, and inject mild humor where appropriate. Your coworkers will look forward to their exchanges with you.

> Paralegal Perspective <

I do not like a coworker to approach me for help if that person has not first tried to research the answer.

CLIENTS: DON'T ASSUME ANYTHING

A new paralegal normally has limited exposure with clients. As the firm becomes more comfortable with your ability, you will come into contact with clients more often. When you are relatively inexperienced in the legal field and are dealing with clients, it is usually best to play it safe. By that, I mean to be courteous and helpful but not stray from the purpose of your discussions with clients.

For example, if the purpose of your meeting with a client is to prepare rough draft responses to interrogatories for the supervising attorney to review, keep the communications to that subject. Do not talk about other issues the client is facing. Be willing to listen to a client's other concerns and convey them to your supervisor, but avoid discussing them. Avoid anything but the mildest of humor. The same goes for anything that could remotely be considered gossip or inside information about the firm. After you gain more experience, and develop your employer's trust, you will have a better sense of the give-and-take that occurs with clients.

Never assume anything about a client. Perhaps due to the media, we tend to have certain preconceived notions about people based on their appearance. The firm's most valued clients surely are the ones who drive nice cars, live in big houses, and have big egos. Nothing could be further from the truth! I have seen clients who drive beat-up pickups, wear old clothes, and have grade school educations who have a net worth in the millions. I have had clients who wear $2,000 suits, drive expensive European cars, and live in massive homes who have negative net worth because they bought everything with borrowed money.

I once clerked for a law firm in which farmers, often wearing overalls and muddy work boots, came into the office regularly for legal advice. I was still in law school and did not have any experience with clients at that time. I asked one of the secretaries why the firm did so much work for these farmers. She told me most of the farmers were businessmen who owned massive operations or converted farmers who became oilmen after that valuable resource was discovered on their property.

Aside from the belief that all clients are valuable and deserve to be treated accordingly, the fact is that you cannot form judgments about people based on their appearance. When you communicate with any client, the only assumption you should make is that the client is valuable to the firm.

Early in my career, I attended a meeting in which two representatives from a large company were interviewing law firms to decide which one would receive their considerable legal business. The senior attorney and I, who attended what amounted to an interview, were excited about the prospect. When the two company representatives introduced themselves, they were a contrast in appearance. One of the representatives was a large, gray-haired, distinguished-looking man dressed in a dark pin-striped suit. He carried an expensive black briefcase. The other representative appeared to be in her mid-thirties, disheveled, diminutive, and carrying a purse and notepad. The partner proceeded to tell the gentleman for the next thirty minutes about the great legal service we could offer, rarely losing eye contact, while the female took notes. After the presentation was over, the senior attorney asked what his impressions were. He paused, looked at the woman, and said "Well, maybe you should ask her. She is the one who will be making the decision about which firm to hire." Needless to say, we did not succeed in landing a new client that day. The assumptions here resulted in a lack of communication and, in this example, irreparable harm.

When you make assumptions like the situation just described, you are usually following stereotypes about people. Those types of assumptions will harm your legal career. That is why many colleges require classes that teach students the fallacy of stereotypes. While communication based on stereotypes is inherently poor communication, it is especially dangerous when directed toward those outside the firm's employ because you don't have frequent opportunities to interact.

When you communicate with a client, ask yourself if your message is based on the client's needs or based on an assumption you made that may be false. Going back to the example about meeting with the client to prepare draft responses to interrogatories, when you ask the client if she needs help understanding the questions, is that something you would ask any client, or something you asked because the client does not appear educated? While messages like this may seem minor to you, the client may view them in a totally different way.

THE COURT: COURTESY AND HELPFULNESS ARE THE KEYS

In your capacity as a new paralegal, you will at times come into contact with court personnel. Some court personnel are assigned to a particular judge, sometimes called the judge's staff. Others are not assigned to a judge but work for the court at large.

In all of your communications with the judge's staff, remember that they are likely to have the full support of the judge they work for. A bond almost forms between the judge and staff. The best policy is to communicate with any member of a judge's staff as if you were speaking with the judge herself. This means being professional, respectful, and helpful. Most of the judicial staff I have come into contact with are extremely dedicated public servants who understand the importance of their position.

Occasionally, you will come into contact with staff who seem to try to make your life difficult. In those situations, it is important to exercise restraint in your communications. I once tried a case out of town in which it seemed that the judge's staff did everything in its power to make life miserable for me. If an exhibit wasn't stapled correctly, they told me "the judge won't accept it." I knew better but was not about to get into an argument of this type in the middle of trial. Although it took great effort, I exercised restraint.

The same type of professionalism in communication that needs to be exercised with a judge's staff also needs to be directed toward court personnel not assigned to a particular judge. The people who accept your court filings are a good example. They do not necessarily have the authority that comes from working for a judge, but they have authority of their own. Those people who accept your court filings can choose to close the doors at 5:00P.M. or 5:01P.M. Sometimes it can make a difference, such as when your brief is due today.

We earlier discussed how "please" and "thank you" are important. When communicating with court staff, other important phrases include, "How can I help?" "Would you like anything further?" "What can I do for you?" and "I would be glad to do that for you!" Get into the habit of making statements like these. You will find that court personnel will want to be helpful to you in return.

>Paralegal Perspective<

The legal community is small. All news, whether good or bad, travels fast. So think things through; continue to improve your knowledge; be courteous, open, and friendly at all times; and get involved with the legal associations in your community.

OTHER FIRMS:
MINEFIELDS
EVERYWHERE

When communicating with personnel from other law firms, the best policy is to always be on your guard. There are ethical requirements at work here. Rules of Professional Conduct in all jurisdictions generally require fairness to the opposing party, truthfulness in representation, noncommunication with represented parties, refraining from practicing law without a license, zealous representation of a client, the supervising attorney to take responsibility for conduct of employees, and confidentiality of client information. This list is not exhaustive; it is illustrative of the many ethical requirements attendant to legal representation of a client by a law firm. Your ethical obligations extend to all facets of your job as a paralegal, not just when you are communicating with another law firm. However, the minefields are especially present when you engage in this type of communication. Paralegals are agents of the law firm, and thus their ethical violations may be attributable to the firm. This is known as *respondeat superior*.

Know ahead of time exactly what it is you want to communicate to the other law firm if you initiate the contact. As a new paralegal, it is best not to interact with another law firm without your supervising attorney's approval. When you initiate the contact, do not be thrown off-course. If the opposing firm brings up other issues, defer until you have the opportunity to discuss the new issues with your supervising attorney. Similarly, if the opposing law firm initiates contact with you, defer all but the most routine decisions. By "routine," I am referring to decisions where there is no chance of committing any ethical violation, compromising the client's interests, or compromising the firm's interests. As you become more experienced, your employer will usually be comfortable giving you more latitude.

If you find yourself in a situation where your employer is giving you more latitude than you think you should have in communicating with opposing firms, discuss it with the supervising attorney. If the situation is still not resolved after speaking with your supervising attorney, remember that cases have held that you may be personally liable when you act without adequate supervision.[1] Make it a point to become extremely familiar with the ethical obligations in your jurisdiction as a paralegal, as well as those required by attorneys.

In addition to the ethical considerations when communicating with another law firm, remember the practical implications. You are new to the paralegal profession and trying to establish a good reputation. When you violate ethical requirements, are reckless with information, and generally act in an unprofessional manner while engaged in discussion with another law firm, you are causing potential damage to your reputation.

CHAPTER SUMMARY

Good communications with those inside and outside the law office are essential to success. When communicating with coworkers, use direct, plain language; be truthful; become a good listener; think before responding; limit your response; know the purpose of the communication; and always keep a sense of humor. Keys to becoming a good listener are to eliminate distractions that cloud the message, maintain eye contact, repeat the message in your own words, make a conscious effort to listen, and practice your listening skills. With clients, remember not to assume anything; appearances can be deceiving. Treat every client with courtesy and respect. Try to be helpful when communicating with court personnel. Remember that court employees are in a position to have a significant impact on your firm's effectiveness. Always keep ethical standards high when communicating, including communications with opposing firms.

> ## > Web Research Exercise <

Use a search engine on the Internet to find an article on "employee communication." You will find many articles on this topic. Additionally, your school library may have a database specifically for finding magazine articles that you may find helpful. Bring a particularly useful article to class and share it with your classmates.

> ## > Chapter Exercises <

1. Assume you are a new paralegal in a law office. How would you most effectively go about doing each of the following.
   a. Ask a fellow paralegal in the office for assistance in helping you to write a legal memorandum.
   b. Discuss with your supervising attorney a problem you are having getting

a client to cooperate in finding the documents you need to respond to a request for production.

c. Ask a legal secretary to type a brief that you just learned has to be filed today.

d. Call the court five minutes before the clerk's office closes and let a clerk know your brief is due today and someone from your office will be there in a few minutes.

e. Tell a client that the documents she found are not responsive to the request to produce which the opposing law firm recently served.

2. A clerk from the local court calls you and asks if you can do her a favor. She knows your office filed a motion that was due yesterday, just before the clerk's office closed. She was in the process of taking the court file to the judge who will hear the motion when she noticed that she "misplaced" the motion. She asks you to bring another "original" to the courthouse and will stamp it for the prior day so "no one will know the difference." How would you respond to this request? In responding to the clerk's request, what issues should you consider?

3. You are a new paralegal working in a private law firm that is handling a divorce case. You are going over an accounting provided by the opposing law firm and notice that several assets have been omitted. To be sure, you check a confidential disclosure of assets provided by your firm's client, which appears to confirm the discrepancy. Coincidentally, a paralegal from the opposing firm calls and asks if you received the accounting. What do you say to the paralegal from the opposing firm? How would you go about resolving the apparent discrepancy? Are there ethical considerations that apply to this situation?

> ## > Ethical Discussion <

Assume you are a paralegal in a law firm that has a trial scheduled in the local courthouse. A former classmate of yours is now employed as a clerk for the judge who will preside over the trial. You call the clerk to ask if the judge would like a courtesy copy of a pretrial motion your firm is about to file. During the course of your conversation, the clerk asks you about the case and the motion. How much can you ethically tell the clerk?

> Suggested Reading <

Douglas Stone, Bruce Patton, and Sheila Heen, *Conversations: How to Discuss What Matters Most*, Viking Press, 1999.

> Note <

1. See, for example, *Tegman v. Accident & Med. Investigations, Inc.*, 107 Wn.App. 868, 30 P.3d 8 (2001).

Chapter 12
Office Politics: Danger Lurking Around Every Corner

Key Success Points

> *Office politics is inevitable.*
> *Generally you should become involved in office politics only when it directly affects you.*
> *When you do become involved, stay positive regardless of the temptation to attack.*

> > > > > > > > >

You're a paralegal for celebrities? What's it like?

The usual. Copyrights, contracts, loads of criminal indictments.

POLITICS EXIST IN EVERY OFFICE

What exactly is office politics? Most of us recognize when politics takes place in the office. There are no universal and entirely encompassing definitions, including the one provided here. For our purpose in learning how to handle politics in the law office, it is two or more people combining informally in a workplace to accomplish a common and mutually agreed-on personal objective. We are not talking about two or more people combining to complete an assignment, such as a trial brief, because that involves a formal combination of skills to accomplish an objective of the law office, not a personal objective. We are also not talking about gossip, which is talk that does not have a purpose other than its own sake. Anyone who has worked in a setting involving more than two people has experienced office politics. Sometimes the objective of office politics is a good one; more often, the objective is of dubious character. An example of a positive purpose would be employees combining their efforts to have the firm owners reconsider the denial of a pay raise to a co-employee. Of course, what is positive is in the eye of the beholder. The firm owners may not appreciate such an effort. Usually office politics comes into existence for less than positive reasons. The examples are as numerous as the personalities involved are able to conjure up. Anyone who feels he or she has been unfairly treated by a combination of the efforts of at least two coworkers has been the victim of office politics. It is safe to assume just about everyone has felt victimized in this manner, since politics exists in every work setting.

The situations in which a new paralegal can become involved in office politics are numerous. For example, your supervising attorney asks you to give a secretary not normally assigned to your cases an extra duty, perhaps to contact witnesses for an upcoming trial. The secretary objects and enlists the support of your supervising attorney's secretary to persuade your supervising attorney that you really do not need the help. Now both secretaries are unhappy with you for "throwing your weight around" by giving one of the secretaries "extra work." You feel as if you are between a rock and a hard place: you want your work to be done on time and believe the extra secretarial help is necessary, yet you understand that having good relationships with the legal secretaries is important to your success.

Another example would be when a paralegal and attorney, with whom you have no direct contact, come to the conclusion that the managing partner is assigning the best new cases to your supervising attorney and you. They decide to point out to the managing partner your supervising attorney's lack of experience, which they feel is reflected in the quality of the work your supervising attorney is producing. You believe your supervising attorney is being unfairly pilloried.

One more example would be when several people in the office come to the conclusion that one of the paralegals leads a lifestyle that these people do not approve of—perhaps overindulgence in alcohol. These people in the office therefore begin a campaign to undermine the other paralegal by reading into every action some kind of adverse consequence of the paralegal's lifestyle. Every time the paralegal is a few minutes late from lunch, looks red-eyed, or calls in sick, others are quick to seize the opportunity to attribute it to lifestyle and let the bosses know.

Do you see any differences in each of the three examples? The first example directly affects you. The second example affects you indirectly through your supervising attorney. The last example has no connection to you. We will see that how you respond to politics in the office should depend on the directness of its affect on you.

First, there are a few attributes of office politics that will help you understand and address it where you work.

Office Politics Will Always Exist

Politics exists wherever three or more people are employed. The perfect law office in which politics does not exist isn't a reality. There are differences in the nature and prevalence of politics in each office, but no place is immune from the effects of politics.

Being treated unfairly as a result of office politics is inevitable. If you work in a place long enough, you can expect to be treated unfairly at some point as the result of office politics. There are ways you can and should minimize the effects of politics, but you will never go completely untouched by politics. While I am a strong advocate of avoiding office politics in most cases, there will be times when you do not have a choice in the matter.

Relationships Are Important

Building strong relationships in the law office is important when you inevitably come into contact with the potentially adverse effects of office politics. Some relationships are obvious in their importance. Having a strong professional relationship with your supervising attorney is foremost. You want to have a relationship with your supervising attorney that engenders loyalty on his or her part. How do you build such a strong relationship with your supervising attorney? When you have consistently sacrificed for the attorney's success, you create loyalty. For example, when you work through lunch to get the job done on time, do the tasks others avoid, and consistently support your attorney in business and social settings, you are working for your supervising attorney's success. Make sure you do everything within reason to create a strong relationship between you and your supervising attorney. When office politics rears its ugly head, you will be a step ahead of the game by having a loyal boss.

Although the relationship between you and your supervising attorney is usually the most important relationship in the office, it isn't the only one you should be cultivating at all times. Focus initially on all of those in your office with whom you have direct contact in doing your work. Depending on how your office is managed, this may include another attorney from whom you receive assignments even if that person is not technically a supervising attorney, another paralegal with whom you work, and a legal secretary.

Make sure you do not wait until you are the victim of office politics to forge strong relationships. You would be amazed at how others in the firm will assist you in dealing with unfair treatment when they feel you share more than just office space together. Without forgetting to act professionally, become a friend of those with whom you have direct contact in the office. The only way to have friends in the office is to be a friend. Make reasonable sacrifices for others in the office, and they will usually do the same for you when necessary. When I refer to "sacrifice" I mean making relatively small sacrifices that cumulatively build a strong relationship over time. For example, whenever I had to have a brief done, I knew that my legal secretary would work through lunch, come in early, and stay late if necessary—whatever it took to get the work done. Although I rarely took advantage of her generosity, knowing she was willing to make that sacrifice made me an advocate on her behalf.

Once you have been in the office long enough to establish strong relationships with those you have direct contact in your role as a paralegal, slowly begin to branch out. Get to know others in the firm and establish strong relationships. You may not work directly with the senior paralegal in a firm, but she is in a position to help should politics in the office come into play. You can't establish strong relationships with everyone; you will never have the time. However, if you focus first on those with whom you directly work and later with others who can influence your future in the firm, you will have invested your time wisely.

Office Politics Ebb and Flow

Relationships and loyalties change over time. This happens in part through attrition as employees leave the firm and new ones are hired. Relationships also change because interests change. You may have built up a strong relationship with your supervising attorney only to be assigned to another attorney at some point. While you are probably best off not working for a firm that makes reassignment a common practice, to some extent it occurs in nearly every law firm. What this means is that you should always be working on establishing new relationships as well as maintaining existing ones.

> Paralegal Perspective <

I believe that as a new paralegal, office politics should not occupy too much of your attention and energy. Just keep in mind that in law offices, as well as many other professional settings, less speech and more action, less politics and more techniques, will almost always be appreciated by your employer.

DON'T BE A GAMBLER; PLAY IT SAFE

When it comes to office politics, it is best to play it safe as a new paralegal. Don't take unnecessary chances by becoming involved in politics. As a general rule, you are much better off to simply go about your work and not delve into the jungle of office politics to the extent you can. As a new employee, you do not know the full extent of the relationships that preceded your employment, and even if you did, you are not experienced in perceiving the impact of those relationships. Don't take sides; stay neutral whenever a controversial issue presents itself and your coworkers are lining up on one or the other side. The old adage, "The enemy of my enemy is my friend," does not apply here. The enemy of your enemy may be hostile to you too.

When It Is Necessary to Be Involved

You should get involved in office politics only when the issue at hand directly affects you. In the three examples of office politics earlier in this chapter, the first situation is the only one that directly affects you. Recall the two secretaries who combined their efforts to let your supervisor know you really did not need extra help. Although you would probably rather not get involved, you *are* involved because the issue is about how much work you are producing and how quickly you will be able to get it done. The secretaries may give your supervisor the incorrect impression that you are not producing enough work to warrant extra secretarial help. If your supervising attorney buys into this argument yet you truly do need the help, the quantity and quality of your work will suffer. If you are not producing the best work product of which you are capable, your job security may suffer too. You cannot afford to simply sit back and ignore this situation.

In order to handle a situation that directly affects and involves you, realize, and therefore anticipate, that there are going to be inescapable situations in the office in which you cannot avoid politics. If you understand that politics is relationship based, you may already have developed a strong relationship with your secretary such that she is lukewarm to her fellow secretary's attempts at undermining you.

When it is necessary to be an advocate for yourself, always be positive. Since politics is malleable, you don't know if your supervising attorney in this situation will be the ally of someone you just insulted in the current situation. Further, even if the insult took place in private, information like this has a way of filtering out. Although you may have won the current battle by putting down the other secretary, you may now find yourself in a long-term war with that person. You might tell your supervising attorney something to the effect of understanding how hard the other secretary works but that you agree with the supervising attorney's original assessment that you need additional secretarial help, on a temporary basis, because of the amount of work that is being produced.

If this doesn't work for some reason, do not become negative. Simply keep your supervising attorney apprised of the situation and hope that his or her analysis of it will change after there is additional time to assess the workload. You do not want to make enemies in the office. Where you believe that potential exists, it is best not to burn bridges. Talk with the other person. You don't necessarily need to apologize unless you were clearly wrong or unfair. Apologizing when you were not wrong simply gives the offended person confirmation that you deserve the ill will directed toward you. You *should* apologize when it would be clear to any reasonable person that you were wrong or unfair. Whether you apologize or not, you do need to let the other person know you value him or her as a coworker.

When Not to Become Involved

As for the other two example situations, you should not get involved. In the situation involving other workers' wanting the choice assignments, it would be tempting to conclude this is one of those situations that involves you and you should thus get involved. Although it may be a close call here, the best policy is not to become involved absent direct impact, as in the first example. Here, your supervising attorney's work, not yours, is being criticized. By implication, your attorney's work is to some extent a reflection of the quality of work you do for him, but there is no direct criticism of you here. No one is advocating that you should not receive assignments, just what they perceive to be choice assignments. It is best to err on the side of noninvolvement in office politics when you are not directly affected, even in these gray areas.

The final example, involving the co-employees who are critical of another paralegal's lifestyle, is the easiest in terms of whether to become involved. Clearly there is no direct link to you here, and not even an indirect link. You should not become involved. This isn't always easy when you perceive an injustice is being done, but right now your focus needs to be on your own success in the office. There is a limit to everything. I would not advocate that you remain uninvolved regardless of the circumstances, but you should do so only when the situation clearly contravenes your ethical values, you understand the potential negative effect on your success, and you believe the price is worth paying. An example would be racial injustice in the office. If that is occurring due to office politics, you are best working for someone else anyway. For the great majority of office politics situations, you are better off staying away altogether.

CHAPTER SUMMARY

Politics exists in every office. Politics can directly affect you, indirectly affect you, or not affect you at all. Common to all office political situations are their inevitability, occasional unfairness to you, the need to develop certain relationships to combat them, and their malleability. It is important, especially for the new paralegal, to play it safe when dealing with these situations. In general, get involved only when you are directly affected. When you are directly affected by office politics and must become involved, make sure you are always positive in advocating for yourself. Never become negative even when it may be justified. In rare instances, you may choose to become involved even when you are not directly affected when your ethical values are compromised, you fully understand the potential negative affects on your job and career, and you choose to accept those consequences anyway.

>Web Research Exercise<

On the Internet, go to www.paralegals.org and click "search." If you type in the words "office politics" you will usually find at least one article on this topic. If an article on office politics is not currently posted, try the same search with a general search engine. Find a particularly useful article to share with your classmates.

>Chapter Exercises<

1. You have just heard from your secretary that another paralegal in the office wants to be assigned to your supervising attorney because she is considered the best to train with. You have been assigned to your current supervising attorney for six months and are just beginning to feel comfortable working with her. What specifically would you do to address this situation, if anything?

2. Assume you are a new paralegal in a private law firm and do not know any of your coworkers yet. With whom would it be important to establish strong relationships in the first six months? First year? First three years? How would you go about establishing those relationships? What reasonable sacrifices on your part would you be willing to make for each relationship described?

3. This chapter recommends that you generally not become involved in office politics as a new paralegal unless you are directly affected. One of the exceptions involves your own personal ethical values concerning unfairness that results from office politics. What level of unfairness would have to exist for you to become involved in office politics when you are not directly affected? Describe specific situations that would violate your ethical standards sufficiently that you would become involved.

> Ethical Discussion <

Does participation in office politics have the potential to lead to unethical behavior? How? What can you do to guard against participation in office politics that may lead to an unethical situation? Explain.

> Suggested Reading <

Kathleen Kelley Reardon, *The Secret Handshake: Mastering the Politics of the Business Inner Circle*, Doubleday, 2002.

Chapter 13
How to Know What You Are Worth

Key Success Points

> *It is important not to equate your worth as an individual with your success as a paralegal.*

> *Your worth to a law firm is a function of your economic contribution to the firm, the demand for paralegals with your training and experience, and intangible qualities that you possess.*

> *When asking for a raise, be prepared, don't be confrontational, ask at the right time, don't put it off, be positive, and persist.*

> > > > > > > > >

Reading the Will

"To my loyal paralegal,
I leave my caseload in utter chaos
so you'll have total job security."

ECONOMICS—A DISMAL BUT NECESSARY SCIENCE

When we talk about "worth" here, we are not referring to your value as a person. How you view yourself should not be determined by your job. Those who cannot divorce their value as a person from their value as an employee are likely to view job failure as personal failure. Your employer tells you that your work is not up to par, and you begin to wonder if your entire life is what you hoped it would be. Although career success is important in life, it is not how you should define your life. The irony is that having this attitude will take some of the pressure off and allow you to perform better at work. The whole idea is to keep this very important part of your life—your career—in perspective.

What we are referring to in this chapter is your worth to your legal employer, much of which is dependent on cold, hard dollars. What does the employer look at when determining whether it makes economic sense for you to be employed? As a paralegal you are a fee-producing part of the firm just like the attorneys in the office. Analyzing a paralegal's economic worth is more complex than analyzing an attorney's economic worth because of your wider variety of job skills. In other words, because you have skills that generate fees directly and indirectly, determining how much you bring to the firm economically usually involves more than simply adding up the fees you bill and deducting what it costs to employ you. However, any analysis of what you are worth begins with an analysis of your direct financial impact on the firm. If the fees you generate yourself and those you assist others in generating do not exceed the cost of employing you (usually by a certain margin determined by your employer), it does not make economic sense for the firm to employ you. How does a firm determine your direct economic impact?

The first part of the equation is relatively simple. What are the billable hours you generate times your hourly rate? If, for example, you generate 1,200 billable hours per year at $80 per hour, you have generated $96,000 for the firm in one year.

If you are working on contingency fee cases instead of billable hour cases, determining the fees you generated is a little more difficult. One way a firm tracks this information is for attorneys and paralegals to keep track of the time they spend on each contingent fee case and then divide the total amount of the fee generated on the case by the individual's time on the case. You are writing down the time you spend on the case that you could have billed if you were working on a billable hour case. Therefore, you would record your time for preparing a deposition summary, but not for some task considered more administrative in nature, such as addressing an envelope. Let's assume you are working on a personal injury case with an attorney. The attorney and you both record the time spent on the case. When the case settles, it turns out the attorney spent a total of 60 hours on the case and you spent a total of 40 hours. If the fee (not the settlement amount) is $10,000, you have generated 40 percent of that fee, or $4,000.

As a paralegal, you have skills that also allow you to assist others with their work so they can bill the client. Sometimes you may bill for this time, but often you cannot ethically do so. Sometimes you may ethically be able to bill for a certain task, but your employer asks that you not do so for other reasons; perhaps the client does not feel she or he should pay for that kind of a task. I once had a very good client who refused to pay for my paralegal's presence in a deposition. He did not believe it took two of us to "take notes." Although I believed the paralegal performed a vital function in attending depositions for this client, the firm did not bill the client for the paralegal's time in depositions for the client. This decision was based on the realistic decision that it was not in the firm's interest to disagree with the client on a relatively small matter and risk losing the client—and a large amount of legal fees—in the process. Decisions in law firms are often based on their practical effect, so it is important for the paralegal to have that mind-set. In other words, the big picture is important.

In a situation such as asking the paralegal to be present at a deposition even though she did not generate any fees herself, it would be unfair for her not to receive credit for her time. Certainly, the paralegal who attended all those depositions contributed to the success of the case by keeping the attorney organized, taking accurate notes, assessing the deponent's effectiveness as a witness, and keeping track of questions to be asked as well as exhibits to be examined. This is an example of the *indirect* generation of fees.

There are many other situations where paralegals make it possible for others to generate fees. Sometimes those situations involve tasks that are strictly legal in nature, such as attending a deposition; sometimes they do not. Examples of the latter include attending lunches with an important client, representing the firm as a guest speaker before a civic organization, preparing a PowerPoint show for the supervising attorney's presentation to a potential client, filing an appeal that the supervising attorney will trust only to you, proofreading a legal document that someone else has prepared, and a whole host of administrative tasks that may be necessary in a crunch.

You should keep track of all your time spent on indirect fee generation, whether your employer asks you to do so or not. Your employer should be able to use this information in determining your overall fee generation for the firm. If you spent 20 hours on a case for which you were not able to bill but which allowed others to bill, the firm should know this. Suppose the fees generated by everyone who worked on the case were $15,000 and the total time spent by attorneys and paralegals was 75 hours, of which you contributed 15 hours. You should receive credit for having generated 20 percent of the fees, or $3,000. Be sure not to pad your time. Just because the client isn't being billed doesn't mean it is ethical to mislead your employer. Most employers review billing carefully and will know if you recorded more time than you actually spent. Once you lose your employer's trust, it is difficult to repair the damage.

A caveat is in order at this junction. Legal employers vary markedly in how they track your economic impact. Some are extremely meticulous, to the point of being obsessive by any reasonable definition. Indeed, I know of a firm that keeps a running total of each employee's billable hours and posts it! Other firms assume that if everyone is working hard and the firm is making a profit, there is no need to keep close track of the amount of fees each individual employee generates. Some firms keep track of direct billing but not the indirect fees generated by helping others on a case. Many, if not most, law firms keep track of your economic impact similarly to what has been described in this chapter.

Regardless of the manner in which your employer keeps track of your economic impact, you should do so carefully, as I have described. This information will give you a stronger bargaining position with your employer when you ask for additional pay or benefits. And it will allow you to demonstrate your worth to the firm should the firm have to downsize.

Now let's assume your firm has determined that in the past year, you generated 1,200 billable hours at $80 per hour, $7,000 for the hours spent on contingency cases, and $5,000 for indirect tasks that allowed for others to generate fees. That is a total of $172,000 you generated for the firm. However, the analysis is not quite complete.

Every firm has what is known as an *overhead factor*. The adage that it takes money to make money is essentially what the overhead factor is about. Think for a moment about the costs associated with keeping the law firm's doors open: office rent, insurance, book and on-line legal subscriptions, stationery, photocopying, phone bills, salaries, and utilities, to name just a few of the expenses a law firm typically incurs. That $172,000 you generated came at a cost. If that cost was less than $172,000, the firm made a profit (at least on having employed you). When the firm adds up all of its fees and compares it with all of its costs, the difference is either a profit or a loss, depending on which figure is greater. The ratio between fees and costs is the overhead factor.

Why is that important to you? It determines the profit (or loss) the firm experienced by employing you.

Let's say that on average, the firm has an overhead factor of roughly 60 percent, a figure that is reasonable in many firms. This means that for each dollar of fees generated, it took $.60 in costs to generate that dollar. The profit is $.40 for every $1.00 in fees generated. Applying the 60 percent overhead factor to a paralegal who generated $172,000 means that the paralegal generated $54,800 more in fees than she cost the firm to generate those fees. How much of that $54,800 you are paid and how much of that figure the firm keeps depends on several factors, such as the market demand for your skills, and some noneconomic factors. The figures used in this illustration, including the overhead factor, vary from firm to firm. Some paralegals bill at higher hourly rates, some at lower rates. Some bill more hours and others less. The overhead factors vary by law firm. The point is the process by which a firm determines your worth. Knowing this process is invaluable information when asking for a raise or increased benefits.

THE MARKET'S INFLUENCE ON PAY AND BENEFITS

It does not take an economist to understand that the demand for all employees, including paralegals, fluctuates. When demand is down, there are more workers willing to take less in pay and benefits. Fortunately, you have chosen a profession where the overall demand for paralegals is expected to increase in the long term.[1] This explains in part the upward trend in salaries for paralegals. The demand for paralegals in general, and for paralegals with your skills specifically, plays a large role in determining your worth to the firm. If demand is low, the portion of the $54,800 the firm is willing to share with you is less than if firms are having a difficult time finding people with your skills. But if you would be difficult to replace because of high demand for those with your skills, you can command a higher salary. It should be obvious that the best time to ask for a raise is when times are good.

Determining the demand for paralegals is not just a matter of looking at the overall demand for paralegals. Paralegals with certain types of training may be in greater demand than paralegals in general. During the boom times in the high-tech field, paralegals with training in intellectual property were in shorter supply than paralegals in general. The same can be said for paralegals whose practice emphasis was corporate law during the mergers and acquisitions frenzy of corporations in the 1990s.

Localities vary in their demand. Some areas of the country have a greater need for paralegals than other areas. Therefore, in determining the level of demand for purposes of determining your worth to a firm, consider the overall demand for paralegals, the demand for paralegals with your training, and the demand in your geographical location. The *Occupational Outlook Handbook* is a good source of information concerning the overall demand for paralegals nationwide.[2] Local and state paralegal associations are a good source of information about demand for paralegals with certain training or practice emphasis, as well as local demand for paralegals in general. Practicing paralegals, paralegal instructors, and those in your inner circle of advisers are also excellent sources of information concerning the demand for paralegals. As a new paralegal, your college paralegal instructors are a particularly great source of information. They are in a position to know about the local demand for paralegals, especially as it pertains to paralegals with little or no experience. In addition, if you recently completed your paralegal certificate or degree, chances are you are still in close contact with your instructors.

> Paralegal Perspective <

For new paralegal graduates, I really don't think salary standards should play a big role in turning down or accepting a job offer. I don't mean that we should all volunteer at our first jobs. The market standard is there, and the gap between salaries and benefits offered by different employers for similar positions usually won't be incredibly big. To me, working with supervisors with great personalities and professionalism at a place where I can utilize my knowledge and skills, and constantly learn something new, is much more important than salary differences. And don't be obsessed by the fact or idea that you can earn more somewhere else. Instead of paying tuition, you are getting paid at this "on-the-job training institute." After all, you are the lifetime beneficiary of all the expertise and skills obtained, which could be worth much more or even be priceless later.

NONECONOMIC FACTORS FIRMS CONSIDER

With most firms, determining your worth is more than just adding up the numbers, though those numbers are probably most important. Firms do want to know how much you are contributing to their bottom line; after all, the firm exists primarily to make a profit. No profit means no law firm; no law firm means no job for an aspiring paralegal like you. Law firms are about more than mere numbers; they are about people. There is a synergy that firms strive for that means the collective efforts of the whole are greater than the sum of individual efforts. You are part of a team. We have seen certain sports teams that have great individual players but the team is mediocre. The chemistry for success is lacking. We have also seen sports teams with few, if any, great individual players that seem to win more than their fair share of games.

Where do you fit in your law firm team? Are you good at your job? Do you make those around you better? Do you bring energy and enthusiasm that help firms stay motivated during those inevitable rough times when difficult people and difficult cases want to get the best of others in the firm? Do you seem to perform especially well when the pressure is on? Do you go the extra mile and do the things that others would rather not do in order to help the firm be successful? Are you constantly trying to improve your skills, including taking the opportunity to cross-train so you will be more valuable to your firm? Do you have a good relationship with the firm's clients? Do you make your supervising attorney's job less stressful than it would be without your presence? Would the thought of your absence be untenable, even painful, to your supervising attorney?

These are the types of intangibles that factor into your worth to the firm; they do not easily translate into dollars and cents, but their value is unquestioned. Law firms are willing to pay more to paralegals who possess these qualities. You can develop these qualities by following the suggestions in this book. These qualities become even more valuable when you consider that most of your fellow employees do not possess these qualities. It is one thing to know what it takes to be successful; it is another thing entirely to follow through. Employers know this through their own experience with employees. If you possess all the qualities described in the preceding paragraph, there is a good chance that your employer will strive to accommodate you. Knowing you possess these intangibles makes asking for more pay or benefits a lot easier, and you are dealing from a position of strength.

These intangible qualities are always valuable to a law firm. However, the amount of value depends on the firm's circumstances. If the firm is making a healthy profit, there is a tendency to be more forgiving to the paralegal who may not have stellar billing figures but has these important intangible qualities. If the firm's financial situation is more fragile, the amount of billing generated is of utmost importance. Of course, your goal should be to have both stellar billing figures and all the intangibles that a firm values.

Earlier in this book, we discussed how self-assessment can be difficult. Within the context of determining the extent to which you possess the intangible qualities alluded to in this chapter, be careful about relying solely on your own assessment. Your assessment of the intangible qualities you possess may differ from your employer's assessment. It is vital that you obtain constant feedback from your employer. Ask your employer how you are perceived. There is absolutely nothing wrong with asking not only whether you possess the qualities described in this chapter, but also what you can do to improve on them. How many times does an employer get asked these questions? The answer is not nearly enough. You will stand out in a positive way by wanting to know how your employer feels. Another benefit to asking for feedback is that if your employer perceives any shortcomings, it is better that you, rather than the employer, bring up the subject. You will likely bring it up in time to have an opportunity to correct the situation before it becomes a detriment to further advancement. By taking the initiative, you also remove much of the sting that would occur if your employer felt forced to discuss the issue. Your inner circle is also an excellent source of advice about how you are likely perceived by your employer.

HOW TO ASK FOR A RAISE

Asking for a raise, especially if you are relatively new to the legal profession, is one of the most difficult experiences you will have with your employer. It can be downright unnerving at times. I recall a coworker had once not received a raise in over two years. He could not bring himself to ask. Finally, he got the nerve to ask and received a raise immediately. He asked the partner why he did not receive a raise earlier, and the reply was, "You didn't ask." Some firms have a regular salary review, which makes the subject of a pay raise easier, but even in those situations, the paralegal may not feel the proposed raise is adequate. The fact is that there will be times when you have to let your employer know you feel you deserve more. How do you go about doing this without seeming greedy or ungrateful yet getting what you think you deserve? Here are some suggestions.

Be Prepared Before You Ask

Know how much you have billed, both directly and indirectly. You may not be privy to the firm's overhead factor, but anything more than 60 percent would be unusual. Know what intangible qualities you bring to the firm, and be specific about them. Give examples of the strong relationships you have with clients, how you've helped coworkers, taken on difficult tasks that others avoided, strived to learn more about your job, made extraordinary efforts when the situation required it, and all the other things you did to make the firm more successful. Know the national and local markets. Be able to discuss, if appropriate, the demand for paralegals with your skills and training. Find out what other paralegals in your legal community are paid, as well as their benefits. One of the least impressive ways I have seen to ask for a pay raise is for someone to tell me they're "not sure" why they should be paid more other than that they haven't had a raise for awhile. Make sure you are armed with knowledge, and use it judiciously. In other words, be prepared to answer any question your employer may ask about a possible raise, but don't give your employer information he or she does not want to hear. You could start out by stating you believe you deserve a raise and would be glad to answer any questions about why you feel you deserve one.

Don't Confront

You are not engaging in an oral argument. You are looking for a solution to what you perceive to be a potential problem. Keep a friendly, professional, matter-of-fact attitude. Don't argue with your employer, but point out any disagreements you may have. For example, if your employer says something to the effect that you are being paid what the local market will bear, point out that your information differs and where you obtained that information. It will be hard for the supervising attorney to say no when you have a good response to every issue raised. It is possible the attorney will be confrontational. If that occurs, ask if there is a better time to discuss it, but above all else, do not get into anything resembling a confrontation. Attorneys are confrontational by nature in many cases; their work often involves confrontation. Many of them have a difficult time turning off the switch.

>Paralegal Perspective<

> Don't ask for more money if you don't deserve it. You should be able to demonstrate why you deserve the raise.

Good Timing Is Essential

How well your request for a pay raise or increased benefits is received depends on when you ask. Ask at the wrong time, and all the preparation in the world will not matter. Ask at the right time, and it can be a very pleasant experience. In an ideal world, you would ask precisely when the demand for paralegals nationwide is great, the local demand is high, the firm is doing very well financially, and you have recently done something extraordinary for the firm—perhaps worked hard on a difficult case that settled for a large amount. Of course, it is very difficult for the timing to be perfect. Before you ask for a raise or more benefits, be methodical about when to ask. Do you anticipate the firm's settling a large case that you worked on so soon? Did the supervising attorney recently win an important trial? Has another paralegal left recently for a higher-paying job? Once you determine the best time to ask, make an appointment. This is a subtle way of telling your employer you consider this an important matter. It also makes it more likely your employer will not be distracted by other responsibilities instead of focusing the attention on you.

Make sure the timing is good for you too. Don't fall into the trap of the boss's saying, "Why don't you come in now while I have a few minutes?" unless you are adequately prepared and your boss truly has the time to give your request the attention it deserves. Simply reply, "Thank you. I appreciate your offer. I have to finish this project I'm working on but I checked your calendar, and it looks as if next Thursday at 9:00 A.M. works"—or words to that effect.

Don't Procrastinate

If you have done your homework and truly believe a raise is in order, determine the best time to ask, and then follow through. Make the appointment now. Waiting will only increase your anxiety and, perhaps, your resentment. Anxiety and resentment are not productive feelings when asking for a raise. There is a greater chance for confrontation, which is the last thing you want. While it is important not to procrastinate, it is equally important not to rush. Make sure you really do deserve a raise and you have the time to prepare to show your employer why you have reached this conclusion.

Be Positive

Asking for a raise is not the time to complain about your coworkers, the clients, or how you are treated. There is a time for complaining about that type of thing, but this is not it. Put a positive spin on everything. You were able to bill all of these hours because of a great support staff and your wonderful working environment. You have developed excellent working relations with the firm's clients. You have taken on tasks that others avoided because it was an opportunity to learn something that makes you more valuable to the firm. Everyone, including your boss, likes to be around positive people. Being positive is a subtle reminder of the fact that you are not a complainer. If you are not a complainer, you must truly deserve a raise.

Be Persistent

Since asking for a raise is so difficult, the tendency is to view anything but an unequivocal yes as rejection. There may be several reasons that you would not hear the resounding affirmation you seek right away, and they probably have little, if anything, to do with you. The attorney may need more information before deciding. She may not need more information but needs to think it over. She may need to discuss it with the other firm owners. She may even purposely want to give you a negative impression in the hopes that the issue will go away, not necessarily because she has anything against you but she simply has too much going on now to address your issue. It is important not to become discouraged when you don't hear what you want to hear immediately. Be patient. Tell the supervising attorney you understand he may need time to think it over. After a reasonable amount of time, raise the subject again in a polite, professional manner. Don't give up too soon.

At some point if it looks as if the issue of a raise is hopeless, try to understand why. It is possible you were wrong. Be open-minded about your employer's reasons. Then ask your employer what you need to do the next time. If you do all your employer asks and still receive a negative response to what you believe is a reasonable request, it is time to assess your employment situation. And take a long-term view. Is this just a small bump in the road to your success with the firm? All jobs have disappointments that need to be worked through instead of running away from. In the whole scheme of things, will leaving this employer seem shortsighted when you look back on the situation a few years later? Is the situation reflective of the employer's attitude toward you and unlikely to change? If so, it may be best to find another employer while you can still do so under positive circumstances. These are all questions that need to be asked if you don't receive the response you had hoped.

CHAPTER SUMMARY

Remember not to confuse your worth as a person with your worth as a paralegal. Your worth as a paralegal is determined by several factors, starting with your economic worth. The amount of revenue you generate for your employer, both direct and indirect, is an important factor in determining worth. There are intangibles that also factor into your worth to the firm. These are considerations such as your attitude toward your paralegal position, how well you fit in the firm environment, clients' opinions about you, and your level of skill. The market demand for your skills is also an important factor. This demand fluctuates and can vary depending on geographical location.

When you do ask for a raise, be prepared by knowing what you are worth to the firm and being ready to discuss how you arrived at your conclusion. Do not be confrontational about asking for a raise. Confrontation is hardly ever effective when asking for an increase in pay. Be professional and courteous when asking for a raise, even if you do not get what you want. Asking at the right time can make a tremendous difference. Once you determine your worth and the right time to ask, do not procrastinate. Being positive and persistent will make it more likely you will receive a raise.

>Web Research Exercise<

On the Internet, go to www.monster.com This Web page is a source of information on job finding and career information. Click on "Career Marketplace." Next, click "Personal Salary Report." Then complete the survey, which is designed to assist you in determining your correct salary. What information did the report contain? How can this information be helpful to you? Was the result what you would have expected, or were you surprised? How convincing would this survey by itself be to an employer? Be ready to discuss your results with others in your class.

> Chapter Exercises <

1. To what extent do you define your worth as an individual with your success at work? Should there be no overlap at all between success as a paralegal and feelings of self-worth? Should success as a paralegal and a person's self-worth be identical? Should there be a middle ground between feelings of self worth and success as a paralegal? If so, where is the middle ground?

2. Assume you have been a paralegal in a law firm for about eight months. When you accepted the position, you were told that you would receive a salary review in "about six months" after you began the job. You have not received a salary review. There is supposed to be a salary review after 12 months also. You like everything about your job except you have determined you are probably underpaid by about 10 percent compared with others in your community with similar experience doing similar paralegal work. How would you handle the situation? Be as specific as possible.

3. This chapter discussed the intangible factors law firms consider in determining your worth to the firm. What can you do now to improve on those intangibles? What can you do in the next 3, 6, and 12 months? If you are not yet employed as a paralegal, what will you do to improve on the intangible factors?

> Ethical Discussion <

You suspect that you are being paid less than the average paralegal of similar ability and experience in the local legal community. In order to confirm your suspicion, you call several paralegals working for private and public legal employers to ask what pay they are receiving. Are any ethical issues presented by contacting these paralegals for wage information? Explain.

> Suggested Reading <

Robin L. Pinkley and Gregory B. Northcraft, *Get Paid What You're Worth*, St. Martin's Press, 2000.

≻ Notes ≺

1. Bureau of Labor Statistics, U.S. Department of Labor, *Occupational Outlook Handbook, 2002–03 Edition*, U.S. Government Printing Office.

2. Ibid.

Chapter 14
The Importance of
Growing Professionally

Key Success Points

> *Professional growth is a multidimensional undertaking.*

> *The goal of professional growth is to develop state-of-the-art skills and increase job satisfaction.*

> *Your inner circle can assist in identifying professional growth opportunities.*

> > > > > > > > >

"And while the lawyers argued,
the King's paralegals got all
the real work done."

WHAT DOES IT MEAN TO "GROW PROFESSIONALLY?"

Quite a lot of people express the desire for "professional growth" in a general way, but give little thought to exactly what the phrase means and how to achieve it. The phrase has come to mean different things to different people. For some, it means joining a professional organization. For others, it is taking a class. Others believe it means accepting new and challenging job duties. None of these definitions is necessarily incorrect. However, growing professionally today is a multidimensional undertaking. We live at a time when job skills (and thus those who possess those skills) can become obsolete in a very short period of time. That trend is not going to change any time soon. This means growing in your profession has taken on a whole new sense of importance. There has always existed the potential of becoming obsolete or outdated in this profession, but the rapidity of change today is unlike anything that has preceded it. In addition to the need to keep skills updated, professional growth has always been a source of increased job satisfaction. The fact is that the better you are at what you do, the more you enjoy the work. Recognition of your peers in the paralegal profession is an immensely satisfying career experiences.

Professional growth is the constant effort to do all of the things necessary in your career to maintain state-of-the-art job skills and increase job satisfaction. This means that growing professionally is a continuous undertaking; you do not grow for a little while, take a rest, and then start back up again. The danger with intermittent effort is that the "rest" becomes habit. Bad habits can be hard to break. You wouldn't take a break from showing up to work on time or filing a motion by its deadline because these are essential to your job as a paralegal. Professional growth is equally essential. It is important to make the idea of growth a way of life and incorporate it into everything you do in your profession as a paralegal. You should have the attitude that you will look for the opportunity to grow with each task you undertake. Going to the law library? This is a good time to learn how to use another legal resource. Writing a brief? What a great opportunity to increase your legal vocabulary by learning words that may give a more precise meaning than the words you normally use. These are examples of fairly small efforts that can amount to an incredibly successful career in the aggregate.

This definition also means that simply growing one way is not enough. Taking a class is fine as far as it goes, but there is more to it. You are involved in a multifaceted undertaking. Joining a professional organization, taking part in panel discussions, speaking to a classroom full of paralegal students, becoming active on a professionally related committee, and taking on added job duties are also examples of growing professionally. There are two questions you can ask yourself that will help you decide whether you should undertake a new task to grow professionally: Is this making me better at what I do? and Will this make my career more satisfying? If you can answer yes to both questions, you should do it. If you can answer yes to one of the two questions (a yes-no situation), you should do it if there are no yes-yes situations available to you at the present. If you answer no to both questions, avoid it if possible.

While professional growth is multifaceted, this does not mean you will undertake all of the growth opportunities available to you simultaneously. That would be foolish, not to mention almost impossible. Growing in a multifaceted way means taking the best opportunities available to you at any given time. You need to prioritize your opportunities. List all of the professional growth opportunities available to you now. The yes-yes opportunities go at the top of your list, followed by the yes-no opportunities. The no-no opportunities do not go on your list at all. Choose from the yes-yes opportunities first. Which one (or ones) do you have time for right now without unreasonably compromising your immediate job responsibilities and your personal life? If you find you are able to undertake more opportunities than you have on your yes-yes list (which would be a rare situation), go to your yes-no list. There will be times in your career when you can undertake more in the way of growth and times when the best you can do is take advantage of opportunities that are strictly intertwined with your specific job tasks (such as learning a new legal resource while at the library). The point is that over the course of your career, you will need to grow professionally in a variety of different ways.

JOB SECURITY AND ADVANCEMENT

Although the long-term trend is for growth in the paralegal profession, there will always be ups and downs in hiring. No profession is immune to the effects of the economy. Even if the economy is doing well, certain employers need to downsize for various reasons, such as when a major client takes its business elsewhere. Never take job security for granted. The days are over when you can obtain a position with an employer and expect to work there indefinitely. Yet there are those who seem to have no trouble staying employed; in fact, these people manage to advance in their careers while others have a hard time holding onto their jobs. What is the secret to job security and advancement? It boils down to the ability to grow professionally.

If you have the attitude that you will look for the opportunity to grow professionally in everything you do, some very good things will occur. All of them make it less likely you will have to be concerned about job security or advancement in the paralegal profession.

First, you will have the positive attitude that legal employers desire. Law firms are stressful enough without having to work with those who always see the cup as half-empty. When you look at each new task as an opportunity to grow as a paralegal, you are focusing on the positive. When you see a task that needs to be done, and do it without being asked because you recognize how it helps you to be better at what you do, you are focusing on the positive. Legal employers will go out of their way to retain employees with this kind of attitude. When a more senior position becomes available, someone who is known as a positive contributor to the success of the firm is in a good position to be selected for advancement.

Second, taking advantage of professional growth opportunities gives you extra energy and enthusiasm. When you become better at what you do, you enjoy your job more. When you enjoy your job more, you don't become tired as easily. Have you ever had a job you didn't enjoy? How tired were you at the end of the day? Words like *exhausted*, *fatigued*, and *worn out* may come to mind. Yet how tired do you get when you're doing something you enjoy? There is no comparison in the energy level. Working as a paralegal requires lots of energy to be successful. It follows that if you have more energy, you will be more successful.

Third, having the attitude that you are always looking for more ways to grow professionally makes it painful for your employer to contemplate professional life without you. You are the person who takes on new challenges when others shun them. You learn the new software that makes for better presentations at trial. You enhance the firm's reputation by the work you do in paralegal organizations. You are your own toughest critic when it comes to your ability to write well. In other words, without you, life at the office is substantially more difficult for your employer. If you have reached this point in your career, job security is not going to keep you up at night. In fact, you will probably not spend a lot of time worrying about job security and will focus on job advancement instead. In my own law practice, my paralegal became so valuable that I simply could not imagine the firm without her. I would rather do without anyone else in the office if I ever had to make that choice.

Even in the unlikely event that you have reason to be concerned about job security despite taking every opportunity of professional growth you could, you are not likely to be out of work long, if at all. For example, sometimes large clients decide for reasons totally unrelated to a firm's performance that they wish to cut back on the legal business they give a firm. This could occur if a company decided, for financial reasons, to have more legal work done in-house. When this happens, jobs in the firm could be in jeopardy. If you're the rare paralegal who has taken every reasonable opportunity to grow in your profession, you should be in a strong position to find similar work with another legal employer. Do you think if Oprah Winfrey's show went off the air, she could find work elsewhere? She is a star in the media (and deservedly so), and numerous companies would welcome the opportunity to use her enormous skills. There are stars in every profession, though they are less well known than those we see on TV or in movies. Making professional growth an unrelenting pursuit will eventually make you a star in the paralegal profession.

> Paralegal Perspective <

Growing professionally is the key to longevity and maintaining a high demand for your paralegal skills. Take the attitude that there is no limitation to the difficulty or level of task you are willing to undertake. Show the attorney that time invested in teaching you is a worthwhile investment in his or her practice and that it will yield great returns.

USING YOUR INNER CIRCLE

Professional growth opportunities are not always apparent, especially when you are new to the paralegal profession. In an ideal world, you would have plenty of time and resources to take advantage of anything with a remote possibility it would make you better at being a paralegal or increase your job satisfaction. Of course, we live in a world in which there is too little time and too much to do. It is apparent that opportunities have to be judiciously selected. Wasting your energy on matters that have at best marginal benefits in terms of professional growth is counterproductive.

For example, a former student of mine once asked me if she should take a night course in physics because the firm in which she worked handled car accident cases and it often hired "scientific experts" to analyze their cases. I applauded Amy's desire to improve. With an attitude like that, she was bound to be successful. When I discussed what it is her law firm employer does, it became apparent that the firm often worked with accident reconstructionists who usually had an engineering or physics background. Was it worth committing two evenings a week for ten weeks for this endeavor? I told Amy there were more efficient ways to learn even better information and directed her toward classes for legal professionals who wanted to learn more about accident reconstruction. I also told Amy that there were very good personal reasons to take a physics class, such as a natural curiosity about the nature of our world. At this point in Amy's career, however, committing two evenings a week, along with the outside study required, would have precluded her from having time for other worthwhile professional opportunities. As a member of Amy's inner circle, I was able to give her the guidance necessary to make a good choice.

Another former student asked me if he should join a state paralegal organization. I not only strongly recommended it, but had suggestions about which people within that organization would be in a position to assist him with his professional growth goals. Without those suggestions, this former student may well have attended meetings rather aimlessly for quite a while before determining who in the organization could be most helpful to him.

If you are not sure whether a particular opportunity to grow in the paralegal profession is the right one for you, ask members of your inner circle for guidance. They will help you make a good decision. Also, if you find yourself unable to discover any yes-yes opportunities, members of your inner circle will have ideas and suggestions that you should find helpful.

CHAPTER SUMMARY

Professional growth is multidimensional in nature. It is the constant effort to do all of the things necessary in your career to become a more capable paralegal with the intention of maintaining state-of-the-art job skills and increasing job satisfaction. You are not usually able to take advantage of all of the professional growth opportunities available. Therefore, you need to prioritize these opportunities. Ask whether a particular opportunity both makes you better at what you do and increases job satisfaction. These yes-yes situations are the professional growth opportunities that have the highest priority. Your inner circle can assist you in identifying these opportunities and determining how to take advantage of them. Professional growth is essential to job security and advancement.

>Web Research Exercise<

On the Internet, go to the Web page for your state paralegal organization or a national paralegal organization, such as http://www.paralegals.org. On the Web page, identify three opportunities for professional growth that would be useful to you in your paralegal career. Write down each opportunity, a brief description of each one, and how it could result in professional growth for you. Be ready to discuss your findings with others in your class.

>Chapter Exercises<

1. Take an inventory of what you have done in the past year to grow professionally. How useful will those professional opportunities be in the future? Did any of those opportunities prove to be not as productive professionally as you would have liked? Why? Were any of the opportunities more productive than you anticipated? In what regard? How will this information help you be selective about your participation in future professional opportunities?

2. Make a list of all the opportunities you have now to grow professionally. Divide them into three columns: "yes-yes," yes-no," and "no-no." Remember, yes-yes opportunities help you become a better paralegal and make your job more enjoyable. Yes-no opportunities satisfy one, but not both, of these descriptions. No-no opportunities satisfy neither of these descriptions. In other words, they do not make you a better paralegal and do not make your job more enjoyable. Are you satisfied with the opportunities for professional growth you have identified? Which opportunities are you going to take, and when? What can you do right now to identify further opportunities for professional growth?

3. Make an appointment to discuss the topic of professional growth with at least one member of your inner circle. Ask this person to help you identify the professional growth opportunities that would be most advantageous for you right now and the best manner in which to pursue those opportunities.

Before the appointment, identify several opportunities you are considering, and obtain the inner circle member's opinions and advice about these opportunities when you meet.

> Ethical Discussion <

You decide that you want to take on more responsibility for handling cases as part of your goal to grow professionally. What are the ethical limits to which you can handle a case for the firm? What should you do if you are unsure whether a particular task on a case crosses the line into unethical behavior?

> Suggested Reading <

Terry L. Hull, *The Paralegal Handbook*, Delmar Learning, 2002.

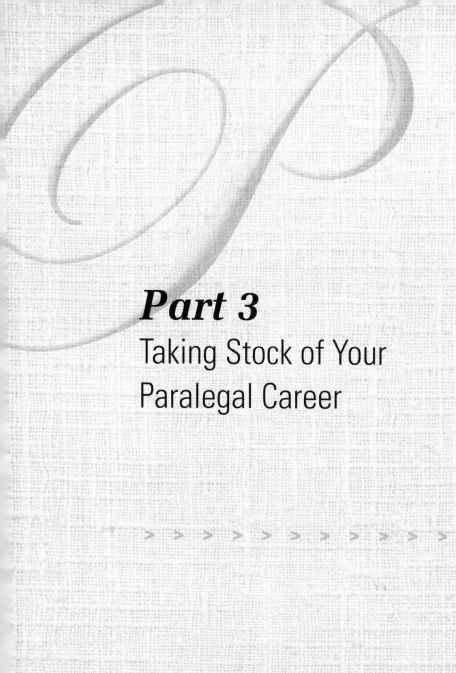

Part 3
Taking Stock of Your Paralegal Career

> > > > > > > > > > > > > > >

Chapter 15
Achieving Professional and Personal Balance

Key Success Points

> Employees work for more than just a paycheck.
> There are five steps you can take to find the job that allows balance in your life.
> Your paralegal career is like a marathon: you are in it for the long term.

> > > > > > > > >

"Us? No, we're not in disguise.
We're paralegals who do pro bono."

IS IT JUST ABOUT MONEY?

Have you ever had a job where you said the money was "just too good" for you to quit, even though you didn't like the job? Have you known others, perhaps a family member or friend, who felt the job was just too good to quit? How happy can anyone be in a situation where work represents little more than a paycheck? The answer to the last question is obvious.

Yet new paralegal graduates usually don't stop to think about how happy they will be in a job before they accept the offer. When paralegal graduates finish their schooling, they often wonder why anyone would hire them. Often they are unsure of their ability. The feeling among many new graduates is that the day of reckoning has finally come when they'll have to prepare an actual pleading, discovery request, or contract. These are documents prepared not for a letter grade but for a client. When someone does offer the paralegal a job, the thought of turning down the offer is anathema to most recent graduates. There is the fear that the next offer may not come right away, and there is no guarantee it will be as good as the one that is on the table now. Why not jump at the first job offer?

The answer is that we work for more than money. Most employees want to be respected by their coworkers and supervisors. They want to feel as if they are contributing to the organization's success. Employees also have the need to believe they are making the world a better place. They want to believe that their hard work and loyalty will be appreciated. Of course, there are many other reasons that people work other than the money. If all you wanted in a career was a paycheck, there are easier ways to make a living. If the first offer you receive is ideal for you, by all means accept it. However, you have earned the right to be selective. You are part of a profession that is in demand and is expected to remain so for quite some time. You have training in a complex subject matter whose complexity will only increase in the future. And not everyone has the ability that you possess to learn this demanding profession. Many paralegal school graduates are working on their second or third careers and have already worked at jobs they did not enjoy. Indeed, many paralegal school graduates chose their new profession precisely because they did not enjoy their prior careers. You are worthy of spending most of your waking hours at a workplace that fulfills you professionally and allows you to pursue the important goals you have set in your personal life.

>Paralegal Perspective<

> My employer is a very good person, and I feel very lucky to be working for her. She was flexible and supported my every effort to earn my paralegal certificate. She has given me generous raises and bonuses as she can, and has shown she values me professionally too. I was so complimented when she put my name and title on her business cards and letterhead after I earned my paralegal certificate. This is important daily recognition for me.

Few things in life are sadder than feeling anchored to a job you do not enjoy. Minutes seem like hours. Days seem like weeks. That achy feeling you used to get when you felt the onset of the flu is how you feel all the time at work. Your dissatisfaction at work spills over into your personal life. You are in a bad mood when you prepare to go to work and when you get home. You are too preoccupied with worry about work to engage in meaningful conversations with those who are important to you. The result? The lack of a fulfilling personal life adversely affects your attitude at work. It is a dangerous cycle you are on when you work at a job you do not enjoy.

STEPS TO A HAPPY, SUCCESSFUL, AND BALANCED CAREER

You need not find yourself in this situation. There are five things you can do today that will help you achieve a happy, successful, and balanced career as a paralegal.

Step 1. *Know what you want in a paralegal career and in your personal life.* That is why a major portion of this book explored how to go about setting goals as well as determining what those goals should be. If you have not invested quality time determining what your professional and personal goals are and writing them down, *get started today*. There is nothing you can do for yourself as important as setting goals and having a plan to attain them.

Step 2. *Do your homework.* You have done painstaking research of all kinds of legal problems during your training. Often the research you did during paralegal school was a struggle. You wondered: Did I find the right law? Do I understand the law correctly? Did I explain the law correctly in my memorandum? Think about the most difficult legal problem you have worked on and the effort on your part it required to solve the problem. Now apply the same effort to searching out the paralegal jobs that meet your professional and personal goals. The right job for you exists. You must be unrelenting in your pursuit of that job. In actuality, there are probably several jobs that would be ideal for you, but many more that would not meet the goals you have set for yourself. Since the best jobs tend to be filled by word of mouth, ask your inner circle to keep you in mind when a new job is opening up. Find out who outside your inner circle may know about job openings that meet your requirements, and ask for their advice and assistance. If you're still in a paralegal program, use your internship opportunity wisely to advance your goal of finding the ideal job. Ask those whom you consider knowledgeable to direct you to any reading material or any person who may possess information that could help you find your ideal job.

Step 3. *Apply for that job today, whether it is currently available or not.* What do I mean by this? Once you have identified the job (or jobs) you want, don't wait for an opening to occur to begin the application process. Find out the quailities sought in the ideal candidate for the job if an opening existed. Work toward making yourself that ideal candidate so you will be ready when the job becomes available. Does the job require expertise in particular software? Make sure you are an expert. Does the job require the applicant to be bilingual in a certain language? Take courses in that language. You get the idea. Don't be one of the 99.9 percent who do not think about their qualifications for a particular job until they see an advertisement. I tell my paralegal students to prepare the "dream resumé." What do you want your resumé to reflect by the time you graduate? Work toward making the dream resumé your own resumé by the time you graduate.

Step 4. *Be disciplined about your job approach.* Don't give into the temptation of settling for a job you know will not achieve your professional and personal goals. If you have set out long-term goals for yourself and a plan to achieve them, you are less likely to find yourself in a situation where finances require you to accept a less-than-ideal job. If you find yourself in that type of a job, redouble your efforts to find the ideal job for you. Keep in mind that a disciplined approach may mean turning down what may be a good paralegal position but may not allow you to achieve the balance in your life you have determined is necessary to maintain your mental, emotional, and physical well-being. The goal is balance between your job and everything else in your life. It can be extremely difficult to turn down an offer, but your purpose isn't to get any job. If you have followed the recommendations in this book, you are not likely to apply for any jobs that you would not be willing to accept. However, sometimes the job turns out to be something other than what you expected at the time you applied. Your purpose is to achieve the balance in life you have determined will maximize your happiness. That is a goal worth pursuing.

Step 5. *Recognize that an ideal job is not one without any flaws.* In a perfect world, your job would never have any aspect to it that didn't appeal to you. You would like every minute component of every task you undertake. The people you work with would always be part of the solution to any challenge at work. Each assignment would be highly interesting. Your supervisor would be engaging and never fail to compliment you for a job well done. You would never have to do anything that conflicted with a personal goal. That job does not exist, of course. People will let you down. Assignments sometimes are not interesting. At times, the job will take precedence over the personal life. That is the nature of work generally and the legal profession in particular. What really matters is whether the overall aspects of your job allow you to balance professional and personal goals. The day-to-day ups and downs of any job should not be determinative of whether the job is ideal for you. When you consider your job as a whole, does it meet the goals you have set for yourself both at work and elsewhere? That is the important question to ask yourself.

> Paralegal Perspective <

> Is it just about the money? No. It is about challenging yourself as a paralegal, self-satisfaction, and having a fulfilling career on the basis of knowing that your work makes a difference to someone.

YOU ARE IN A MARATHON

The question is whether your job and personal life achieve balance from a long-term perspective, not on a daily basis. Will your current job allow you to achieve the professional and personal goals you have set for yourself over a reasonable period of time? If not, you are not in the job for you. What is "reasonable" in terms of the time it takes to achieve your goals is highly subjective, but in no event should the amount of time be so long as to compromise those goals substantially. Further, reasonableness also depends on the nature of the goal itself. For example, having to wait 10 years to go on a world cruise is probably not unreasonable because the experience will be as fulfilling in 10 years as it would be today, and maybe even more so. However, having to wait several years before you can devote much attention to important relationships may forever alter those relationships. In the first example, 10 years was not an unreasonable period of time to wait because of the nature of the goal (a world cruise) and the fact that waiting that long usually would not be a substantial compromise of this personal goal. In the second example, waiting years before giving personal relationships the attention they deserve is a substantial compromise, maybe even a complete elimination, of an important personal goal (having meaningful personal relationships).

A marathon is a good metaphor for your career as a paralegal. You do not run a marathon without a lot of very difficult training that takes place well before you begin the race. There are others who help you get ready to run. You must be highly disciplined to be successful. You start the race alongside your competitors, but you cross the finish line according to your ability and desire. It is a long race, so you must pace yourself, keeping in mind there are hills and valleys along the way. There are times during the race that you feel like quitting, but you nevertheless press forward. You are just a number when the race starts; nobody knows you. If you do well in the race, you will be individually recognized. There is nothing quite as exhilarating as crossing the finish line. Despite the pain, tedium, and occasionally running yourself ragged, you really like running marathons; it is practically in your blood.

Since you are in a "race" that may last decades, it is crucial that you find the right paralegal job. A balance between professional and personal life will keep you around to complete the race. Any imbalance weighted toward your job is not likely to result in career success any more than starting out in a full sprint is likely to result in finishing first in a marathon. You will burn out before you get to the finish line. Likewise, an imbalance toward your personal life is like running five miles a day to train for a 26-mile marathon. It is nice to have a shorter workout, but you will likely finish in the back of the pack when the real race takes place.

You have worked too hard, and invested too much, to find yourself in a job that doesn't fulfill the professional and personal goals you have set for yourself. This balance is extremely important to your long-term success as a paralegal since professional and personal lives are intertwined. You deserve to have not just a fulfilling career but a happy life.

CHAPTER SUMMARY

New paralegals usually do not stop to consider how happy a new job makes them much further than what the job pays. This is understandable. Those new to the profession are often glad to have any paralegal job that comes with a paycheck. However, money alone will not bring enjoyment to a job. There are many nonmonetary factors that are important in determining job satisfaction and overall happiness. Further, balance between a satisfying job and your personal life is important. To have a happy, successful career, you must do five things. First, know what you want in your paralegal career and in your personal life. Second, do your homework by researching the right jobs for you. Third, apply for the perfect job today even if it is not currently available. This means setting a goal of obtaining a particular job by beginning to prepare now. Fourth, be disciplined about your approach, and do not settle for something that will not achieve what you think is important in your career and life. Fifth, recognize that the ideal job is not without flaws. Achieving balance between a satisfying paralegal position and your personal life is a long-term proposition, similar to a marathon. It may take years to achieve the balance you are looking for, but it is well worth the effort.

> Web Research Exercise <

On the Internet, go to www.selfgrowth.com. This is an excellent source of articles about many topics, including those about achieving balance in career and life. Find an article you find particularly useful. Bring the article to class, and be prepared to discuss it.

> Chapter Exercises <

1. Think back to any jobs you have had where you worked just for a paycheck. What were the circumstances that brought you to that situation? What was

your attitude about that job or jobs? What can you do to avoid being in that situation again?

2. Review the five steps in this chapter to find a job that balances your work life and your personal life. For each of the five steps, write down as many actions you are taking, or can take today, to complete each step. Make a reasonable timetable for completing these actions, and place them on your calendar. Make sure to take all steps necessary to complete each action by the date you have set.

3. This chapter discusses the similarities between running a marathon and your career as a paralegal. Review that section of this chapter. What are the similarities between what you anticipate as your own career projection as a paralegal and being in a marathon? For example, what "hills and valleys" do you anticipate? What training have you undergone to prepare for the "race"? Are you susceptible to sprinting too early and thus tiring too soon? What will you do to finish ahead in the marathon?

> Ethical Discussion <

In preparing for the "marathon" of your paralegal career, what measures should you take to include ethical guidelines and requirements in your "training"? Why is it important to continue the study of ethics throughout your paralegal career? Does achieving balance between personal and professional goals contribute to ethical behavior? Explain.

> Suggested Reading <

Robert K. Johnston and J. Walker Smith, *Life Is Not Work, Work Is Not Life: Simple Reminders for Finding Balance in a 24-7 World*, Wildcat Canyon Press, 2001.

Chapter 16
Staying Motivated: Keeping Your Career Interesting

Key Success Points

> *The two most important antidotes to burnout are balance and variety.*

> *Many opportunities exist within a law firm to achieve the type of variety in your paralegal career that will help avoid burnout and maintain high motivation.*

> *It is important to seek opportunities outside the law firm that help you maintain your motivation.*

> > > > > > > > >

BALANCE AND VARIETY ARE IMPORTANT

Staying motivated about being a paralegal is easier than in most other professions. The job by its nature is interesting. Every client brings in a new set of facts. Solving the clients' problems is a lot of what being in the legal profession is about. Every new problem is, in essence, a mystery to solve. No two situations are identical. The law is constantly changing. Most major social issues have some connection with the law.

Nevertheless, any career is subject to periods when keeping a high motivation is a challenge. Although you like your career as a paralegal, there are only so many medical records and deposition transcripts you can do before the process becomes routine. While just about every aspect of paralegal work is interesting, there can be too much of a good thing at times. What can you do to keep your level of enthusiasm high? The two most important antidotes to what is commonly known as burnout are balance and variety.

Balance refers to a lifestyle that recognizes both personal and professional goals, something that we have already explored. *Variety* refers to the professional portion of your balanced life. Your job will remain interesting if you learn new skills and take on new challenges. It is hard to imagine as a new paralegal that you would want to take on more professional challenges; the challenge of learning a new profession is enough right now! However, there will come a time when you have mastered your job and are ready for something new. How quickly you reach this point varies widely among paralegals, but in almost every career, there comes a time in which the job seems flat without new challenges. What can you do to create the variety in your job as a paralegal that will keep you motivated to come to work and perform at a high level?

TAKE ADVANTAGE OF OPPORTUNITIES WITHIN YOUR LAW FIRM

Your current legal employer is the best place to start to increase the variety of challenges in your professional life that keep your job interesting. Think of your firm as a collection of experts and resources available to teach you what you need to know to become extremely good at what you do and to learn new information that makes you more interested in your job while making you more valuable to an employer at the same time. Think about your coworkers. All of them have something they can teach you that will make you a better paralegal and contribute to making your job more interesting. Most of them will be flattered if you tell them you have noticed how good they are at some aspect of their job and would appreciate their showing you how they achieved that competence.

As time permits, ask a coworker if you can shadow her while she performs some aspect of her job that you want to learn. You would like to know what takes place at an escrow closing, so you ask a coworker (who may or may not be a paralegal) to sit with him the next time the legal papers that close escrow are executed by a client. You have always wanted to learn employment law, so you ask a paralegal in the office if you can attend the initial client interview for a wrongful-termination case. You are interested in learning what takes place at an expert inspection of a damaged vehicle, so you ask to attend the inspection. You think accounting malpractice would be an interesting area of the law to learn, so you ask to attend the deposition of a witness in an accounting malpractice case. You would like to learn litigation, so you ask to attend a trial being handled by your employer. Better yet, you ask if you can help out rather than merely attend all of the foregoing events. These are all tremendous learning experiences that many people do not take advantage of, though they are often available.

Just about every legal employer has some legal research resources available to it in the form of books or on-line databases. Most of the time, legal employees use those resources only to the extent required to complete specific tasks. However, these resources are often useful for learning about an unfamiliar area of the law. Pull a book off the shelf that has nothing to do with any current assignment you have and read it. Click on a link on a Web page that you haven't looked at before. You will learn something. If you are consistent about this, you will learn a lot over the course of a career. That knowledge will allow you to assist your employer with new responsibilities that contribute to the variety you are seeking in your job.

When a vendor visits your firm, attend her presentation. These are essentially free classes about what the vendor is trying to sell the firm. Your current paralegal position may not involve accounting, but knowing something about the latest law firm accounting software will give you a better understanding of how law firms operate. If you think you want to be a law firm administrator or at least take on some administrative duties in your paralegal position, this knowledge will be helpful. Of course, vendors sell many products and services. Judiciously choose the right presentations to attend.

Where it is appropriate, ask to meet with experts the firm hires. Most firms hire experts to assist with their clients' needs, such as engineers, medical doctors, psychologists, and financial consultants. The variety of experts a firm hires is usually quite wide, especially if the firm's practice emphasizes litigation. These experts have a wealth of knowledge. Attending a meeting with an expert is often like having a college professor tutor you. Experts tend to be well respected in their area of expertise. Knowing a little more about medicine or engineering may cause you to write a better brief or demand-to-settle letter. Or the knowledge you gain may have little or nothing to do with your current job duties but may pique an interest in areas that you would like to incorporate into your job.

Another way to bring variety into your professional life is to organize classes for your coworkers taught by you, a coworker, or even a guest speaker. Check with your employer about the usefulness of classes and appropriate topics. How about a "brown bag" lunch one Friday afternoon a month on a topic of interest to you and those you work with? Your employer will be impressed with your initiative. You will sharpen both legal and organizational skills. To the extent you have a guest speaker from outside the firm, you have the perfect excuse to establish another professional contact that may be useful later. Potential topics are practically endless, but include changes in the local court rules, a review of ethical requirements for paralegals, how to handle difficult clients, software demonstrations, an important new appellate court decision, effective brief writing techniques, and current events of particular interest to the law firm. Guest speakers can be found by asking the state bar association, state paralegal association, specialty bar associations, nonprofit organizations, and vendors. Don't necessarily limit yourself to legal or legally related organizations as a source of guest speakers. There are numerous nonlegal organizations that provide speakers who may be of interest to those in your firm, such as local realtor or accounting societies. A local paralegal program may have someone who can discuss the program's internship program with your firm. There are organizations of retired professionals, who have much to offer.

> ## >Paralegal Perspective<

> I enjoy crafting a letter or trying my hand at drafting a trial brief. I am flexible and patient when meeting the challenges and variety of communicating with clients and other professionals each day.

A newsletter, for internal or external use, may help you develop more variety in your job. Ask your employer about creating a newsletter—either one that you write or, more likely, one that you oversee but is written by numerous contributors in the firm. Since preparation of a newsletter involves an ongoing commitment of time, you will want to discuss with your employer the extent to which the time you spend on the newsletter is credited toward the billable hour requirements that may exist. If done right, the newsletter can be an excellent way to communicate with the firm's clients. Even an internal newsletter for the sole benefit of employees can be useful in developing cohesiveness, especially in larger firms.

SEEK OUT CONTINUING- EDUCATION OPPORTUNITIES

Opportunities are available through local, state, and national paralegal associations. There are also courses and workshops available through bar associations. A number of private companies also provide educational courses. Some firms are generous about sending their paralegals to continuing legal education (CLE). Other firms send paralegals on a case-by-case basis. Some firms do not usually send their paralegals to CLE opportunities, usually due to concerns about losing productivity while the paralegal is away, as well as the cost of the CLE itself. If your legal employer does not usually send paralegals to CLEs, be ready to explain in detail how sending you to a particular CLE will benefit the firm. Offer to teach others in the office what you learned. Bring back the course materials, and make them available to your coemployees.

Many CLE courses take place on weekends and evenings. You may want to volunteer to assist as either an instructor or organizer. Volunteering your time will ensure your attendance at the CLE. You can volunteer directly through one of the presenters or by way of the organization that sponsors the CLE, such as the local chapter of a paralegal association.

There is a whole world wanting what you have. Many opportunities exist outside your legal employer to add variety to your career as a paralegal.

VOLUNTEER

Consider volunteering your time to the many organizations that can use your legal, analytical, and organizational skills. There is likely an organization whose mission coincides with a cause you believe in. There are organizations that address domestic violence, unethical treatment of animals, veterans' affairs, party politics, elder abuse, school funding, and many other issues. The purpose of this list isn't to suggest which organization you should volunteer your time with but to demonstrate the wide variety of interests that exist. Although you cannot give legal advice as a paralegal, your legal knowledge will help you understand the issues these organizations face.

> Paralegal Perspective <

> I volunteer my time at a local women's legal center. My time there has made me realize I have skills that can make a difference in someone's life, in addition to giving me more training as a new paralegal.

BE A REGULAR GUEST SPEAKER

I routinely ask guest speakers to the paralegal courses I teach. Often the guest speakers are paralegals. Practicing paralegals bring a perspective and level of knowledge to the classroom that a textbook cannot replace. For example, I teach a paralegal course in employment law. Each time I teach the class, I ask a paralegal who has worked on hundreds of employment law cases to speak with my class. The students think she's great. I also ask a paralegal who has worked on many civil rights cases to speak with my civil rights class.

There are likely numerous guest speaking opportunities available to you. A local paralegal program is but one such opportunity. Serving on a panel discussion at a paralegal CLE is another idea. Teachers of middle and high school courses in government may want someone to explain the court system or how litigation proceeds to trial. Speaking to a group usually requires that you learn more about your topic because you have to anticipate the questions those in the group may ask. In the process of preparing for your presentation, you will often discover that you enjoy your discussion topic more than you realized.

TEACH A CLASS

Consider teaching a class as a way to bring more variety to your paralegal career. You could teach a class at a local paralegal college, an adult education program, or a private trade school. All of these institutions have night courses that are not likely to conflict with your paralegal job duties. My recommendation is that you teach a class one quarter or one semester each year. Having to work all day and teach at night continuously can throw your life out of balance. Teaching a class three or four months a year is much easier to manage. Your quest for the variety that continues to motivate you should maintain the balance between professional and personal life that you seek.

CHAPTER SUMMARY

Staying motivated in your career requires balance and variety—balance between your personal and professional lives and variety in your paralegal career by learning new skills and taking on new challenges. If you do not achieve variety, you will eventually lose motivation and experience burnout. Variety in your career can be achieved by taking advantage of the opportunities within the firm where you work, such as learning new skills from coworkers, using the firm's legal research resources to their full potential, having vendors teach you how to use new products and services, talking with experts the firm hires, arranging classes and guest speakers for the firm, and writing a newsletter. Outside the firm, you can take classes, volunteer your expertise to needy organizations, be a guest speaker, or teach a class. All of these activities add to your skill level and make your job more interesting.

> Web Research Exercise <

On the Internet, go to www.ali-aba.org, the Web site of the American Law Institute–ABA Committee on Continuing Professional Education. You will find numerous professional legal courses offered in a variety of formats, such as audio/video, on-line, satellite, in-house, and a traditional classroom setting. Find three courses that you believe would offer you the chance to develop new skills that would bring variety to your paralegal career. What is it in particular about the courses you selected that you find appealing? Can you find any other sources of information on the Internet that would help paralegals stay motivated? What information did you find? Be prepared to discuss all of your findings with your classmates.

> Chapter Exercises <

1. Have you ever experienced burnout in a career or known someone who did? Why did the feeling of burnout come about? What could have been done with the benefit of hindsight to avoid reaching that state? How can you use this information to help you avoid burnout in your paralegal career?

2. At what time in your new career as a paralegal do you anticipate needing to feel more challenged in your job? When that time comes, what specifically will you do to create more challenge such that your job remains interesting and you continue to feel motivated about being a paralegal? Even as a relatively new paralegal, are there things you can begin to do now in anticipation of the day when you need more challenge and variety in your career?

3. Assume you work in a law firm that customarily does not send its paralegals to professional courses. The firm says that it cannot afford to have you away from your job because there is too much work to be done. The firm specializes in civil litigation. You notice that the local chapter of a paralegal organization is sponsoring a class on trial preparation. What will you do to convince your employer that you should attend this class? How important is it to you that your employer send you to professional classes? Are the types of concerns that your employer has expressed legitimate? What should you do if you like your job generally but disagree with your employer's position about sending you to professional classes?

> Ethical Discussion <

A student paralegal association asks you to speak at a membership meeting about your experience as a new paralegal. Are there any topics that ethically you should not discuss? What are those topics, and why is it unethical to discuss them? How should you handle a situation when a paralegal student asks about a topic that you believe would be unethical for you to discuss?

> Suggested Reading <

Steve Chandler, *100 Ways to Motivate Yourself*, Career Press, 2001.

Chapter 17
Mission Accomplished: Now What?

Key Success Points

> *Success requires daily effort.*
> *The key to moving forward in your paralegal career is implementing what you have learned.*
> *The challenges of the profession for an experienced paralegal are different than they are for a new paralegal.*

> > > > > > > > > >

Actually, Daddy is a "paralegal".
That's totally different
from a "paratrooper".

LOSING THAT "NEW" TAG

There will be a time in which the tag *new* or *inexperienced* no longer applies to you. There is no magical moment when you are suddenly transformed to an experienced professional; it is a gradual process. The time it takes to no longer be considered new at your profession varies from paralegal to paralegal. It depends on what you do for yourself. If you are like the majority of people who wander aimlessly through their careers without much thought to where they want to go, you may never be considered a complete legal professional that others look up to. However, the fact that you are reading books like this one indicates that you want more in your career. You are serious about making the most of the considerable positive features a paralegal career has to offer.

What you have learned in this book for the most part is not particularly hard to understand. The key is going forward by implementing what you have learned. Your situation is akin to learning to play a piano. It's fairly easy to understand what the music you are reading requires you to do; each note tells you which key to strike. The difficult part is putting all the notes together so that a song is created. Your paralegal career is no different.

You now know that you should set long-term, intermediate, and short-term goals, with plans to accomplish those goals. You know that certain people, both within and outside your inner circle, can help you accomplish your goals. You know about the importance of managing your workload properly, communication, handling office politics, billable hours, and what a law firm values in its paralegals. You have read throughout this book about always taking the ethical high road. Balancing work and the rest of your life is critical. In fact, you now know substantially more than the average paralegal about what it takes to be successful at the outset of a career.

How do you take all of the paralegal career "notes" mentioned in the prior paragraph, and throughout this book, and turn them into the beautiful song of your paralegal career? Like someone learning to play the piano, you must work at professional success consistently. Remember that success is not just about money. To achieve what you want from your career requires daily effort. There will be days when you wonder why you got into the profession and you want to quit. If you have your career grounded with goals and plans to achieve them, you will be able to overcome those difficult days that everyone experiences sooner or later. With constant effort, you will eventually lose that "new" label and become the professional you set out to be.

> Paralegal Perspective <

Check out books and seminars that will assist you in being the best problem solver there is. Just because you graduated with a degree does not mean you have to stop learning. Continue to absorb as much information as possible to become the best you can be.

NOW WHAT HAPPENS?

Now that you are no longer considered inexperienced, what happens next? The challenges become different, but they do not go away. The good news is that these challenges are ones you are prepared for and make your career more interesting.

As an experienced paralegal, the more rudimentary aspects of your job are not as difficult. What seemed overwhelming when you began your job now seems manageable. Your confidence level should have increased proportionate with your ability. Instead of being on the receiving end of advice in the office, you now find you are giving more of it than you receive.

Your challenges as an experienced paralegal often have more to do with people than the law. A client or court staff member is upset; you are asked to rectify the situation. You may be asked to manage other staff in your office. Your coworkers ask you to intervene on behalf of someone they feel is being treated unfairly. The attorneys ask you to train new paralegals. These are but a few examples of the "people" challenges placed on an experienced paralegal; there are many more. It is easy to understand why possessing interactive social skills is important.

You will be asked increasingly for your opinions about law office management decisions. Should we hire this new associate? Should we replace our current billing software? Is a satellite office a good idea for the firm? What will the client think if we take this approach to the case? Are we growing too fast? Not fast enough? Although the final decisions about these issues rest with the firm management, an experienced paralegal's input is often important.

As an experienced paralegal, you will find that your knowledge is in demand outside the office, as well as within the office where you are employed. You may be asked to teach a continuing-education seminar, make a speech, write an article, attend a conference, or any one of numerous other requests. Here, you will have to make sure you make an effort to keep balance in your life.

You will do all of this in a profession that has changed dramatically over the years and will continue to change. It is likely that issues such as paralegal certification requirements, what constitutes "the practice of law," requirements to enter the paralegal profession, and many more will need to be addressed during your paralegal career. As someone experienced in your profession, you may take part in the resolution of these issues.

It is likely that as more employers recognize the value of paralegal training, paralegals will be increasingly employed in nontraditional careers where skills can be useful, such as insurance claims, human resources, civil and criminal investigation, and government research. This trend toward nontraditional careers will give you more career options. There are many jobs other than a paralegal that can use your skills effectively.

Another trend likely to continue is the utilization of contract paralegals. Employers, often through placement agencies, hire paralegals on a contract basis for relatively short periods of time, perhaps to complete a certain project or to meet a temporary staff shortage. There is debate whether this phenomenon is good for the profession.

Another trend that is likely to continue is the option of working from home. Technology now makes the requirement that work be performed in an office less important than it used to be. Home-based paralegal work has its limits, though. Even with telephones, fax machines, and the Internet, it is difficult to replace the personal interaction that is required to accomplish many job duties. For example, you probably wouldn't want to meet with a client in your home. Some combination of home-based and office work is increasingly popular in the legal profession, however.

LOOKING BACK AND LOOKING AHEAD

When you look back at your experience as a new paralegal someday, what do you expect to see? The hope is that you will see someone who succeeded rather than just survived and can look back on the experience as a positive one. You have chosen an outstanding career. Taking time to reflect on what you have done in your career will make you appreciate all you have accomplished. By becoming a member of this profession, you have already accomplished a lot. Looking ahead, the best is yet to come.

CHAPTER SUMMARY

You will eventually reach a point in your paralegal career where you are no longer considered inexperienced. In order to become a respected legal professional, you must not only learn the lessons from this and other career advice books, you must work at them consistently throughout your career. Once you become an experienced, respected paralegal, the challenges are different but always present. Often those challenges have less to do with the rudimentary knowledge of law than with dealing with people in a variety of situations. Your knowledge and opinions become in demand both within and outside the firm. By constantly working at achieving success, which is not merely economic in nature, you will be prepared for the dramatic and positive changes ahead in the paralegal profession.

> Web Research Exercise <

On the Internet, go to www.homeworkersnet.com. This Web page is a source of information about home-based jobs, including those in the paralegal profession. Click to the Web page on "home-based paralegals." After reviewing the information provided, does working out of your home appeal to you? Why or why not? What are the advantages and disadvantages of working as a paralegal out of your home? Be prepared to share your responses with your classmates.

> Chapter Exercises <

1. What will you have to accomplish as a paralegal in order for your coworkers to no longer consider you a new paralegal? When do you anticipate no longer being thought of by coworkers as a new paralegal? Is there anything you can do now that will expedite the process? How important is it to you to become a seasoned veteran in the paralegal profession?

2. Find an article about trends in the paralegal profession. How will those trends affect you personally? What can you do now to prepare for those trends and use them to your advantage? Be as specific as possible.

3. Talk with a paralegal who has at least 10 years of experience. Ask this person what challenges experienced paralegals face and how he or she is addressing those challenges. Ask what challenges the experienced paralegal anticipates for someone relatively new in the profession and what you can do to meet those challenges.

> Ethical Discussion <

As the paralegal profession changes, what new ethical guidelines will be necessary to address these changes? For example, if paralegals are permitted to give limited legal advice in the future, what can be done to encourage ethical behavior while giving advice? In responding to these questions, think about the implications of changes that are likely to affect the paralegal profession.

> Suggested Reading <

Linda Dominguez, *How to Shine at Work*, McGraw-Hill, 2003.

Appendix A
Model Code of Ethics and Professional Responsibility and Guidelines for Enforcement* [of the National Federation of Paralegal Associations, Inc.]

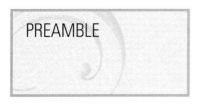

PREAMBLE

The National Federation of Paralegal Associations, Inc. ("NFPA") is a professional organization comprised of paralegal associations and individual paralegals throughout the United States and Canada. Members of NFPA have varying backgrounds, experiences, education and job responsibilities that reflect the diversity of the paralegal profession. NFPA promotes the growth, development and recognition of the paralegal profession as an integral partner in the delivery of legal services.

In May 1993 NFPA adopted its Model Code of Ethics and Professional Responsibility ("Model Code") to delineate the principles for ethics and conduct to which every paralegal should aspire.

Many paralegal associations throughout the United States have endorsed the concept and content of NFPA's Model Code through the adoption of their own ethical codes. In doing so, paralegals have confirmed the profession's commitment to increase the quality and efficiency of legal services, as well as recognized its responsibilities to the public, the legal community, and colleagues.

Paralegals have recognized, and will continue to recognize, that the profession must continue to evolve to enhance their roles in the delivery of legal services. With increased levels of responsibility comes the need to define and enforce mandatory rules of professional conduct. Enforcement of codes of paralegal conduct is a logical and necessary step to enhance and ensure the confidence of the legal community and the public in the integrity and professional responsibility of paralegals.

In April 1997 NFPA adopted the Model Disciplinary Rules ("Model Rules") to make possible the enforcement of the Canons and Ethical Considerations contained in the NFPA Model Code. A concurrent determination was made that the Model Code of Ethics and Professional Responsibility, formerly aspirational in nature, should be recognized as setting forth the enforceable obligations of all paralegals.

The Model Code and Model Rules offer a framework for professional discipline, either voluntarily or through formal regulatory programs.

§1. NFPA MODEL DISCIPLINARY RULES AND ETHICAL CONSIDERATIONS

1.1 A PARALEGAL SHALL ACHIEVE AND MAINTAIN A HIGH LEVEL OF COMPETENCE.

Ethical Considerations

EC-1.1(a) A paralegal shall achieve competency through education, training, and work experience.

EC-1.1(b) A paralegal shall aspire to participate in a minimum of twelve (12) hours of continuing legal education, to include at least one (1) hour of ethics education, every two (2) years in order to remain current on developments in the law.

EC-1.1(c) A paralegal shall perform all assignments promptly and efficiently.

1.2 A PARALEGAL SHALL MAINTAIN A HIGH LEVEL OF PERSONAL AND PROFESSIONAL INTEGRITY.

Ethical Considerations

EC-1.2(a) A paralegal shall not engage in any ex parte communications involving the courts or any other adjudicatory body in an attempt to exert undue influence or to obtain advantage or the benefit of only one party.

EC-1.2(b)   A paralegal shall not communicate, or cause another to communicate, with a party the paralegal knows to be represented by a lawyer in a pending matter without the prior consent of the lawyer representing such other party.

EC-1.2(c)   A paralegal shall ensure that all timekeeping and billing records prepared by the paralegal are thorough, accurate, honest, and complete.

EC-1.2(d)   A paralegal shall not knowingly engage in fraudulent billing practices. Such practices may include, but are not limited to: inflation of hours billed to a client or employer; misrepresentation of the nature of tasks performed; and/or submission of fraudulent expense and disbursement documentation.

EC-1.2(e)   A paralegal shall be scrupulous, thorough and honest in the identification and maintenance of all funds, securities, and other assets of a client and shall provide accurate accounting as appropriate.

EC-1.2(f)   A paralegal shall advise the proper authority of non-confidential knowledge of any dishonest or fraudulent acts by any person pertaining to the handling of the funds, securities or other assets of a client. The authority to whom the report is made shall depend on the nature and circumstances of the possible misconduct, (e.g., ethics committees of law firms, corporations and/or paralegal associations, local or state bar associations, local prosecutors, administrative agencies, etc.). Failure to report such knowledge is in itself misconduct and shall be treated as such under these rules.

1.3   A PARALEGAL SHALL MAINTAIN A HIGH STANDARD OF PROFESSIONAL CONDUCT.

Ethical Considerations

EC-1.3(a)   A paralegal shall refrain from engaging in any conduct that offends the dignity and decorum of proceedings before a court or other adjudicatory body and shall be respectful of all rules and procedures.

EC-1.3(b)   A paralegal shall avoid impropriety and the appearance of impropriety and shall not engage in any conduct that would adversely affect his/her fitness to practice. Such conduct may include, but is not limited to: violence, dishonesty, interference with the administration of justice, and/or abuse of a professional position or public office.

EC-1.3(c) Should a paralegal's fitness to practice be compromised by physical or mental illness, causing that paralegal to commit an act that is in direct violation of the Model Code/Model Rules and/or the rules and/or laws governing the jurisdiction in which the paralegal practices, that paralegal may be protected from sanction upon review of the nature and circumstances of that illness.

EC-1.3(d) A paralegal shall advise the proper authority of non-confidential knowledge of any action of another legal professional that clearly demonstrates fraud, deceit, dishonesty, or misrepresentation. The authority to whom the report is made shall depend on the nature and circumstances of the possible misconduct, (e.g., ethics committees of law firms, corporations and/or paralegal associations, local or state bar associations, local prosecutors, administrative agencies, etc.). Failure to report such knowledge is in itself misconduct and shall be treated as such under these rules.

EC-1.3(e) A paralegal shall not knowingly assist any individual with the commission of an act that is in direct violation of the Model Code/Model Rules and/or the rules and/or laws governing the jurisdiction in which the paralegal practices.

EC-1.3(f) If a paralegal possesses knowledge of future criminal activity, that knowledge must be reported to the appropriate authority immediately.

1.4 A PARALEGAL SHALL SERVE THE PUBLIC INTEREST BY CONTRIBUTING TO THE IMPROVEMENT OF THE LEGAL SYSTEM AND DELIVERY OF QUALITY LEGAL SERVICES, INCLUDING PRO BONO PUBLICO SERVICES.

Ethical Considerations

EC-1.4(a) A paralegal shall be sensitive to the legal needs of the public and shall promote the development and implementation of programs that address those needs.

EC-1.4(b) A paralegal shall support efforts to improve the legal system and access thereto and shall assist in making changes.

EC-1.4(c) A paralegal shall support and participate in the delivery of Pro Bono Publico services directed toward implementing and improving access to justice, the law, the legal system or the paralegal and legal professions.

EC-1.4(d) A paralegal should aspire annually to contribute twenty-four (24) hours of Pro Bono Publico services under the supervision of an attorney or as authorized by administrative, statutory or court authority to:

1. persons of limited means; or
2. charitable, religious, civic, community, governmental and educational organizations in matters that are designed primarily to address the legal needs of persons with limited means; or
3. individuals, groups or organizations seeking to secure or protect civil rights, civil liberties or public rights.

The twenty-four (24) hours of Pro Bono Publico services contributed annually by a paralegal may consist of such services as detailed in this EC-1.4(d), and/or administrative matters designed to develop and implement the attainment of this aspiration as detailed above in EC-1.4(a) (c), or any combination of the two.

1.5 A PARALEGAL SHALL PRESERVE ALL CONFIDENTIAL INFORMATION PROVIDED BY THE CLIENT OR ACQUIRED FROM OTHER SOURCES BEFORE, DURING, AND AFTER THE COURSE OF THE PROFESSIONAL RELATIONSHIP.

Ethical Considerations

EC-1.5(a) A paralegal shall be aware of and abide by all legal authority governing confidential information in the jurisdiction in which the paralegal practices.

EC-1.5(b) A paralegal shall not use confidential information to the disadvantage of the client.

EC-1.5(c) A paralegal shall not use confidential information to the advantage of the paralegal or of a third person.

EC-1.5(d) A paralegal may reveal confidential information only after full disclosure and with the client's written consent; or, when required by law or court order; or, when necessary to prevent the client from committing an act that could result in death or serious bodily harm.

EC-1.5(e) A paralegal shall keep those individuals responsible for the legal representation of a client fully informed of any confidential information the paralegal may have pertaining to that client.

EC-1.5(f) A paralegal shall not engage in any indiscreet communications concerning clients.

1.6 A PARALEGAL SHALL AVOID CONFLICTS OF INTEREST AND SHALL DISCLOSE ANY POSSIBLE CONFLICT TO THE EMPLOYER OR CLIENT, AS WELL AS TO THE PROSPECTIVE EMPLOYERS OR CLIENTS.

Ethical Considerations

EC-1.6(a) A paralegal shall act within the bounds of the law, solely for the benefit of the client, and shall be free of compromising influences and loyalties. Neither the paralegal's personal or business interest, nor those of other clients or third persons, should compromise the paralegal's professional judgment and loyalty to the client.

EC-1.6(b) A paralegal shall avoid conflicts of interest that may arise from previous assignments, whether for a present or past employer or client.

EC-1.6(c) A paralegal shall avoid conflicts of interest that may arise from family relationships and from personal and business interests.

EC-1.6(d) In order to be able to determine whether an actual or potential conflict of interest exists a paralegal shall create and maintain an effective recordkeeping system that identifies clients, matters, and parties with which the paralegal has worked.

EC-1.6(e) A paralegal shall reveal sufficient non-confidential information about a client or former client to reasonably ascertain if an actual or potential conflict of interest exists.

EC-1.6(f) A paralegal shall not participate in or conduct work on any matter where a conflict of interest has been identified.

EC-1.6(g) In matters where a conflict of interest has been identified and the client consents to continued representation, a paralegal shall comply fully with the implementation and maintenance of an Ethical Wall.

1.7 A PARALEGAL'S TITLE SHALL BE FULLY DISCLOSED.
Ethical Considerations

EC-1.7(a) A paralegal's title shall clearly indicate the individual's status and shall be disclosed in all business and professional communications to avoid misunderstandings and misconceptions about the paralegal's role and responsibilities.

EC-1.7(b) A paralegal's title shall be included if the paralegal's name appears on business cards, letterhead, brochures, directories, and advertisements.

EC-1.7(c) A paralegal shall not use letterhead, business cards or other promotional materials to create a fraudulent impression of his/her status or ability to practice in the jurisdiction in which the paralegal practices.

EC-1.7(d) A paralegal shall not practice under color of any record, diploma, or certificate that has been illegally or fraudulently obtained or issued or which is misrepresentative in any way.

EC-1.7(e) A paralegal shall not participate in the creation, issuance, or dissemination of fraudulent records, diplomas, or certificates.

1.8 A PARALEGAL SHALL NOT ENGAGE IN THE UNAUTHORIZED PRACTICE OF LAW.
Ethical Considerations

EC-1.8(a) A paralegal shall comply with the applicable legal authority governing the unauthorized practice of law in the jurisdiction in which the paralegal practices.

§2. NFPA GUIDELINES FOR THE ENFORCEMENT OF THE MODEL CODE OF ETHICS AND PROFESSIONAL RESPONSIBILITY

2.1 BASIS FOR DISCIPLINE

2.1(a) Disciplinary investigations and proceedings brought under authority of the Rules shall be conducted in accord with obligations imposed on the paralegal professional by the Model Code of Ethics and Professional Responsibility.

2.2 STRUCTURE OF DISCIPLINARY COMMITTEE

2.2(a) The Disciplinary Committee ("Committee") shall be made up of nine (9) members including the Chair.

2.2(b) Each member of the Committee, including any temporary replacement members, shall have demonstrated working knowledge of ethics/professional responsibility-related issues and activities.

2.2(c) The Committee shall represent a cross-section of practice areas and work experience. The following recommendations are made regarding the members of the Committee.

1) At least one paralegal with one to three years of law-related work experience.

2) At least one paralegal with five to seven years of law-related work experience.

3) At least one paralegal with over ten years of law-related work experience.

4) One paralegal educator with five to seven years of work experience; preferably in the area of ethics/professional responsibility.

5) One paralegal manager.

6) One lawyer with five to seven years of law-related work experience.

7) One lay member.

2.2(d) The Chair of the Committee shall be appointed within thirty (30) days of its members' induction. The Chair shall have no fewer than ten (10) years of law-related work experience.

2.2(e) The terms of all members of the Committee shall be staggered. Of those members initially appointed, a simple majority plus one shall be appointed to a term of one year, and the remaining members shall be appointed to a term of two years. Thereafter, all members of the Committee shall be appointed to terms of two years.

2.2(f) If for any reason the terms of a majority of the Committee will expire at the same time, members may be appointed to terms of one year to maintain continuity of the Committee.

2.2(g) The Committee shall organize from its members a three-tiered structure to investigate, prosecute and/or adjudicate charges of misconduct. The members shall be rotated among the tiers.

2.3 OPERATION OF COMMITTEE

2.3(a) The Committee shall meet on an as-needed basis to discuss, investigate, and/or adjudicate alleged violations of the Model Code/Model Rules.

2.3(b) A majority of the members of the Committee present at a meeting shall constitute a quorum.

2.3(c) A Recording Secretary shall be designated to maintain complete and accurate minutes of all Committee meetings. All such minutes shall be kept confidential until a decision has been made that the matter will be set for hearing as set forth in Section 6.1 below.

2.3(d) If any member of the Committee has a conflict of interest with the Charging Party, the Responding Party, or the allegations of misconduct, that member shall not take part in any hearing or deliberations concerning those allegations. If the absence of that member creates a lack of a quorum for the Committee, then a temporary replacement for the member shall be appointed.

2.3(e) Either the Charging Party or the Responding Party may request that, for good cause shown, any member of the Committee not participate in a hearing or deliberation. All such requests shall be honored. If the absence of a Committee member under those circumstances creates a lack of a quorum for the Committee, then a temporary replacement for that member shall be appointed.

2.3(f) All discussions and correspondence of the Committee shall be kept confidential until a decision has been made that the matter will be set for hearing as set forth in Section 6.1 below.

2.3(g) All correspondence from the Committee to the Responding Party regarding any charge of misconduct and any decisions made regarding the charge shall be mailed certified mail, return receipt requested, to the Responding Party's last known address and shall be clearly marked with a "Confidential" designation.

2.4 PROCEDURE FOR THE REPORTING OF ALLEGED VIOLATIONS OF THE MODEL CODE/DISCIPLINARY RULES

2.4(a) An individual or entity in possession of non-confidential knowledge or information concerning possible instances of misconduct shall make a confidential written report to the Committee within thirty (30) days of obtaining same. This report shall include all details of the alleged misconduct.

2.4(b) The Committee so notified shall inform the Responding Party of the allegation(s) of misconduct no later than ten (10) business days after receiving the confidential written report from the Charging Party.

2.4(c) Notification to the Responding Party shall include the identity of the Charging Party, unless, for good cause shown, the Charging Party requests anonymity.

2.4(d) The Responding Party shall reply to the allegations within ten (10) business days of notification.

2.5 PROCEDURE FOR THE INVESTIGATION OF A CHARGE OF MISCONDUCT

2.5(a) Upon receipt of a Charge of Misconduct ("Charge"), or on its own initiative, the Committee shall initiate an investigation.

2.5(b) If, upon initial or preliminary review, the Committee makes a determination that the charges are either without basis in fact or, if proven, would not constitute professional misconduct, the Committee shall dismiss the allegations of misconduct. If such determination of dismissal cannot be made, a formal investigation shall be initiated.

2.5(c) Upon the decision to conduct a formal investigation, the Committee shall:

1) mail to the Charging and Responding Parties within three (3) business days of that decision notice of the

commencement of a formal investigation. That
notification shall be in writing and shall contain a
complete explanation of all Charge(s), as well as the
reasons for a formal investigation and shall cite the
applicable codes and rules;

2) allow the Responding Party thirty (30) days to
prepare and submit a confidential response to the
Committee, which response shall address each
charge specifically and shall be in writing; and

3) upon receipt of the response to the notification,
have thirty (30) days to investigate the Charge(s). If
an extension of time is deemed necessary, that
extension shall not exceed ninety (90) days.

2.5(d) Upon conclusion of the investigation, the Committee
may:

1) dismiss the Charge upon the finding that it has no
basis in fact;

2) dismiss the Charge upon the finding that, if proven,
the Charge would not constitute Misconduct;

3) refer the matter for hearing by the Tribunal; or

4) in the case of criminal activity, refer the Charge(s)
and all investigation results to the appropriate
authority.

2.6 PROCEDURE FOR A MISCONDUCT HEARING BEFORE A TRIBUNAL

2.6(a) Upon the decision by the Committee that a matter
should be heard, all parties shall be notified and a
hearing date shall be set. The hearing shall take place
no more than thirty (30) days from the conclusion of
the formal investigation.

2.6(b) The Responding Party shall have the right to
counsel. The parties and the Tribunal shall have the
right to call any witnesses and introduce any
documentation that they believe will lead to the fair
and reasonable resolution of the matter.

2.6(c) Upon completion of the hearing, the Tribunal shall
deliberate and present a written decision to the parties
in accordance with procedures as set forth by the
Tribunal.

2.6(d) Notice of the decision of the Tribunal shall be
appropriately published.

2.7 SANCTIONS

2.7(a) Upon a finding of the Tribunal that misconduct has occurred, any of the following sanctions, or others as may be deemed appropriate, may be imposed upon the Responding Party, either singularly or in combination:

1) letter of reprimand to the Responding Party; counseling;
2) attendance at an ethics course approved by the Tribunal; probation;
3) suspension of license/authority to practice; revocation of license/authority to practice;
4) imposition of a fine; assessment of costs; or
5) in the instance of criminal activity, referral to the appropriate authority.

2.7(b) Upon the expiration of any period of probation, suspension, or revocation, the Responding Party may make application for reinstatement. With the application for reinstatement, the Responding Party must show proof of having complied with all aspects of the sanctions imposed by the Tribunal.

2.8 APPELLATE PROCEDURES

2.8(a) The parties shall have the right to appeal the decision of the Tribunal in accordance with the procedure as set forth by the Tribunal.

DEFINITIONS

"Appellate Body" means a body established to adjudicate an appeal to any decision made by a Tribunal or other decision-making body with respect to formally-heard Charges of Misconduct.

"Charge of Misconduct" means a written submission by any individual or entity to an ethics committee, paralegal association, bar association, law enforcement agency, judicial body, government agency, or other appropriate body or entity, that sets forth non-confidential information regarding any instance of alleged misconduct by an individual paralegal or paralegal entity.

"Charging Party" means any individual or entity who submits a Charge of Misconduct against an individual paralegal or paralegal entity.

"Competency" means the demonstration of: diligence, education, skill, and mental, emotional, and physical fitness reasonably necessary for the performance of paralegal services.

"Confidential Information" means information relating to a client, whatever its source, that is not public knowledge nor available to the public. ("Non-Confidential Information" would generally include the name of the client and the identity of the matter for which the paralegal provided services.)

"Disciplinary Hearing" means the confidential proceeding conducted by a committee or other designated body or entity concerning any instance of alleged misconduct by an individual paralegal or paralegal entity.

"Disciplinary Committee" means any committee that has been established by an entity such as a paralegal association, bar association, judicial body, or government agency to: (a) identify, define and investigate general ethical considerations and concerns with respect to paralegal practice; (b) administer and enforce the Model Code and Model Rules and; (c) discipline any individual paralegal or paralegal entity found to be in violation of same.

"Disclose" means communication of information reasonably sufficient to permit identification of the significance of the matter in question.

"Ethical Wall" means the screening method implemented in order to protect a client from a conflict of interest. An Ethical Wall generally includes, but is not limited to, the following elements: (1) prohibit the paralegal from having any connection with the matter; (2) ban discussions with or the transfer of documents to or from the paralegal; (3) restrict access to files; and (4) educate all members of the firm, corporation, or entity as to the separation of the paralegal (both organizationally and physically) from the pending matter. For more information regarding the Ethical Wall, see the NFPA publication entitled "The Ethical Wall—Its Application to Paralegals."

"Ex parte" means actions or communications conducted at the instance and for the benefit of one party only, and without notice to, or contestation by, any person adversely interested.

"Investigation" means the investigation of any charge(s) of misconduct filed against an individual paralegal or paralegal entity by a Committee.

"Letter of Reprimand" means a written notice of formal censure or severe reproof administered to an individual paralegal or paralegal entity for unethical or improper conduct.

"Misconduct" means the knowing or unknowing commission of an act that is in direct violation of those Canons and Ethical Considerations of any and all applicable codes and/or rules of conduct.

"Paralegal" is synonymous with "Legal Assistant" and is defined as a person qualified through education, training, or work experience to perform substantive legal work that requires knowledge of legal concepts and is customarily, but not exclusively performed by a lawyer. This person may be retained or employed by a lawyer, law office, governmental agency, or other entity or may be authorized by administrative, statutory, or court authority to perform this work.

"Pro Bono Publico" means providing or assisting to provide quality legal services in order to enhance access to justice for persons of limited means; charitable, religious, civic, community, governmental and educational organizations in matters that are designed primarily to address the legal needs of persons with limited means; or individuals, groups or organizations seeking to secure or protect civil rights, civil liberties or public rights.

"Proper Authority" means the local paralegal association, the local or state bar association, Committee(s) of the local paralegal or bar association(s), local prosecutor, administrative agency, or other tribunal empowered to investigate or act upon an instance of alleged misconduct.

"Responding Party" means an individual paralegal or paralegal entity against whom a Charge of Misconduct has been submitted.

"Revocation" means the recision of the license, certificate or other authority to practice of an individual paralegal or paralegal entity found in violation of those Canons and Ethical Considerations of any and all applicable codes and/or rules of conduct.

"Suspension" means the suspension of the license, certificate or other authority to practice of an individual paralegal or paralegal entity found in violation of those Canons and Ethical Considerations of any and all applicable codes and/or rules of conduct.

"Tribunal" means the body designated to adjudicate allegations of misconduct.

Appendix B
Sample Resumé
with Comments

Jane Smith[1]
Tel: 000.000.0000
jsmith@delmar.com
111 Court Street
Anytown, NY 00000

Summary of Qualifications:[2]
- Able to prepare pleadings, discovery, motions, and legal correspondence.
- Proficient in on-line legal research, including Westlaw and Lexis.
- Skilled in use of legal and data management software.
- Capable of summarizing complex material, such as depositions and medical records.
- Knowledgeable in use of investigative techniques.

Legal Experience:[3]
- Paralegal Intern, Law Office of Thomas Jefferson, Anytown, NY, from 08/2003 to 12/2003. Responsible for interviewing clients, conducting legal research, summarizing discovery, and preparing legal documents.
- Volunteer, Indigent Law Center, Anytown, NY, from 6/2003 to 12/2003. Gained valuable practical experience in law center by frequently meeting with clients, telephoning personnel at law firms, local courts, and aid organizations.

Education:[4]
- Associate of Applied Science Degree, State College Paralegal Program, Anytown, NY. GPA of 3.2 in ABA-approved paralegal

program. Courses include civil litigation, torts, contracts, legal research, family law and employment law.
- Graduate, Anytown High School, Anytown, NY.

Personal Interests:[5]
- Reading novels, writing poetry, travel

References:[6]
- Available on request.

Comments

Experts differ on the appropriate length of a resumé. Rather than arbitrarily limiting the length, the rule of thumb I apply is whether all the information is helpful in allowing the employer decide whether you deserve an interview. Never place "filler" in a resumé.

1. Make sure your name and contact information are easy to find on your resumé. Employers will normally contact you by telephone if they are interested in your application. Many firms communicate by e-mail today, so make sure you have a professional-sounding e-mail address, not something like silly@email.com. Use bullets throughout your resume to facilitate reading. If your resumé is easy to read, it is more likely to catch an employer's attention.

2. Early in your paralegal career, you will have to overcome a lack of experience when applying for a paralegal position. One effective method of overcoming inexperience is to summarize the practical legal skills you already have. Experience is important because it is an indicator of a certain skill level. Point out to the potential employer that you have developed many legal skills that can be used now.

Have at least three bulleted points but not more than five. Fewer than three are not enough to impress the employer. More than five may cause the employer to skip over some of the information. To develop a list of practical legal experience, think back to all of the paralegal classes you took. What practical skills did you obtain in the course that relate to the job for which you are applying? If you did an internship, what practical skills did you learn there that relate to the job for which you are applying? Use "power" verbs such as *able, proficient,* and *knowledgeable* to describe your skills.

The "Summary of Qualifications" section is near the top of the resumé, where it is easily noticed by someone who may be reviewing dozens of resumés in a short period of time. Notice that no "Objective" section was included. While there are differing opinions about the use of an "Objective" section, my impression is that they normally are not useful because they tend to be overlooked and written in such a way that the employer's objectives are not addressed.

3. Chances are you will not have much more than what you see here as a new paralegal. Make sure you indicate any skills you obtained or experiences you had that would benefit the potential employer. Try to learn as much as you can about the job for which you are applying. Match the skills needed for the job with skills you obtained through an internship or volunteer work; the closer the match, the better your chances.

4. If your GPA is impressive, be sure you include it. If your GPA is not impressive, omit it. If your paralegal school was ABA approved, note it. List classes you took that relate to the job for which you are applying instead of listing all your classes or none. If you won any awards or scholarships, put them here unless they are so numerous that a separate section is warranted.

5. Opinions differ about the merits of listing your personal interests. However, I find them helpful in determining whether you would fit in the particular office environment. If you have interests that directly relate to the job, list them. For example, if you like to work on cars and you are applying for a position in which you will handle automobile accident cases, list it. Otherwise, list interests that show attributes all paralegals should have, such as the ability to read and write.

6. References should not be included in a resumé. At the job interview, ask the employer what kinds of references she would like. This will also allow you to refresh the reference's recollection about the job you applied for.

Appendix C
Sample Cover Letter
with Comments

(address)[1]
(telephone)
(email)
(date)

Shirley Williams, Hiring Partner[2]
Law Firm of Davis and Williams
1234 Main Street
Anytown, NY 00000

Dear Ms. Williams:[3]

I was referred to you by Jane Doe,[4] who indicated your firm was recruiting a litigation paralegal.[5] I am a graduate of Anytown Paralegal School and worked in a local law firm recently while completing my paralegal internship.[6] I have the legal, writing, and technology skills to be a productive employee for your firm.[7]

While at Anytown Paralegal School, I took courses in civil litigation, contracts, torts, and legal investigation.[8] Further, I developed skills in legal research and writing by taking courses in that subject and completing my internship at the Jones Law Firm.[9] While at the Jones Law Firm, I worked on several litigation cases.[10] My technology skills include proficiency in [list all technology skills related to the job].[11] The professionalism and efficiency required in a law firm are consistent with the high standards I have set for myself.[12]

I would appreciate the opportunity to discuss a paralegal position with your firm.[13] I have enclosed my resumé for your review. If you would like additional information about my qualifications, such as references or a writing sample, please do not hesitate to request it.[14] I can be reached by telephone or e-mail. Thank you for your consideration.[15]

Sincerely,

Paula Paralegal

Enc: Resumé

Comments

1. Cover letters should be brief. Three to four paragraphs are usually sufficient. Make sure all contact information is at the top of the letter even though it is also on your resumé, since resumés can become separated from cover letters.

2. Try to address your cover letter to a specific person instead of "Hiring Partner" or "To Whom It May Concern." You can call the law firm and ask a secretary to whom the letter should be addressed. If that does not work, law directories often identify the hiring partner, supervising paralegal, or managing partner who may oversee the hiring process. Even if this person doesn't have the specific task of hiring for the position, he or she will forward it to the right person in the firm, thus giving your application a little more attention. However, if a job announcement gives specific directions about how to address the application, follow those directions.

3. Be sure to address females with "Ms." and males with "Mr." unless given specific instructions to use a different title. If it is not apparent from the name whether the addressee is male or female, call the employer and ask.

4. If you have a personal contact, make sure you mention that person in the first sentence. This will get the employer's attention.

5. Make it clear in the first or second sentence specifically what position you are applying for.

6. Here and in the next sentence, you are giving an overview of what makes you qualified for the position.

7. You are indicating to the employer you understand, and possess, the skills necessary to be successful in the position, including productivity.

8. Name the courses you took that relate to the position. If you did exceptionally well in any of the courses, note it. For example, "in torts, I scored 98 out of a possible 100 for my final grade." Your primary goal in the second paragraph is to elaborate on the qualifications you indicated you possess in the first paragraph. Since a cover leter needs to be brief, you will have to be selective about what to put in the second paragraph.

9. Research and writing skills are universally important. Be sure to mention them in any job application. In this letter, you are telling the employer that you have put your knowledge to work in a law office, helping to overcome the issue of inexperience.

10. If you have any experience that relates specifically to the job for which you are applying, perhaps in an internship or volunteer capacity, be sure to mention it.

11. Paralegals today need to be proficient in technology. Make sure you indicate in the cover letter your technological know-how.

12. You are telling the employer about your personal work habits here. Most employees do not succeed because of poor work habits, not lack of knowledge or skill. Employers know this.

13. You are telling the employer you want an interview. Some advise being more aggressive by making statements such as, "May I call you?" or "I will call you next week." Law firms tend to be fairly subdued and conservative institutions. It is usually best to be subtle; you can send a follow-up letter later if you don't hear from the employer after a reasonable amount of time.

14. Be sure to let the employer know you are willing and able to provide additional information. This is a reflection of your preparedness, which is a positive attribute for any paralegal.

15. Although it should be obvious, it is important to thank the employer for considering your application.

Appendix D
Sample Thank You Letter with Comments

(address)
(telephone)
(e-mail)
(date)

Shirley Williams, Hiring Partner
Law Firm of Davis and Williams
1234 Main Street
Anytown, NY 00000

Dear Ms. Williams:

Thank you for the opportunity to interview with you on [date] for a paralegal position. After our discussion, I am confident that I can be an effective member of your litigation team. I appreciate that your firm has high standards for its employees.[1]

I found your explanation of the firm's practice very interesting.[2] In particular, cases such as Smith v. Jones, which your firm took to the Court of Appeals, are the kind of challenge I appreciate.[3] As you know, I have taken courses in civil litigation, and my paralegal internship was completed in a civil litigation law firm.[4]

You indicated at the interview that references with knowledge of my skills as a civil litigation paralegal would be most helpful. The enclosed list of references should meet those qualifications and are expecting your call.[5] I welcome any further requests for information about my application.

Sincerely,

Paula Paralegal

Encl: References
Resumé[6]

Comments

1. In your interview, one of the questions you will want to ask is when a decision about the position will be made. Make sure you send your thank-you letter well before that deadline since the letter may float for awhile until it is read.

Some also recommend a follow-up letter if there is no action on your application after a reasonable period of time. If you haven't heard from the employer after a decision was to have been made, I recommend you call the employer's office and speak with someone in an administrative capacity about the status of your application. If your application is still pending, ask if further information would be helpful. If your application has been rejected, try to find out why; this information will help for the next application.

In the first paragraph, after thanking the employer for the opportunity to interview, remind her of what position you interviewed for and when. Be extremely positive and upbeat. By telling the employer you appreciate its "high standards" or "professionalism" or "challenging work environment" (or something similar to these examples) you are indicating you identify with the firm.

2. During the interview, make note of anything of particular interest that you want to remember later. It is acceptable to bring a professional-looking notepad or folder, but nothing too large, to the interview. Be careful not to look down too much as you take notes; just jot down key words or phrases. Later, when you write your thank-you letter, you can refer back to your notes.

3. Mentioning a specific case, or other situation concerning the firm, in your thank-you letter shows you pay attention to detail. Also, if you can tie the case or situation to your own qualifications and interests, the employer is more likely to believe you are a good fit for the position.

4. Remind the employee that your training has prepared you for the position.

5. It is a good idea to tailor the references to the position. Therefore, waiting until the interview to ask what types of references the employer wants is a good strategy. You are also demonstrating that you were listening carefully during the interview and initiative by contacting the references to let them know they may be contacted.

6. Enclose another copy of your resume. When an employer has numerous resumés, along with the usual other written material in a law office, yours can become misplaced.

Appendix E
Alternative and Nontraditional Career Resources

Books

Carol Adrienne, *When Life Changes or You Wish it Would: A Guide to Finding Your Next Step Despite Fear, Obstacles, or Confusion*, Quill, 2003.

Deborah Arron, *What Can You Do with a Law Degree? A Lawyer's Guide to Career Alternatives Inside, Outside and Around the Law*, Niche Press, 1997. Contains ideas that also apply to paralegals.

Hindi Greenberg, *The Lawyer's Career Change Handbook: More Than 300 Things You Can Do with a Law Degree*, HarperCollins, 2002. Contains ideas that also apply to paralegals.

Carole Kanchier, *Dare to Change Your Job and Your Life*, 2nd ed., JIST Publishing, 2000.

Dorothy Secol, *Paralegal's Guide to Freelancing: How to Start and Manage Your Own Legal Services Business*, Aspen Publishers, 1996.

Karen Treffinger, *Life Outside the Law Firm: Non-Traditional Careers for Paralegals*, Delmar Learning, 1995.

Web Sites

ParalegalGateway.com: This site contains numerous links that may be useful to paralegals, such as career information, use of technology, and Continuing Legal Education.
http://www.paralegalgateway.com

Martindale-Hubbell: This is the well-known legal directory whose online version contains law firm profiles that may be useful in a job search. http://www.martindale.com

Palidan Legal Resources: This site contains a wide range of information that may be useful to legal professionals, such as classifieds, recruiters, news, and legal research links. http://www.palidan.com

Index